DATA PROCESSING
IN ARCHAEOLOGY

CAMBRIDGE MANUALS IN ARCHAEOLOGY

Series editors

Don Brothwell, *University of London*
Barry Cunliffe, *University of Oxford*
Stuart Fleming, *University of Pennsylvania*
Peter Fowler, *Royal Commission on Historical Monuments (England)*

DATA PROCESSING
IN ARCHAEOLOGY

J. D. Richards

Department of Archaeology,
University of Leeds

and

N. S. Ryan

Computing Laboratory,
University of Kent

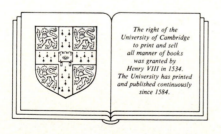

The right of the
University of Cambridge
to print and sell
all manner of books
was granted by
Henry VIII in 1534.
The University has printed
and published continuously
since 1584.

Cambridge University Press

Cambridge
London   New York   New Rochelle
Melbourne   Sydney

Published by the Press Syndicate of the University of Cambridge
The Pitt Building, Trumpington Street, Cambridge CB2 1RP
32 East 57th Street, New York, NY 10022, USA
10 Stamford Road, Oakleigh, Melbourne 3166, Australia

First published 1985

Printed in Great Britain at the University Press, Cambridge

Library of Congress catalogue number: 84-9523

British Library Cataloguing in Publication Data
Richards, J.D.
Data processing in archaeology.
(Cambridge manuals in archaeology) 1. Archaeology -
Data processing
I. Title II. Ryan, N.S.
930.1′028′5   CC80.4

ISBN 0 521 25769 7

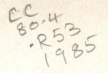
ACKNOWLEDGEMENTS

This book is not just the product of our own attempts to apply computers in archaeology. It is the outcome of the experiences of all those who have had a hand in this continuing learning process, and of those who believe in the routine application of computers to archaeological problems.

In particular we are grateful for the environment for research and debate provided within the Research Centre for Computer Archaeology under its founder John Wilcock, and for the contributions of each of our colleagues: Mike Attwell, Malcolm Cooper, Gary Lock, Paul Reilly, Dan Smith and Dick Spicer. Many individuals gave us advice on particular topics; Malcolm Cooper and Dan Smith deserve special mention for having valiantly read, and commented upon, earlier versions of the entire text.

We are also indebted for the help generously given by Tony Whitehouse and the staff of the Computing Services Unit of North Staffordshire Polytechnic, especially the chief operator Eric Halliday. Terry Coombes, technician to the Computing Department, and David Heath of the Audio-Visual Aids Unit also provided practical support for the production of the book.

We have also been the beneficiaries of guidance and constructive criticism from Ian Hodder, but whilst all the above mentioned may have been responsible for improvements to the text, needless to say we must bear the responsibility for those faults which remain.

Finally, Kate Owen at Cambridge University Press should be thanked for her support and constant faith in the idea of this book.

PREFACE

The aim of this book is to provide an introduction to current computer applications in archaeology. It should be of interest to all archaeologists, whether working in the field or in an academic environment. No previous computer experience is expected of the reader, but it is anticipated that the book will be of equal value to both the newcomer and those whose involvement has so far been limited to the use of published program packages.

At present, the prospective computer user has available a number of books and conference proceedings covering a variety of specialist applications, many of which have been found to be somewhat daunting for those with little previous experience in this direction. Furthermore, most of what is available was written before the so-called 'Microprocessor Revolution' and the widespread introduction of micro-computers. The impact of these machines, especially in the fields of graphics and word processing, is now beginning to be appreciated by archaeologists.

Introductory texts on computing in the humanities and social sciences are available, but it is not always apparent how applicable these may be to the problems faced by archaeologists. This volume is intended as a practical guide, although a certain amount of theory is inevitable. It provides the information necessary to enable the archaeologist to decide how best to deal with problems which may, at first, appear to be specific to the research objectives, but with further knowledge can be seen to be capable of solution using standard computing techniques. Nevertheless, no attempt is made to turn the archaeologist into a computer scientist, or to make an unnecessary burden of the inner workings of the machine. Nor does this book teach programming, for which there are a large number of texts available.

Data processing in archaeology may be read from cover to cover, or it may be regarded as a manual and dipped into according to individual requirements. The sections are hierarchically organised, with more detailed information indicated by subdivisions of the section number. Where possible the reader is referred to appropriate computing texts for more information. Whenever terms which may be unfamiliar are used for the first time they appear in bold type. Specialised computing terms are also defined in the glossary.

We have attempted to provide archaeological examples throughout the text but rather than burden the reader with detailed and distracting case studies we would ask each reader to consider how the ideas discussed relate to particular archaeological problems with which they are familiar. No one case study can be made to appear relevant to more than the small proportion of readers familiar with such material. Each would tend to involve discussion of problems related to the material, rather than to the data processing techniques being illustrated.

Chapter 1 ('Introduction') introduces the basic concepts of data processing, gives a brief history of automatic data processing in archaeology, and looks at its current role.

Chapter 2 ('Data') examines what we mean by data in more detail, and investigates ways of measuring it. It is inevitably a theoretical chapter, but sections 2.2 and 2.7 at least should be considered as essential reading as they establish the terminology used throughout the book.

In chapter 3 ('Hardware') we consider the computer equipment. This is not a chapter about electrical engineering, but rather it describes the items of equipment likely to be encountered by archaeologists, and contains the information required to make effective use of them.

In chapter 4 ('Software') we look at all the types of program which can be used on a computer system. In particular we consider programs written by the user to solve specific problems. The benefits of learning a programming language are discussed, and several of the more popular languages are described.

In chapter 5 ('Data capture') we return to the data. Before data can be processed by a computer it must normally be coded, by which we mean only that it must be categorised in some systematic way. This chapter explores the best ways of coding data and of getting it onto a computer.

Chapter 6 ('Files and file management') examines a number of techniques of data storage and retrieval. The later sections of this chapter introduce some relatively advanced computing concepts; they will not initially be essential to most readers' requirements.

A wide range of tasks may be performed with existing applications programs by those with little computing experience. Chapter 7 ('Packages') surveys the packages available which are likely to be useful to archaeologists.

In conclusion, in chapter 8 ('The future') we take up some of the themes examined in the introduction, and develop them in the light of the intervening chapters. We ask where the archaeologist goes from here, both in terms of individual computing requirements, and in terms of where developments in computers are likely to lead archaeology in the immediate future.

Finally, it should be noted that at the risk of chastisement by strict grammarians we have regarded 'data' as both a singular and a plural noun throughout the text. A datum in archaeology is usually taken to mean something completely different.

CONTENTS

1

INTRODUCTION

1.1 Data processing

Our first task must be to indicate what we mean by data processing. Archaeological **data** consists of recorded observations. These might be measurements of the size of a handaxe, the stratigraphical relationship between two layers or the geographical location of a site. Whilst archaeological data is frequently numeric, it can equally well be non-numeric, such as the name of the material or colour of an object. It also comprises visual data, such as photographs, plans or maps.

Data **processing** is the name given to the manipulation of data to produce a more useful form, which we shall call **information**. This is frequently accompanied by a reduction in quantity. Several thousand observations may be processed to produce a few salient points of information.

This sequence of events is known as the **data processing cycle**. It is shown in fig. 1.1. There are three steps in the cycle. Firstly, data must be **input** to the

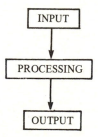

1.1 The data processing cycle

processing system. Therefore it must be selected and prepared in a form which the system can understand. Secondly, it must be processed to produce information. Thirdly, this information must be **output** in a useful form. The actual processing involves one or more operations, which may be carried out in various sequences, according to what information is required:

1) Duplication: reproducing the data in identical, or edited, form.
2) Verification: checking the data for errors.
3) Classification: separating the data into various categories.
4) Sorting: arranging the data in a specified order.
5) Merging: taking two or more sets of sorted data, and putting them together to form a single set of sorted data.

6)   Calculation: by performing numerical operations on (numerical) data.
7)   Selection: to extract specific data items from a set of data.

The sequence of operations required to perform a specific task is known as an **algorithm**.

The output from one data processing cycle may become the input to another cycle. In other words, one person's information may become another's data. The distinction between data and information is not absolute, but is confined to a single cycle. The information produced from an excavation, for example, may provide the data for someone else's research project.

It may also be desirable to store data at any stage in the cycle. Data is generally stored in **files**, which are defined as organised collections of data. It may also re-enter the cycle at any stage. Therefore we can draw an expanded data processing cycle (fig. 1.2).

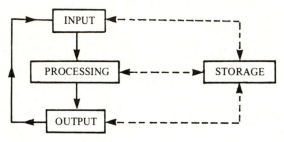

1.2 An expanded data processing cycle

It will be apparent that there is nothing new about data processing as we have so far described it. We have simply formalised a sequence of operations that archaeologists have always performed whenever they have recorded anything and sought to derive information from it. Since archaeologists must frequently deal with large quantities of data, they have long stood to benefit from various mechanical aids to data processing. At its most primitive this mechanisation may consist of no more than methods of rapid retrieval from a card index system, such as the peek-a-boo or edge-notched card systems. At a slightly more advanced level were the early punched card processing machines, which automatically sorted cards punched with holes representing characters.

However, the major developments in data processing have come about through the advent of the electronic computer, a machine capable of performing algorithms automatically. The term data processing has therefore gained a more restricted meaning, implying especially that the operations are performed by computer. This book is concerned with the archaeological applications of computers; to find out more about pre-electronic data processing techniques, which are now generally of antiquarian interest only, the reader may refer to Jolley (1968) or Foskett (1970).

Electronic data processing is performed through the operation of the two components of a computer system: **hardware** and **software**. Hardware is the term given to all the electronic and mechanical equipment used. Software is the general name for the sets of instructions which express algorithms in a form which the computer can execute. A set of instructions to perform a particular algorithm is known as a computer **program**. Programs are written in a computing **language**, of which there are many. Like data, programs are generally held in files.

1.2 **The development of automatic data processing in archaeology**

The history of computer applications in archaeology may be traced in a series of review articles, including Cowgill (1967a; 1967b), Chenhall (1968), Burton *et al* (1970), Wilcock (1971), Gardin (1971), Whallon (1972b), Wilcock (1973a), Gaines and Gaines (1980), and Scollar (1982).

For those with an interest in causality this provides an illuminating case study. The history of computer applications may be characterised as one of accelerating growth, driven by developments in technology. As new equipment and programs have become available they have been applied in archaeology, with a varying time lag, and have even determined the archaeological questions being asked. For example, the resurgence of archaeological interest in classification in the late 1960s and early 1970s (cf. Clarke 1968; Dunnell 1971) may be linked to the availability of powerful computers capable of performing multivariate statistical analyses.

It was the increasing availability of computing facilities that preceded the first archaeological applications of computers in the late 1950s. The accumulation of large quantities of data, and an increasing archaeological awareness of the contribution to be made by the sciences, may be cited as contributory causes, but both these factors can also be seen in the work of earlier archaeologists, such as Flinders Petrie (1899).

With the benefit of hindsight four areas of computer applications in archaeology may so far be identified:

    i)   information retrieval;
    ii)   statistics;
   iii) ancillary data processing;
   iv) modelling.

In the past different practitioners have worked on each of these fields, and thus their development has largely been independent. Latterly, however, they have begun to merge as archaeologists have adopted a more comprehensive approach to data processing.

In addition, there are two areas which do not represent specific fields of inquiry, but which may be applied in any sphere of archaeological interest, namely graphics and word processing. The theory of computer graphics is beyond the scope of this book. Readers who wish to find information on the subject are referred to Angell (1981) and Scott (1982). Some graphics software which may be useful to archaeologists is described in section 7.3. Word processing is dealt with in section 7.4.

1.21 **Information retrieval**

One of the simplest things that a computer can do is to act as an elaborate filing system, storing data and producing it on request. **Information retrieval** is the term applied to the branch of data processing relating to the storage and categorisation of large quantities of information, and the automatic retrieval of specific items. Data is frequently stored in large files, which are often described as **data banks** (cf. section 2.76).

Chenhall (1971a,4) describes one of the earliest applications of information retrieval techniques in archaeology. In the 1950s Gaines recorded data relating to pottery of the American South West on punched cards, and used conventional punched card machines to sort and list it. Gardin (1956) was another early user of mechanical punched card systems.

However, according to Cowgill (1967b, 331) the earliest uses of a real computer to record archaeological data were probably by Ihm, and by Gardin and Garelli in France, around 1958 or 1959. At about the same time in the United States, Deetz also recorded pottery data on punched cards which were processed by computer (Deetz 1965; 1967, 110).

Archaeological data banks may be classed in one of four groups, ranging from the particular to the general. In increasing order of generality they are:

    i)   research project data banks;
    ii)   specialist data banks;
    iii)   excavation or survey data banks;
    iv)   general purpose data banks.

At the lowest level, the research project data bank is a collection of data relating to a particular project, and usually gathered by an individual researcher with specific questions in mind. It may comprise, for example, data about an artefact type, aspects of a site, or about several sites in one region. The data relating to the cemetery at Munsingen-Rain (Doran and Hodson 1975, 309–15) is probably the best known example of this class. This is a rapidly accelerating growth area of archaeological applications. In our own department there are data banks of Irish megalithic tombs, Scandinavian Bronze Age razors, Roman coins, Anglo-Saxon cremation urns, Christian sites on the Isle of Man and quern stones.

At the second level is the specialist data bank. This contains data of a specific type, but intended for general usage. For example, a data bank of radiocarbon dates (Moffett and Webb 1982) would fall into this category.

Data banks containing data on an excavation, or from a field survey, constitute the third class of data bank. The Teotihuacan Mapping Project (Cowgill 1968), and the mesolithic excavation at Bergumermeer in the Netherlands (Newell and Vroomans 1972) are early published examples in this sphere. In the United States a computerised data processing and information retrieval system was developed to aid the investigation of the Koster site in Illinois from 1972 to 1978 (Brown *et al* 1981). More recently, data on several large excavations in the United Kingdom, notably Danebury (Lock forthcoming), Mucking (Catton, Jones and Moffett 1982), and Maxey (Pryor 1980; Booth 1982), has been transferred to computer. Such data banks are often intended as an aid to writing the site report, and as a means of archiving the excavation records so that they may be used by future archaeologists. Graham (1980) has outlined some of the advantages of this approach. These include direct production of microfiche reports, indexing and sorting, and a permanent record on magnetic tape. In addition, the excavation record is available for statistical analysis, examination of the relationship of finds and stratigraphy, with automatic production of the site matrix (Bishop and Wilcock 1976; Wilcock 1982) and automatic plotting of distribution maps.

Finally, at the highest level are what we have described as general purpose data banks. These are collections of data covering a large field, gathered with no particular research objectives other than that they may be used by all archaeologists. The general purpose or 'universal' data bank therefore represents a rather dubious concept, for as we shall see in chapter 2, any computer recording involves some selection of data, and the selection criteria should be explicit. At one level, namely as a means of finding data required for particular projects, such data banks are completely satisfactory. Thus computerised museum records (Orna and Pettitt 1980), or county sites and monuments indexes, such as that in use by the North Yorkshire County Council (NYCC 1983), are useful sources of data for all archaeologists. The papers in Gaines (1981a) include several comparable examples from the United States, particularly the SARG (Plog 1981) and AZSITE (Rieger 1981) projects. Such data banks may also be of primary value in indexing existing manual filing systems, and referring the user to maps, photographs and so on.

On the other hand, systems which attempt to record all data about every artefact in an area, such as the Arkansas Archaeological Survey (Chenhall 1971b), will probably be of less value to future generations of archaeologists. The problem is that such general purpose data banks seek to record archaeological data at a level of detail at which there is little agreement on what should be recorded, and nor should there be:

> Archaeology is not yet sufficiently scientific to establish any immutable variables, attributes, or classes in our data other than perhaps some very simple ones, useful more for cataloging than for analysis. A possible danger of data banking done too

> soon and on too all-encompassing a scale is that it is not likely to prove particularly
> useful to innovative, experimental, and exploratory researches and may
> actually tend to stifle active questioning and thought about the basic nature and
> meaning of the units of data, variables, and attributes which we use in our work.
> (Whallon 1972b, 38)

In conclusion it seems likely that there will be an accelerating growth of
data banks for individual research projects, for specialist needs and for site
recording. However, the general purpose data bank will not gain wide
acceptance, apart from those containing a minimum of descriptive detail, and
used to locate sources of data. Consequently, standardisation of data bank
recording is not an important question for archaeology, apart from matters of
uniformity of sites and monuments indexing and museum cataloguing, where
the work of the Museum Documentation Association has been valuable
(Stewart 1982a; 1982b). We wholeheartedly agree with Doran and Hodson
(1975, 331) that

> the keynote of the future will be and should be diversity rather than standardisa-
> tion and the giant integrated information system.

Finally, it should be emphasised that the traditional use of data banks need
not lead to any great change in archaeological habits. Gardin (1971, 198)
suggests that the principle of a data bank is contrary to the archaeological
practice of isolated scholars jealously guarding information. Whilst data
banks may be consulted by any number of users, they can equally well be used
by a single individual. Despite popular mythology, if proper precautions are
taken then data held on a computer is secure. The archaeologist can release it
to others only if and when so desired, just as in traditional publishing.

1.22 Statistics

Archaeologists often need to count things, and so by its very nature archaeology is a suitable area for the application of statistical techniques. It is
frequently necessary to deal with large amounts of data, and archaeologists
are typically interested in groups of artefacts rather than single objects.
Hence the use of statistics in archaeology goes back beyond the introduction
of the electronic computer (cf. Orton 1980). Simple tabulated descriptive
statistics may be found in the earliest excavation reports (e.g. Pitt-Rivers
1887-98), but the first application of real statistical method in archaeology is
conventionally regarded as being that of Robinson (1951).

Therefore, as Gardin (1971, 190) observed:

> the use of statistical tools is not basically or even historically linked to the
> computerization of archaeology...

Nevertheless, the computer is an ideal tool for counting and its use has
accelerated the development of statistical applications. Indeed, without it a
lot of the multivariate statistics currently applied would be impossible be-

cause of the time and patience required to carry them out by hand. According to Gardin (1971, 193) the earliest computerised statistical application was by Ihm, who used a computer to apply a classification algorithm to a collection of Bronze Age axes in 1959. For some the use of computers has now become synonymous with statistical techniques (cf. Doran and Hodson 1975) and there has probably been more written on this area than any other. It would be impossible to give a comprehensive list of statistical applications involving computers, and also irrelevant to this book, as the interest of these papers is primarily statistical, and not in the application of a computer.

The areas in which computers have been used to perform statistical techniques include seriation, cluster analysis, principal components and factor analysis, multi-dimensional scaling, and spatial analysis. The papers in Hodson, Kendall, and Tautu (1971) include many examples of seriation and multivariate statistics; Hodder and Orton (1976) include references to spatial applications. Several journals also regularly carry examples of the use of computers for statistical work, including *American Antiquity*, the *Journal of Archaeological Science*, *Science and Archaeology*, and special numbers of *World Archaeology*. Although of variable quality, the annual proceedings of the *Computer Applications in Archaeology* conference represent another useful source.

Whilst the value of the computer for heavy statistics, or **number-crunching**, will continue, it should be stressed that the application of a computer is by no means limited to the use of such statistical techniques, and the proportion of other applications is growing. Frequently simple descriptive statistics, such as averages and percentages, are sufficient, and should always be used as a preliminary to any further more complex analysis. As Whallon (1972b, 31) emphasises:

> One of the simplest yet most important uses of the computer in archaeology is the generation of descriptive statistics and the manipulation of quantities of data too large to be easily managed by hand.

Clark and Stafford (1982) stress the growing importance of quantification at the level of exploratory data analysis, rather than for confirmatory data analysis.

The use of statistical techniques in archaeology has highlighted three problems. Firstly there is the question of sampling, and whether archaeological populations are representative samples:

> do the nature and extent of the 'populations' studied ... justify the use of a particular statistical tool? (Gardin 1971, 190)

Linked with this is the second problem of confirmation. The use of computational and statistical tools does not automatically confer validity on the results of an analysis, which can be only as good as the initial assumptions. Thirdly, the use of computers to execute automatic classification algorithms has highlighted the problem of taxonomy. It has reinforced the absence of a 'natural' classification, stressed the crucial effect of the choice of variables, and highlighted the question of resemblance. When can we say that two artefacts are identical? These problems are also important when computers are used for information retrieval and we shall return to them in chapter 2.

1.23 Ancillary data processing

Ancillary data processing covers the application of computers in the areas ancillary to archaeology, including dating, prospecting, and aerial photography.

It is likely that the first application of a real computer to archaeological data was not made in mainstream archaeology, but in one of the ancillary sciences. According to Scollar (1982, 189), Cook and Belshé (1958) used a computer program in 1957 to evaluate readings taken from kilns for magnetic dating.

The use of computers in the ancillary fields is now routine. The techniques employed in these areas frequently result in vast quantities of data which must be reduced, and the background noise eliminated. Computers are therefore an obvious choice, both for the heavy statistics commonly involved, and the graphical presentation of results.

Scollar used a computer to calculate and filter a resistivity plot in 1959, and has subsequently processed magnetometer data (Scollar and Krückeberg 1966; Scollar 1959; 1968; 1969; 1974). Wilcock (1970a) used a computer to process survey data from South Cadbury.

As mentioned above, computers were used in dating techniques in 1957, and Scollar (1982, 194) also refers to their use in radiocarbon and tree ring dating. Computers are now a standard fitment in many laboratories. Wilcock, Short and Greaves (forthcoming) describe the automatic logging of measurements at the Harwell radiocarbon laboratory as part of a micro-computer network. Whallon (1972b, 40) records the use of computers in statistical analysis of pollen data.

In aerial photography, computers have been valuable in the transformation of oblique photographs. The first attempt was by Scollar (1975), followed by Palmer (1976; 1977; 1978), and Chamberlain and Haigh (1982). Scollar has also worked on image processing of aerial photographs, and there have been applications to x-ray images, and to ultra-violet and infra-red pictures (Scollar 1977; Scollar and Weidner 1979).

In conclusion, computer applications in these areas will undoubtedly continue to be of importance. Nevertheless, these are specialist techniques beyond the scope of this book.

1.24 Modelling

The term modelling describes the **simulation** of the structure and behaviour of a complex system. The definition of the parameters of such a system and their articulation may well be a valuable manual exercise, aiding clarity and precision of thought. However, in order to observe the operation of the system it generally becomes necessary to run the simulation on a computer. Whether the results of a computer simulation have any predictive value depends upon how well the input parameters may be defined. In a recent guide to simulation in archaeology, Aldenderfer (1981a) stressed the conceptual utility gained from attempting to model a system and the developmental utility derived from translating it into a simulation model; the output utility gained from the operation of the model was seen as being of less importance.

Some of the parameters of a simulation model may take constant values; others may take one of a range of values, sampled from a frequency distribution. In the latter case the model is described as **stochastic** since it incorporates random elements. It is necessary to run such models many times in order to observe the range of possible outcomes.

The verification of a simulation model should be distinguished from its validation. In this context verification simply means that the simulation program is a correct translation of the algorithm. Validation, on the other hand, involves examining the goodness-of-fit of the data generated by the model to the real world. The lack of suitable data with which to validate a model is a major difficulty in archaeology, but as Aldenderfer (1981a, 41) comments, an incompletely validated model may still be a useful predictor of systemic behaviour.

It will be apparent that simulation modelling may be regarded as the practical equivalent of systems theory, requiring the definition of the parameters and boundaries of the system. It has therefore found its greatest popularity with the proponents of the systems theory approach (e.g. Doran 1970a).

The archaeological applications of modelling have ranged from the simulation of site formation processes to that of the evolutionary development of complex societies. The work by Thomas (1972; 1973) on the simulation of Shoshonean settlement patterns was one of the first examples of computer simulation of the archaeological record, although the criticisms of Doran and Hodson (1975, 305) that this simulation was too simplistic to warrant the use of a computer should be borne in mind. More recently, Aldenderfer (1981b) has devised a simulation program called ABSIM to model lithic assemblage production amongst aborigines in the Western Australian Desert.

As examples of simulation of the development of a society we may cite the work of Cooke and Renfrew (1979), and of Hosler, Sabloff and Runge (1977) on the modelling of the Classic Maya collapse. Other early work on simulation has also concentrated on the modelling of past societies. It includes papers by Ammerman and Cavalli-Sforza (1973) on the diffusion of early farming in Europe, Wobst (1974) on the simulation of palaeolithic population growth, Levison, Ward and Webb (1972) on the settlement of Polynesia, and Wright and Zeder (1977) on the simulation of exchange systems.

A further form of simulation extensively discussed by Doran (1970b; 1972a; 1972b; 1973) is the use of the computer to model the archaeologist. Doran's SOLCEM project proposed that the computer might be used as a tool for automatic hypothesis generation. He argued that this would have a twofold benefit: in increasing our understanding of the process of validation of archaeological hypotheses and in providing new interpretative tools derived from archaeological reasoning rather than multivariate statistics.

Doran has also stressed the importance of being able to accommodate a wider range of possibilities in a computer simulation than can be expressed mathematically, and has emphasised (1982) that computational models which exploit the structure of high-level programming languages may be able to take into account the cognition and goals of the actors within a society.

Nevertheless, many of the difficulties inherent in systems theory remain implicit in simulation modelling. Firstly, there is the arbitrary imposition of system boundaries, and secondly the problem of the archaeological black box (Leach 1973). Furthermore, simulations have been criticised as being too limited in scope, and too simplistic to be useful, although it has also been claimed that it is this very simplicity which is the advantage of modelling. Certainly it should be recognised that running a simulation represents a considerable programming investment and may be an expensive use of computer time.

On the other hand, the construction of a simulation model may often illustrate weaknesses in our reasoning. Since parameters must be formally defined implicit assumptions must become explicit theory. Furthermore these parameters may be altered and several alternative hypotheses examined. A number of writers have expressed considerable optimism about the potential application of computers for archaeological simulation (Doran 1970a; Bourelly 1972; Whallon 1972b). Plog (1975, 218) notes:

> Simulation will undoubtedly continue to grow in importance in archaeology as a technique for generating hypotheses, for testing alternative models, and for evaluating alternative archaeological methodologies.

It is probably true that it remains to be seen whether such optimism is well-founded. More recently, Aldenderfer (1981a, 48) has expressed doubts about whether simulation will ever become widely applied in archaeology:

> Present funding levels in archaeology, the fuzzy nature of any archaeological processes, and the structure of the discipline itself ... all combine to present a relatively limited future for simulation in archaeological research.

While much of the information contained in this book should be of value to those interested in archaeological applications of simulation, we do not deal specifically with simulation problems. Two recent collections of papers

(Hodder 1978; Sabloff 1981) include further examples of applications, and the papers by Moore (1978) and Aldenderfer (1981a), in particular, provide practical guides to this aspect of archaeological computer usage, which it is unnecessary to duplicate here.

1.3 **The current role of the computer in archaeology**

Of the four areas of computer applications in archaeology discussed in section 1.2, this book is primarily concerned with those in the growing field of information retrieval, although the emphasis throughout is upon a comprehensive approach to computer usage, including the use of graphics and word processing.

Before we go any further, there are at least three popular misconceptions about computers that it is important to correct. In its worst form the popular view is that computers are black boxes producing magic answers, that they are operated by magicians who have mastered some mystical art, and that these magicians work as mathematical wizards in their spare time. In addition, archaeologists sometimes believe that their data is somehow different from all other types of data and cannot be processed by a computer.

In the first place, it is unfortunate but true that computers are incapable of producing magic answers. A computer is only a tool, and at least for the present it cannot 'think' any more than a ship can swim. The results of any computer analysis can only be as good as the data and programs fed to it. The contribution of a computer is limited to how far one can define and formalise a problem put to it (cf. Borillo 1971). Therefore the primary advantages of the application of computers are administrative rather than intellectual. Computers remove many of the tedious aspects of data management, and offer considerable time savings in areas such as word processing and the production of illustrations. They do not in themselves change the nature of archaeology.

Secondly, it is popularly believed that people who use computers are the practitioners of some mystical black art. This is not helped by many computer specialists themselves who apparently insist in talking in a language which seems designed to perpetuate this myth. Unfortunately, most of this jargon is necessary but it is also fairly easily mastered, and a command of the words in bold type in this book covers much of it. The nature of jargon is such that it is easy to be over-awed by an 'expert', whose knowledge may in fact be little in advance of one's own: there is no need to be.

Whilst the difficulty of computing should not be underestimated, it is a skill just like any other which archaeologists are required to master, and should be taught as such. Although most computing can be tedious and frustrating, it can also be challenging and enjoyable. Furthermore, although optimal usage requires a deeper understanding a computer can usefully be employed by someone with a minimal understanding of how it works. As we emphasise throughout this book, it is not even necessary to learn how to write programs in order to benefit considerably from using a computer.

The third popular misconception is that computer specialists are also mathematicians. The corollary of this is that computers are essentially glorified adding machines. In fact, computers can perform any task which can be exactly specified. The use of computers in archaeology has traditionally been associated with statistical applications but this is just one of many possible uses and there is an increasing emphasis on information retrieval. The innumerate archaeologist should not be deterred.

Finally, it is not true that there is anything special about archaeological data which makes it unsuitable for manipulation by standard data processing techniques. The problems encountered in manipulating archaeological data are identical to those found in the analysis of any other sort of data, from biological taxonomy to payroll accounting, and the answers are also the same.

In conclusion, all kinds of archaeologists stand to gain from using a computer. The automation of a data processing task becomes worthwhile when that task is repetitive, when there are several sub-processes to be carried out in a sequence, and when there is a large quantity of data. Shorter (1971) estimates that the maximum size data set that may be processed manually is about 200 items with no more than ten variables each. This provides an adequate rule of thumb, but there are benefits in approaching any problem as if one were using a computer, no matter how small the data set. The careful definition of a problem required by a computer is invariably beneficial.

The greatest time savings can be made when it becomes necessary to process a data set more than once, for example when it is found that the original questions were inappropriate. Rather than having to go through a card index again and again, if the data is held on a computer, then it can be manipulated in many different ways with a minimum of effort.

Therefore all archaeologists can benefit from using computers. 'Old' archaeologists may use them to give their traditional explanations a greater rigour, and 'new' archaeologists can use them to investigate new questions. Computers do not impose a model of explanation on the user. As Shorter (1971, 5) remarked, in an introductory computer text for historians:

> They will not deviously compel the historian with a quantitative source to embark upon some path of explanation obnoxious to him.

On the other hand, there is one requirement that computers do impose on all their users, which is the necessity to record all data in a uniform way. Artefacts must be described in a standardised manner in order that they may be meaningfully compared. In this sense computers turn all archaeologists into theorists, for they demand a greater degree of thought about the units of data, and the techniques of analysis, than has hitherto been common.

2

DATA

2.1 Introduction

Before we can go any further, we must first establish what we mean by data. In this chapter we shall examine the nature of archaeological data, and the means of measuring it. We shall then put forward a conceptual model of the structure of data on a computer, and suggest how this can be related to the archaeological data structure. Further problems of the representation of data are covered in chapter 5.

Several writers have investigated the nature of archaeological data (e.g. Krieger (1944); Ford (1954); Rouse (1960); Clarke (1968); Dunnell (1971); Whallon (1972a); Doran and Hodson (1975); Gardin (1980)). To avoid unnecessary confusion we shall use the terminology preferred by Clarke (1968), which follows the general convention in data analysis (cf. Jardine and Sibson 1971; Sneath and Sokal 1973). Where helpful, reference will be made to equivalent terms used by other writers in section 2.3.

2.2 An archaeological data structure

Archaeological data consists of observations about artefacts and their contexts. An **artefact** is a material thing made or modified by human action. It includes objects, such as tools, weapons, and ornaments, and features, such as buildings, graves, and pits. It is assumed that the patterned behaviour of human beings is reflected in the form and deposition of artefacts.

All artefacts have **attributes**. An attribute is a variable. The attributes of a handaxe include the material it was made from, its dimensions, and surface treatment. The attributes of a grave include its dimensions and contents.

An attribute may take one of several values or **attribute states**. For example, a handaxe might be made of flint or chert; its length might be 12.5 cm or 15.8 cm. Attribute states are mutually exclusive. A handaxe cannot be made of flint and chert, or be both 12.5 cm and 15.8 cm in length: it must be one or the other. If we regard the attribute as a labelled box then the attribute state is the thing occupying it. There is only space for one state in the box at any given moment. We may construct a **data matrix** (fig. 2.1) in which the rows are artefacts, and the columns are attributes.

Attributes belong to one of two classes, namely contextual or specific. **Contextual attributes** are those derived from the context of the artefact, such as environment, grid reference, height above sea level, date, associations,

ATTRIBUTES

ARTEFACTS	A	B	C	D	E	F	G	H
I	0	1	0	0	1	0	1	1
II	1	1	0	0	0	1	1	0
III	1	0	1	0	1	1	0	1
IV	0	0	0	1	1	0	1	0
V	1	1	0	1	1	0	0	1
VI	0	1	0	1	0	1	0	0

2.1 A data matrix

and so forth. **Specific attributes** are those derived from physical or chemical properties of the artefact itself, such as colour, hardness, shape, size, quantity, and decoration. We may further distinguish **positional attributes**, such as the position of a decorative motif, as a particular class of specific attribute.

In the simplest situation there may be just two possible attribute states, as in the sex of a person buried in a grave. Similarly, the two possible states might be the presence or absence of an individual attribute, as in the presence or absence of a particular decorative motif on a pot, or the presence or absence of a particular artefact in a grave. Alternatively, an attribute may take any one of an infinite number of possible states, as in the case of the length of a handaxe, or the size of a grave. Attributes with many possible states are known as **multi-state attributes**.

So far, then, we have seen that archaeological data consists of artefacts, which have attributes, which may take one of two or more attribute states. This hierarchy can also be expanded upwards to introduce some broader archaeological categories.

Above the artefact is the group of artefacts, often called the **assemblage**, and normally consisting of roughly contemporaneous artefacts from a given area. Most frequently it contains artefacts of several types found on a particular site. Above the assemblage many archaeologists distinguish the **culture**. A culture is minimally defined as a group of assemblages, related by their constituent artefacts, spatially linked, and roughly contemporaneous. Finally, above the culture, Clarke (1968) distinguished the **culture group** as a group of related cultures at the apex of the archaeological data hierarchy. We must pass over the problem of interpretation of these high level archaeological units as being beyond the scope of this book. It is sufficient to be aware that their existence is relevant to the discussion in section 2.6 of the organisation

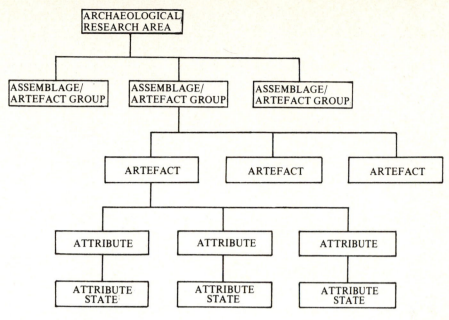

2.2 The structure of archaeological data

of data on the computer. Fig. 2.2 summarises the structure of archaeological data outlined in this section. We shall follow the terminology introduced here throughout this book.

2.3 **Alternative terminologies**

When consulting other works the reader may find that a variety of terms are used to refer to attributes and their states. For those who understandably find themselves confused it may be helpful to relate these to the terminology followed in this text. Otherwise this section may safely be omitted at a first read.

In mathematical jargon an attribute or variable, such as size or material, is known as an **identifier**. The attribute state, such as 15.8 cm or flint, is its **value**. Some archaeological writers have introduced further terminologies. Spaulding (1960), Rouse (1970), and Dunnell (1971) refer to attribute states as attributes, and describe attributes as dimensions (fig. 2.3). We have

	IDENTIFIER	VALUE
Clarke [1968] Doran and Hodson [1975]	ATTRIBUTE	ATTRIBUTE STATE
Spaulding [1960] Rouse [1970]	DIMENSION	ATTRIBUTE

2.3 Terminology for archaeological variables

DERIVED FROM:		
	PHYSIOCHEMICAL PROPERTIES	CONTEXT IN TIME AND SPACE
Spaulding [1960]	FORMAL	NON-FORMAL
Clarke [1968]	SPECIFIC including POSITIONAL	CONTEXTUAL
Gardin [1980]	INTRINSIC	EXTRINSIC

2.4 Terminology for attribute types

defined attributes derived from the physical or chemical properties of an artefact as being specific. Spaulding (1960) describes them as formal; Gardin (1980) as intrinsic. Attributes derived from an artefact's context are contextual. Spaulding calls these non-formal; Gardin terms them extrinsic (fig. 2.4).

2.4 **Recording archaeological data**

In the recording of archaeological data it is necessary to identify the constituent attributes of an artefact. The aim must be to record those attributes which describe the artefact as economically but as completely as possible. This is inevitably a subjective operation influenced by the research design of the recorder (cf. section 2.5). The archaeologist should be aware, therefore, that the initial description of artefacts governs the results of subsequent analyses.

In theory each artefact may have an almost infinite number of attributes. A simple handaxe may be described in terms of its individual minerals, including their fracture, cleavage, and hardness. Each flake scar on the handaxe surface might be recorded, and hundreds of measurements taken.

Obviously, to record every attribute for each artefact would be a practical impossibility. Not only would it take an inordinate amount of time to measure them, but it would be almost impossible to process the data to extract useful information. If every attribute were recorded then each artefact would appear unique, and one would be left with no points of comparison. In excavation recording, where time may be of the essence, it may be especially important to identify the minimum number of attributes which can be recorded with as little loss of information as possible.

In practice then, archaeological recording inevitably involves some selection of those attributes which are considered to be significant by the recorder. However, this need not be a totally arbitrary process; four factors need to be taken into account:

i)   avoidance of duplication;
ii) separation of attribute from attribute state;
iii) identification of deliberate human selection;
iv) frame of reference of the study.

2.41 **Avoidance of duplication**

Clarke defined an attribute as 'a logically irreducible character of two or more states ...' (1968, 138; 665). That is, they are fundamental and cannot be derived from other attributes. There is no need to record several attributes which are each reflections of a single fundamental attribute. For example, if the material from which a tool is made is recorded, then it may be unnecessary to record the hardness, density, etc., for every artefact, if each is dependent upon the material. Similarly, the shape of a rectangular building may be fully described by its length and width; the length of the diagonals and any other measurements are a duplication of data. Where we are dealing with more complex shapes, such as pot profiles, then it may be necessary to identify first those measurements which express most of the variability between pots, such as the height, maximum diameter, height of maximum diameter, and so on (see Richards 1982).

If all tools are made from one material then by the definition of an attribute as a variable of two or more states, material is not an attribute as it can only take one state. Hence it need not be recorded.

There is no law against including non-fundamental properties in the coding of data, but it should be recognised that this involves pre-processing the data, and the loss of some information. For example, a group of buildings may be recorded according to floor area and it may be found that they are all roughly equal. One might conclude therefore that they are all of one type. In fact, this might be disguising the important information that there are some long narrow buildings and some short wide buildings, in reality two types. Similarly, in the case of a cemetery, where the presence or absence of particular grave-goods may constitute attributes, pre-processing the graves by assigning 'wealth-scores' may obscure significant social divisions.

2.42 **Separation of attribute and attribute state**

Archaeologists are frequently careless in their use of attribute and attribute state and fail to distinguish between different attributes and alternate states of the same attribute. Frequently, traits are treated as independent attributes when really they are alternative states of one attribute. Plog (1980) defines this as a problem of 'substitutability'. He emphasises that one must consider variation in elements which are alternatives to each other. For example, if the shoulder of a pot may be decorated with either a chevron or a circle then these may be regarded as alternate states of the same attribute (namely shoulder decoration), as the choice of whether to draw a circle or a chevron represents one decision to the potter. As long as chevron and circle never appear on a pot shoulder together it would be superfluous to define the presence/absence of a circle and the presence/absence of a chevron as independent attributes. Plog describes a well-defined system for classifying the designs of Chevelon Creek pottery consisting of 21 design attributes which emphasise alternative choices made by the potter at different points in the process of decorating a vessel.

2.43 Identification of deliberate human selection

The archaeologist is interested in those attributes which are the product of human action, or selected for by human agency. In some cases these may be self-evident; for example, we can be fairly certain that the presence of decoration on a pot is the product of deliberate human action. We may also be confident that the use of a chevron design reflects a particular style of decoration. But has the actual number of lines in a chevron been deliberately selected by the potter? Similarly, is the colouring of a pot deliberate, or an accident of firing and the clay used? As Clarke (1968, 15) argues, the judgement is '... arbitrary and dependent on the observer and his views or model of the mind of ancient man'. Whilst we cannot record every attribute it is important not to pre-select attributes to the extent that the results of any analysis are predetermined. The recorder should be wary of imposing an ethnocentric view of what is significant on the culture of another society:

> The intuitive and arbitrary 'spotting' of key attributes in a system, before proper analysis, leads to the arbitrary definition of group boundaries based on 'type-fossils'. (Clarke 1968, 138).

By viewing attributes as basic and fundamental units of information, Clarke followed Taylor (1948) and Rouse (1960). Other writers have disagreed as to whether such basic units exist. For example, Hill and Evans (1972, 265) argue:

> No matter how small and minute the attributes are that we wish to consider, they are still further divisible – i.e. each attribute has its own attributes. Presumably even atoms have attributes, and thus are not indivisible or immutable natural units of observation.

Nevertheless, in practice there will generally be a minimum level at which we choose to see human activity as selective. We may safely assume, for example, that the height of a pot may have been deliberately selected but not the number of clay molecules in the fabric.

However, we believe that it is always better to record more data than appears necessary than to pre-select attributes. The help of the computer can then be sought in deciding which are significant.[1] Longacre (1964) illustrates this approach applied to pottery of the American South West, working first with the smallest units of design and combining units later if statistically relevant. One would expect those attributes which are deliberate and non-random to occur repeatedly in regular fashion on several artefacts. This constitutes archaeological information. Those which are not selected for, or are random, will appear as background noise. Of course, certain non-selected attributes, such as hardness or cleavage, may also appear regularly due to natural properties of the raw material. Here the final decision must rest on the subjective analysis of the researcher.

It should be noted that it may be necessary to relate an attribute to external factors in order to decide whether it was deliberately selected. It is unlikely that the use of limestone for the construction of a building in a limestone area represents an act of conscious selection. However, a limestone building in an area where limestone and sandstone are equally available may be evidence for the deliberate selection of material, and building material becomes an attribute we may wish to investigate.

2.44 Frame of reference of the study
That an attribute is 'logically irreducible' does not necessarily mean that it represents a single human action. Each of the grave-goods contained in a burial might be the product of hundreds of actions, whereas pot heights might result from a single movement of the hand on the throwing wheel. The level of complexity of the attributes will depend on the frame of reference of the study. If this were funerary ritual then the presence/absence of an accessory vessel might constitute a fundamental attribute. However, if the frame of reference was the study of pottery then a single vessel might be broken down into hundreds of attributes. In other words, what is regarded as an attribute within one frame of reference may occupy the position of the artefact in another. Chenhall (1968) stresses the importance of defining the level of analysis. The essential point is that comparisons should only be made between attributes of roughly the same level of complexity. A single data set may include attributes of several levels of complexity, but care should be taken when comparisions are made between levels. Generally, one should only compare like with like.

The individual researcher investigating a particular artefact type has a different task in drawing up a list of relevant attributes from someone recording data which is to be used for several purposes. If the research aims are clearly defined then it should be apparent which attributes are required. Yet it may be advisable to record any other data that is readily available, even if it is not immediately obvious how this relates to the problem in hand. Frequently it is later found that this is the vital piece of information required.

On the other hand, excavators, recording data for future researchers, have to guess what their requirements will be. Whilst excavations may be mounted to answer specific questions, their destructive nature means that excavators have a duty to record data that may be useful to others. Of course, whilst recording by individual organisations may vary, a minimum number of attributes that should be recorded in excavation is now established by general convention.

2.5 **Objectivity**

Objectivity should not be confused with precision or accuracy. Precision implies that the degree of measurement of an attribute is refined; accuracy that the measurement taken is correct within the degree of precision indicated. One hopes that all archaeological observations are both accurate and precise. The word 'objectivity', on the other hand, should really only be used when it is intended to imply something external to the observer and so true for all time, including both the archaeologist and the society under study. Obviously, given that it has remained undamaged, a handaxe is the same length today as it was in the Neolithic. In that sense this is an objective measurement. However, the choice of axis to measure and the unit of measurement are subjective decisions by the observer. The simple statement that a handaxe is 15.8 cm in length does not imply that this is the basis of an objective classification. It is possible that length may have had no significance to the maker or user of the handaxe, who selected it for its colour.

Furthermore, an attribute such as the quality of the view from a settlement is no more intrinsically subjective than the size of the buildings. If it could be agreed what constitutes a nice view (e.g. distance to horizon, altitude, direction in which buildings face, etc) then it could be quantified. Colour, for instance, is generally regarded as a difficult thing to measure because of differences in individual perception. However, if it were possible to define a standard, then colour might be quantified. The Munsell soil colour charts used by archaeologists represent an attempt in this direction.

The only difference between the quality of the view and the size of a building, therefore, is the existence of conventions for the measurement of the latter, and there are well-defined units of measurement, e.g. centimetres, metres, etc. However, it may be argued that by measuring the size of a building in metres we may be imposing our ethnocentric view on another society, just as much as when we impose our idea of what is a nice view. Indeed, not only is it unlikely that the building was constructed according to SI units; the builders may even have had a different conception of distance altogether. For example, Fletcher (1977) demonstrates in his examination of an African settlement that buildings, boundaries, and so on , appear to have been laid out according to a logarithmic model of distance.

Of course, so long as the unit of measurement chosen is small enough then it should be possible to work back to the original model, as Fletcher did. This is easier to do for attributes such as size or weight than for attributes such as the view, or artefact decoration. How does one define the basic units in the motifs which decorate a pot, for instance?

Therefore, whilst enabling archaeology to be more precise, and ensuring that the manipulation of data is accurate, the use of a computer does not necessarily make archaeology any more objective. The choice of which data to record, how to measure it, and which manipulative techniques to employ, remain subjective decisions. However, any processing performed by the computer is repeatable, and if attributes are clearly defined, other archaeologists can make the same measurements, perform the same manipulations, and evaluate the results.

2.6 **Data measurement**

The measurement of data involves the assignment of values to attribute states, according to sets of rules. We have already seen that the possible states of an attribute may simply be presence or absence, or one of a large number of possible values. The relationship between attribute states determines the **scale of measurement** which may be employed. In any statistical work it is important to know what the scale or level of measurement is, as this determines whether or not a particular statistical technique is appropriate. Siegel (1956) provides a useful checklist of statistics appropriate at each level of measurement.

The classic formulation of levels of measurement was developed by S.S.Stevens (1946). He identified four levels: nominal, ordinal, interval, and ratio. Other typologies exist and all are summarised and compared in fig. 2.5.

2.5 Scales of measurement

2.61 Nominal level measurement

The nominal is the most basic in the typology as no assumptions are made about the values assigned to the attribute states. Each value is a distinct category, and the value itself simply acts as a name (i.e. is nominal). Artefact colour or material are usually nominal attributes. We may use a numeric system to code nominal categories, but the numbers are simply labels:

RED	1
GREEN	2
YELLOW	3
BLUE	4
......	.

Words or letters would serve equally well. The codes cannot be treated as if they are part of a real number system which can be added, multiplied etc. Therefore, statistics which assume ordering or meaningful distances between categories should not be used, although calculating the number of cases and the mode is permissible.

A distinction is sometimes made between:

(a) The labelling of individual cases for identification, such as by artefact or context number.

(b) The labelling of types or classes, where each member is assigned the same number.

In fact, (a) is just a special case of (b), in which each class has only one member. The simple rule to be followed when measuring attributes on a nominal scale is that the same label should not be assigned to different attribute states, or different labels given to the same state.

2.62 Ordinal level measurement

We are dealing with the ordinal level of measurement when attribute states can be ranked in order according to some criterion, but we do not know the distance between them. The scale of hardness of minerals is the classic example. Graves ranked according to wealth, and archaeological contexts in a Harris matrix, also satisfy this condition. Each category occupies a unique position relative to other categories, but we cannot place it on an absolute scale. Layer A, at the top of the matrix, is later than layer B in the middle, and B is later than layer C at the bottom. Furthermore, this immediately indicates that layer A is later than layer C. However, we do not know how much later B is, relative to C. The distances between layers cannot be tied into an absolute chronology without some other evidence. The only mathematical property involved is the concept of ranking. Therefore, the use of numeric values in coding does not imply that it is meaningful to use the other properties of the real number system.

2.63 **Interval level measurement**

If attribute states are ranked in order and the distances between them are defined in terms of fixed and equal units then one can apply an interval level of measurement. The thermometer is an obvious example, for a degree difference implies the same difference in temperature whether it is at the lower or upper end of the scale. The crucial point about an interval scale, however, is that it does not have an inherently determined zero point. Both Centigrade and Fahrenheit systems have a zero point which is merely a matter of convention. It does not imply absence of heat. Therefore interval level measurement allows one to study differences between things, but not their proportionate magnitudes. It is not true that at 10 degC only half as much heat is present as at 20 degC.

Assigning a date to an artefact is one of the few examples of an interval level measure in archaeology. Unless we follow Archbishop Ussher in believing that the world was created in 4004 B.C. then we cannot give our calendar a true zero point. 0 A.D. was not the start of time and so A.D. 200 is not half as recent as A.D. 400. [2]

2.64 **Ratio level measurement**

Ratio level measurement is at the top of Stevens' typology. Attribute states are ordered with fixed distances between them as for the interval level, but in addition zero is inherently defined by the measurement scale. Therefore if measurements of temperature are taken in degrees Kelvin then a ratio level is employed as an absolute zero point is implied, at 0 degK or -273 degC. Measurements of physical sizes or numbers of artefacts are of this type, as the zero point implies absence of size or quantity. This property means that a meaningful ratio can be computed between two values. For example, a 30 cm high pot is twice as high as a 15 cm one. Ratio level measurements satisfy all the properties of the real number system, and therefore the numbers involved in coding attribute states are more convenient symbols. One may use the attribute value itself: for example, the physical height of the pot expressed in centimetres. Any mathematical techniques suitable for numbers can be applied to ratio level measurements.

In fact, although this is a scale of measurement frequently found in archaeology, most statistical techniques do not require all of its properties. Nevertheless, the essential point is that statistics developed for one level of measurement can always be used with higher level attributes, but not with attributes measured at a lower level. For example, the median is a measure suitable for ordinal data, and it can also be applied to interval and ratio levels, but not to the nominal level.

2.65 **Other scales of measurement**

Coombs (1953) elaborated Stevens' typology with the addition of two intermediate levels. Midway between nominal and ordinal he placed the 'partially ordered' level. This applies when an ordering can be defined between some categories, but not all. Between ordinal and interval levels Coombs placed the 'ordered metric' level. This applies when the relative ordering of inter-category distances is known even though their absolute magnitude cannot be measured. Returning to the Harris matrix example, if it was known that layer C had accumulated over a long period of time (although not the exact number of years), whereas layer A had built up over a few months, then the distances between categories could be ranked. AB would be a much smaller distance than BC.

An alternative typology, which is probably more familiar to archaeologists, simply divides attributes into qualitative and quantitative types. Quantitative attributes are those for which a fixed numeric unit of measurement is defined, namely interval and ratio levels. Qualitative attributes are those at nominal or ordinal level. A **dichotomy** (e.g. male/female) is a special case of qualitative attribute where the attribute can take one of two attribute states. The presence/absence attribute mentioned earlier is a special variant of a dichotomy as the two alternatives are not normally of equal significance. [3] Where only a few out of many possible attributes are likely to be present, presence will generally be more important than absence, although occasionally the reverse may be true. For example, in spatial data the absence of a given type of site in an area may be of greater significance than its presence, although the archaeologist will be aware of the dangers of arguing from negative evidence (cf. Hodder and Orton 1976).

It will be seen that qualitative attributes are discrete entities. Each attribute has a finite number of indivisible attribute states. A bone may be from a cow or sheep or one of several other distinct species. It cannot be part way between two states. On the other hand, quantitative attributes may be discrete or continuous. For example, the number of coins in a hoard or the number of graves in a cemetery is discrete. It corresponds to a whole or **integer** number. One cannot have 501.333 coins or corpses. However, the height of our pot expressed in centimetres will be one value out of a continuous stream of **real** or decimal numbers, such as 33.52. In theory it could be taken to an infinite number of decimal places if we could measure precisely enough. It is worth bearing the distinction between reals and integers in mind as computers store and manipulate them differently, although an integer is really only a special case of a real number. 5 is the same as 5.0 and can be treated as such. Another way round the problem of mixing continuous and discrete variables is to chop the continuous number of attributes into discrete sub-ranges. However, care must be exercised for if the sub-ranges are too broad they may impose types on the data and mask important detail. It is probably reasonable to round our measurements of pot heights to the nearest centimetre without much information being lost. However, if we were to group our pots according to 10 cm bands i.e. 1–10, 11–20, 21–30, 31–40, then we might never discover that there was an important division between two sizes of 22 cm and 30 cm with no pots around the 25 cm size. It is better to code our initial measurements as finely as possible and again seek computer aid in producing real groupings of pot sizes. Generally speaking, it is best to measure data at the highest level that it will support.

2.66 Missing values

Care is also required when dealing with **missing values**, frequent in archaeological data. For some reason it may not be possible to measure a particular attribute of an artefact. For example, a pot may have lost its rim so that we are unable to record its rim diameter, or note if it has a pouring lip. Clarke describes this as a state of No Comparison or 'NC'. It is not the same as the absence of the attribute, but rather a special state with different implications. Most statistical packages, such as SPSS (Nie *et al* 1975) can cope with missing values, but care must be exercised to code them correctly. For example, the presence of a decorative motif is coded as 1 and the absence as 0. An artefact damaged in such a way that one cannot observe if it ever had the motif should not be coded as 0, and nor should the space for this attribute be left blank. A computer may automatically assign a value of zero to a blank field. Therefore it is better to assign a specific symbol to missing values. One solution would be to code presence as 2, absence as 1, and then 0 could be reserved for missing observations.

Sneath (1982) discusses the effect of missing data on classification, concluding that for his test data, serious degradation of the correct solution did not occur until the proportion of gaps was about 50%, or the proportion of errors was about 20%.

2.7 The structure of computerised data

Having examined the structure and hierarchy of archaeological data we shall now look at how it corresponds to the structure of the data held by the computer. We are not concerned here with the physical representation of information. This will be covered in more depth in section 3.21; it is internal to the machine and need not generally concern the archaeological user. Instead we are interested in the conceptual structure of information held on a computer (fig. 2.6).

2.71 Bit

The smallest possible element of information held on a computer is a **bit** (or Binary digIT). It has only two possible states, usually expressed by 0 or 1. Each character in the computer is stored internally as a group of bits. However, the computer user will invariably code data in characters, and

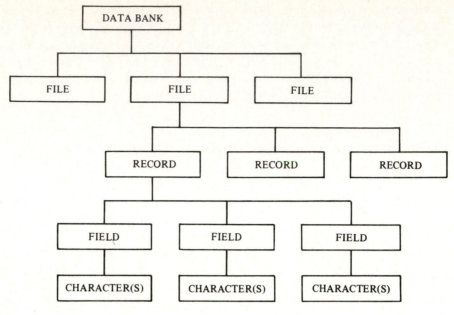

2.6 Data structure

contact with the computer will be through characters, so the bit can safely be ignored.

2.72 **Character**

The lowest level with which the computer user need be concerned is the **character**. The basic character set of a computer consists of the twenty-six upper-case letters of the alphabet, the numbers 0 to 9, and several other symbols (commonly found on a typewriter keyboard), such as the pound sign, the comma, the full stop, and so on. A commonly encountered character set is shown in fig. 2.7. This is known as ASCII (American Standard Code

SP	!	"	#	$	%	&	'	(	)	*	+	,	–	.	/
0	1	2	3	4	5	6	7	8	9	:	;	<	=	>	?
@	A	B	C	D	E	F	G	H	I	J	K	L	M	N	O
P	Q	R	S	T	U	V	W	X	Y	Z	[	\	]	^	_
`	a	b	c	d	e	f	g	h	i	j	k	l	m	n	o
p	q	r	s	t	u	v	w	x	y	z	{	¦	}	~	DEL

Two characters: SP (space) and DEL (delete) are nonprinting.

2.7 The ASCII character set

for Information Interchange). Another set which may be encountered is called EBCDIC (Extended Binary Coded Decimal Interchange Code). An extensive character set will usually provide for both lower-case and upper-case alphabetic characters, and may also comprise Greek symbols used in notation, special symbols, etc.

2.73 Field

A **field** is a group of characters treated as a unit. It corresponds to the attribute in the hierarchy of archaeological data as it is the space in which the particular attribute state of an artefact is entered.

A field has meaning as a data item beyond the meaning of its separate characters, just as a word does. Therefore the height of our pot, e.g. 32.5, may constitute one field in the data; its type, FLAGON, may constitute another. The grid reference of the find spot, TF981195, may be a further field. A field which mixes alphabetic and numeric characters in this way is known as **alphanumeric** or simply, **alphameric**. Note that a field need not just consist of a single word. For example, the field for pot-type could contain two words: STORAGE JAR . In this case the space between the words itself counts as a character. In fact a single field might contain many words. Free comment fields, for data that does not quite fit elsewhere, usually do!

2.74 Record

A **record** is a group of fields treated as a unit. A record contains all fields relating to a single entity. Thus it normally corresponds to the artefact in the archaeological hierarchy. It may also be known as a **case**. A record may be a single line or it may stretch over several lines. It may be split into several sub-records, containing attributes of a similar nature. A single record might comprise one pot with hundreds of fields detailing its attributes. One sub-record might contain those attributes dealing with its dimensions, another those attributes referring to decoration, and so on. In excavation recording, the individual layer or context generally takes the place of the artefact, with one record per context. Its constituents, position, and so on, then comprise its attributes.

2.75 File

A **file** is a group of records treated as a unit. A file usually contains records of similar type representing information with a common purpose. Thus it frequently corresponds to the group of artefacts, or assemblage, in our archaeological hierarchy. For example, all the pots from one site, or all the graves in one cemetery, might be on one file, although this again will depend on the frame of reference of the project. A file might contain several assemblages from one culture or culture group, for example. It might also consist of all artefacts of a particular type, for example all post-built houses, irrespective of assemblage and culture.

2.76 **Data bank**

At the top of the data hierarchy is the **data bank**. Whilst a rigid distinction between file and data bank is not possible, the latter is generally used to refer to a comprehensive file of data or a group of files treated as a unit, and it usually consists of files related in their use or amongst their users. A data bank might consist of one file, or a number of files, for several sites which together comprise a culture; or it might contain all radiocarbon dates for sites of all periods and cultures. Equally, it might consist of files of several different artefact types from a site.

More will be said about characters, fields, and records in chapter 5, and about the management of files and data banks in chapter 6.

NOTES

(1) The statistical search for significant attributes introduces the much debated question of the definition of artefact 'types'. Spaulding (1953; 1960) and Whallon (1972a) describe the use of the chi-square statistic to discover types from lists of attributes. Doran and Hodson (1975, 168) argue that Spaulding's use of the Krieger (1944) formulation of the type as a 'non-random attribute-cluster' is misconceived. One possibility they suggest is to define alternate lists of attributes for the same material and use constellation analysis to choose between them. Brew (1946) argues that there is no single correct classification, and advocates a multiplicity of systems. The whole question is discussed by Hill and Evans (1972).

(2) It may be argued that dating in years B.P. involves a true zero point, as long as the present is taken to mean the present instant in time, and not a conventional point, such as 1950.

(3) Whilst a dichotomy is a qualitative attribute, for statistical purposes it can be treated as a measurement at the interval level. Although an order may not be inherent in the category definitions, either arrangement of the categories satisfies the mathematical requirements of ordering. That is, with only two categories it does not matter which is considered 'high' and which 'low'. The interval-level requirement of equal-sized intervals must also be satisfied because there is only one interval. Therefore, a dichotomy can be treated as a nominal, ordinal, or interval-level measure.

3

HARDWARE

3.1 Introduction

Computer **hardware** is the name given to all of the electronic and mechanical equipment employed in a computer installation. It is distinguished from software which is the collective term for the sequences of instructions, known as programs, which control the operation of the hardware. This chapter aims to provide an introduction to the basic machinery of a computer system while giving more detailed descriptions of those devices which the archaeologist is most likely to encounter. We will examine how these function from the point of view of the user or programmer, and will not be concerned with details of their engineering.

The archaeologist, or indeed any other computer user, who is only interested in using the machine as a tool, may ask whether this is really necessary. In many cases, particularly where existing programs will suffice, it can be argued that knowledge of the hardware need go no further than where to find a terminal, which keys to press and where to collect any printed results. Many potential users may be discouraged by the mistaken belief that they need an extensive knowledge of both hardware and software before venturing near the machine. However, some understanding of the capabilities of the equipment is desirable, in order to make more effective use of a computer system.

In practice, a user may start with a quite minimal understanding of the hardware, but this will usually grow as familiarity with the machine leads to more advanced computing requirements. The reader who has yet to gain **hands-on** experience of using a computer may therefore study sections 3.2 and 3.22 which cover the basic structure of a computer system and the range of types of systems likely to be encountered, before passing quickly over the rest of this chapter. A full understanding of section 3.21 which describes data storage and the binary and hexadecimal number systems need not be considered as essential; indeed, most users rarely need more than a superficial understanding of these topics. In the later sections it will suffice to note simply the functions of the devices which are available and ignore any details of their operation, returning to these at a second reading, or when possible applications are envisaged. The chapter will conclude with a brief discussion of the operating system software which controls the interaction of user, computer and associated devices.

Further details of the operation of the various parts of a computer system may be found in many of the introductory texts on computing science; e.g. NCC (1980) and Fry (1981). For an easily assimilated introduction to this topic see Carey *et al* (1979).

3.2 **The computer**

From the engineering or electronic point of view, all computers are extremely complex machines. This complexity need not, however, concern the user who needs only to visualise the computer as a set of devices which together can perform the basic functions of data processing. The machine must, therefore, be capable of receiving data and programs, processing the data according to the instructions contained in the program, and then producing results in a form which can be assimilated. In addition, it is desirable in any practical machine that there is a facility for storing data and programs which may be used repeatedly.

Fig. 3.1 shows a block diagram of a typical computer system. The machine consists of four elements corresponding to the functions required above. At the heart of the system is the **Central Processing Unit** or **CPU**, where the program instructions are executed. A user's program and some or all of the data may be held in the CPU **memory** unit during execution, but this has a limited capacity. Long term storage requirements are satisfied by the **backing store** using **magnetic tape** and **discs**. Communication between the user and the machine is provided by **Input** and **Output devices**. In some cases these two functions may be combined in one piece of equipment, as in a conventional

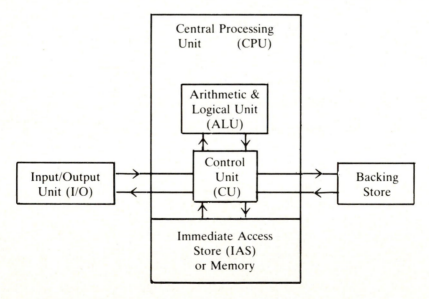

Fig. 3.1 Block diagram of a computer system showing CPU, backing store and input/output units.

terminal, consisting of a keyboard for input and either printer or visual display for output. Both functions are normally grouped under the term **Input/Output** or **I/O** devices.

The devices used for backing storage and I/O are frequently referred to as **peripheral units** or simply **peripherals**. All of these are examples of **on-line** equipment, that is devices which are operated under the control of the CPU. **Off-line** devices for punching cards or recording data on magnetic tape may be available to users at large computer installations. These are independent units, not connected to the CPU, which are used to prepare data for subsequent reading by input devices.

The primary concern of the archaeological computer user will normally be with these I/O devices, and the extent to which users need to be concerned with the backing store will depend on individual requirements and the type of machine used. Rarely, if ever, will the archaeologist require more than the most basic understanding of the CPU. Sections 3.3 ff of this chapter reflect these priorities. First, however, we should consider how a computer holds data and programs in its store.

3.21 Data storage

The devices used by a computer to store data (which in this section should be taken to include programs) are not capable of representing alphanumeric characters (i.e. letters, digits, spaces and punctuation marks) in the same form as we do. It would require some very complex processing for them to do so. Instead, all information held in the machine is stored in **binary** form.

The binary number system uses only two digits, 0 and 1, rather than the ten, 0 to 9, of the more familiar decimal system. Thus the **base** of the binary number system is two rather than ten. To see how this works, consider the decimal number 165. We know that any such number may be broken down into units, tens, hundreds, etc:

$$165 = (1 \times 100) + (6 \times 10) + (5 \times 1)$$

These separate elements are all powers of ten, the base of the decimal number system:

$$100 = 10^2 \qquad 10 = 10^1 \qquad 1 = 10^0$$

So we may express our number, 165, as:

$$165 = (1 \times 10^2) + (6 \times 10^1) + (5 \times 10^0)$$

or, in tabular form:

10^2	10^1	10^0
1	6	5

In the same way, any whole positive number could be used as the base of a number system. Within the computer, numbers to the base two are used, and

Table 3.1

ASCII character set. All 'control' characters are known by a two or three character mnemonic. Those marked with an asterisk are the most frequently used, the remainder are often assigned a new meaning to suit hardware or software requirements. On most keyboards, a control character is made by depressing the control key together with the key for the character in the third column of the table which appears on the same row. For example, BEL is produced by the combination of the 'control' and 'G' keys.

The binary value of any character may be found from the table by combining the two most significant digits from the top of the column with the five least significant shown at the start of each row.

For example the binary value of the character 'T' is found by combining 10 and 10100 to give 1010100.

| 5 least signif. bits | 2 most significant bits | | | | | | | | | | | |
| | 00 | | | 01 | | | 10 | | | 11 | | |
	dec	hex	char	dec	hex	char	dec	hex	char	dec	hex	char
00000	0	00	NUL	32	20	sp	64	40	@	96	60	`
00001	1	01	SOH	33	21	!	65	41	A	97	61	a
00010	2	02	SOT	34	22	"	66	42	B	98	62	b
00011	3	03	ETX	35	23	#	67	43	C	99	63	c
00100	4	04	EOT	36	24	$	68	44	D	100	64	d
00101	5	05	ENQ	37	25	%	69	45	E	101	65	e
00110	6	06	ACK	38	26	&	70	46	F	102	66	f
00111	7	07	BEL	39	27	'	71	47	G	103	67	g
01000	8	08	BS	40	28	(	72	48	H	104	68	h
01001	9	09	HT	41	29	)	73	49	I	105	69	i
01010	10	0A	AF	42	2A	*	74	4A	J	106	6A	j
01011	11	0B	VT	43	2B	+	75	4B	K	107	6B	k
01100	12	0C	FF	44	2C	,	76	4C	L	108	6C	l
01101	13	0D	CR	45	2D	-	77	4D	M	109	6D	m
01110	14	0E	SO	46	2E	.	78	4E	N	110	6E	n
01111	15	0F	SI	47	2F	/	79	4F	O	111	6F	o
10000	16	10	DLE	48	30	0	80	50	P	112	70	p
10001	17	11	DC1	49	31	1	81	51	Q	113	71	q
10010	18	12	DC2	50	32	2	82	52	R	114	72	r
10011	19	13	DC3	51	33	3	83	53	S	115	73	s
10100	20	14	DC4	52	34	4	84	54	T	116	74	t
10101	21	15	NAK	53	35	5	85	55	U	117	75	u
10110	22	16	SYN	54	36	6	86	56	V	118	76	v
10111	23	17	ETB	55	37	7	87	57	W	119	77	w
11000	24	18	CAN	56	38	8	88	58	X	120	78	x
11001	25	19	EM	57	39	9	89	59	Y	121	79	y
11010	26	1A	SUB	58	3A	:	90	5A	Z	122	7A	z
11011	27	1B	ESC	59	3B	;	91	5B	[	123	7B	{
11100	28	1C	FS	60	3C	›	92	5C	/	124	7C	|
11101	29	1D	GS	61	3D	=	93	5D	]	125	7D	}
11110	30	1E	RS	62	3E	‹	94	5E	^	126	7E	~
11111	31	1F	US	63	3F	?	95	5F	—	127	7F	DEL

Key to control character mnemonics

NUL	Null	VT	Vertical Tabulation	SYN	Synchronous idle
SOH	Start of heading	FF	Form feed*	ETB	End of transmission
SOT	Start of text	CR	Carriage return*	CAN	Cancel
ETX	End of Text	SO	Shift out	EM	End of medium
EOT	End of transmission	SI	Shift in	SUB	Substitute
ENQ	Enquiry	DLE	Data link escape	ESC	Escape*
ACK	Acknowledgement	DC1	Device control 1	FS	File separator
BEL	Sound bell or buzzer*	DC2	Device control 2	GS	Group separator
BS	Backspace*	DC3	Device control 3	RS	Record separator
HT	Horizontal tabulation*	DC4	Device control 4	US	Unit separator
LF	Line feed*	NAK	Negative acknowledge	DEL	Delete*

are represented, for instance, by electronic switches being either on or off. Thus presence of a voltage or current may represent 1 and absence, 0. We need not concern ourselves with details of how this is achieved. Instead, let us see how 165 is expressed in the binary number system.

The separate elements of a binary number are all powers of two, the base of the number system:

$$16 = 2^4 \quad 8 = 2^3 \quad 4 = 2^2 \quad 2 = 2^1 \quad 1 = 2^0$$

The largest power of two smaller than 165 is 128 or 2^7. Dividing by 128 we obtain a remainder of 37. The largest power of two smaller than 37 is 32 or 2^5. Dividing by 32 we are left with 5. This we divide by 4 or 2^2 and are left with 1. So we may express 165 as:

$$(1 \times 2^7) + (1 \times 2^5) + (1 \times 2^2) + (1 \times 2^0)$$

or

2^7	2^6	2^5	2^4	2^3	2^2	2^1	2^0
1	0	1	0	0	1	0	1

Thus the binary representation of the decimal number 165 requires eight **binary digits** or **bits**. To avoid confusion when dealing with different number systems, the base value is normally written as a subscript following the number:

$$165_{10} = 10100101_2$$

Eight bits can be used to represent the 256 whole numbers from 0 to 255. Larger numbers require proportionately more bits. Negative numbers can be included by using one bit to indicate the sign. In which case, eight bits can be used to represent the numbers -128 to $+127$. Thus, the range of whole (**integer**) numbers which a computer can store in any one location within its memory will depend on the number of bits available. This number, known as the **word length**, is usually fixed for any one machine and is generally between eight and sixty-four. The word length is frequently a multiple of eight, the unit of eight bits being known as a **Byte**.

The method of storage of **real numbers** is somewhat different to that used for integers. A number such as 248.336 cannot be converted directly into binary form suitable for the machine as there is no means of representing the decimal point. However, if the number is rewritten as 0.248336×10^3, it could be represented as the two integer numbers 248336 and 3. The original number could then be reconstructed when needed, simply by inserting a decimal point in front of the first integer (or **mantissa**) and then raising to the power of the second integer (or **exponent**). The same technique is used in the computer to store any binary real number; both mantissa and exponent are stored as binary integers, either together in different parts of the same word, or in adjacent words. Because of this use of mantissa and exponent form, real numbers are usually referred to in computing jargon as **floating point numbers**. It is important to realise that the arithmetic precision of a machine is not determined by its word length. Instead it is up to the programmer, or more frequently to the programming language being used, to determine how many words will be used to store numeric values. Thus a micro-computer with an eight bit word will usually be programmed to use two, four or eight words in which to store a numeric quantity.

So far we have been concerned only with the storage of numbers, but computers are also capable of storing and processing alphabetic data. How then are alphabetic characters stored? In section 2.72 we introduced the ASCII character set, consisting of upper and lower case letters, the digits 0 to 9, and a number of punctuation marks. This character set has a total of 95 printable characters, including the space. In addition there are 33 non-printable or **control characters**. These allow for functions such as the carriage return, line feed and backspace found on most electric typewriters, together with a number of other functions used in transmitting data between computer and peripheral devices. This total of 128 unique characters is represented in the machine as a seven bit binary number (table 3.1). Thus one or more characters may be held in each stored word depending on the word length. In many systems, especially micro-computers, which use the ASCII code, each character uses one byte for storage. The extra bit is frequently used for some special purpose such as error checking or to allow the use of an extra 128 special characters. Many micro-computers use this facility to allow simple graphical display using 'characters' which consist of basic shapes such as lines, rectangles and triangles, while others allow the user to define a special set of extra characters. Different character sets may be encountered using six, seven or eight bits per character.

As all three of these storage methods, integer, floating point and character, result simply in binary integers, the software must tell the machine how to treat the contents of a word. High-level programming languages (see chapter 4) normally provide for this.

The amount of data which may be stored in any memory device, that is, its storage capacity, is expressed in either bytes or words. In most cases, the numbers involved are very large so it is convenient to use the units **KiloByte** and **MegaByte** (or **Kilo-** and **Megaword**), usually abbreviated to **KB** and **MB** (or **KW** and **MW**). Unlike most other systems of units, the prefixes K and M do not mean exactly one thousand or one million; in computing terms, 1K equals 1024 and 1M equals 1024K. This may at first seem strange, but it should be realised that 1000_{10} is not a round number in binary. The closest binary round number is 2^{10} or $100\ 0000\ 0000_2$ which is 1024 decimal. Note that, just as we often employ commas to make decimal numbers more readable, many programmers prefer to write binary numbers with spaces between each group of three or four digits.

Table 3.2

Equivalent representation of numbers in decimal, binary and hexadecimal notation.

Decimal	Binary	Hexadecimal	
0	0	0	
1	1	1	
2	10	2	
3	11	3	
4	100	4	
5	101	5	
6	110	6	
7	111	7	
8	1000	8	
9	1001	9	
10	1010	A	
11	1011	B	
12	1100	C	
13	1101	D	
14	1110	E	
15	1111	F	
16	1 0000	10	
.	.	.	
32	10 0000	20	
.	.	.	
48	11 0000	30	
.	.	.	
127	111 1111	7F	
.	.	.	
255	1111 1111	FF	
.	.	.	
1024	100 0000 0000	400	(=1K)
.	.	.	
65535	1111 1111 1111 1111	FFFF	(=64K-1)

Whilst binary representation may be necessary to a computer, it is hardly convenient for human use. To avoid this problem, programmers who are concerned with operations at the machine level will frequently use **hexadecimal** notation. This involves numbers with a base of sixteen, represented by the characters 0 to 9 plus A to F. Thus A to F are used to represent the decimal numbers 10 to 15. Sixteen is the range of numbers possible in four bits, thus a byte may be represented by two hexadecimal characters, sixteen bits by four, and so on. Table 3.2 shows equivalent representations of some numbers under all three notations. It will be clear that the use of spaces in binary notation greatly eases translation between binary and hexadecimal forms; each group of four binary digits corresponds directly to a single hexadecimal digit. Readers who are inclined to pursue the topics covered in this section may also encounter the **octal** number system. This has a base of eight and employs the digits 0–7. One octal digit corresponds to three bits.

3.2 An ICL 2966 mainframe computer

3.22 **Types of computer**

Computers come in a wide range of both size and processing power, and are usually grouped under the headings of **mainframe**, **mini-** and **micro-computer**. Whilst the more enthusiastic prophets of modern technology would claim that such divisions are, or soon will be, totally redundant, it is perhaps more realistic to state that the upper limit of processing power in each group is being steadily raised, thus tending to blur the distinctions between them.

To the user, greater processing power is usually apparent as an increase in the speed of execution of programs. Thus, in general, mainframe computers will be found to be faster than mini-computers, which are in turn usually faster than micro-computers. These differences in performance result from two main factors: firstly, the speed at which instructions can be fetched from memory and executed by the CPU, and secondly, the size of the unit of data, the word length, on which the required process can be performed. Whilst the former is largely a matter of electronic technology, computers with a greater word length will generally be able to fetch more instructions at any one time, and will therefore operate more quickly.

3.221 **Mainframe computers**

Fig. 3.2 shows a typical medium-sized mainframe computer, in this case, an

International Computers Limited model 2966, more commonly known as an ICL 2966. Most mainframes are known by similar names comprising a manufacturer's initials and a model number: for example, the IBM 3081 or the DEC 20. The machine is contained within a number of separate cabinets connected by underfloor cables. At the heart of the system are the Central Processing Unit and main memory or **store**. These are located in the plain-fronted cabinets. Also visible in the photograph are **disc** and **tape units** for backing storage and the **operator's console** with **visual display unit** and **keyboard**. The functions each of these units will be described below.

Such machines require purpose-built accommodation with elaborate air-conditioning and special power supplies. A large staff of operators, engineers and systems programmers is needed in order to operate them, together with a number of people to help and advise users. Archaeologists will generally encounter mainframes in the central computing departments of government and educational institutions. They will, therefore, be just one group of many who use such a machine and may find that their requirements conflict with those of others. In some cases the computer professionals may find the archaeological applications sufficiently stimulating for them to devote more time to them than their job strictly requires, but archaeologists should not assume that this will always be true.

Most current mainframe computers employ a word length of between thirty-two and sixty-four bits, although the most powerful machines, such as the Cyber 205, use a variable length word, or **vector**, of up to 64Kbits. The relatively large word size, together with very short memory access times, allows mainframe computers to be extremely fast, thus allowing many users to share the system.

3.222 Mini-computers

Mini-computers are generally of smaller physical size than mainframes, ranging from desk-sized units to a number of cabinets filling a small room (fig. 3.3). Their traditional application has been in scientific laboratories for monitoring experiments and performing complex, repetitive calculations. A well-known example of this type of machine is the Digital Equipment Corporation's PDP-11, which has long been available in a wide range of configurations. Frequently such a machine would serve only a small number of users and perform a limited number of tasks. Users could be accommodated in turn, with no pressure for the machine to be available to more than one person at once. Thus the task of operating the machine would be relatively simple, and would frequently be performed by the users themselves.

More recently, mini-computers have been applied to commercial and administrative data processing tasks. In these latter applications, the need for more extensive backing storage, and the ability to service a number of

3.3 A GEC 4082 mini-computer

individual users at the same time, have made these machines functionally equivalent to small mainframe computers.

Most mini-computers use a sixteen or thirty-two bit word length. Hence the most powerful have similar capabilities to the smaller mainframes, and have tended to supplant them in many applications. However, there is no generally agreed clear distinction between mini and mainframe at this level. Many machines have been called mini-computers simply because they are physically smaller than the functionally equivalent mainframes which they have replaced. Many of the smaller mini-computers will work satisfactorily in any reasonably clean environment with the minimum of special power supply equipment. Those used in data processing applications are frequently provided with some air-conditioning and auxiliary power generators in order to minimise problems with backing store disc units and to protect data during power cuts.

3.223 Micro-computers

The advent of the large scale integrated circuit, in which a very large number of normally discrete electronic components are combined on a small silicon chip, has made it possible to incorporate many of the functional elements of a computer in a small physical space. Such devices also have the advantage of a

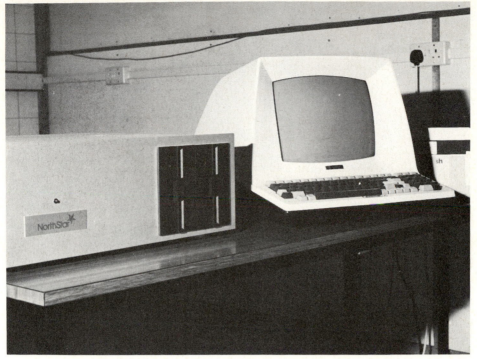

3.4 The North Star Horizon, an 8 bit micro-computer

far lower power consumption than their discrete component equivalents. One such device is the **microprocessor**, a single chip containing the basic elements of a CPU. The major drawback with these complex integrated circuits is that, generally, they are slower in operation than their discrete counterparts.

The first microprocessor was introduced in 1970, but it was not until the second half of that decade that devices suitable for use in a data processing computer became widely available. Subsequently there has been a rapid development of the micro-computer based upon such chips. The small size and low power requirements of micro-computers enable them to be located on a desk top. Their low cost removes the pressure for continuous and efficient usage normally associated with larger machines. Unlike larger computers, micro-computers are within the budget of many archaeological organisations. With these machines available to many people with little or no experience of or interest in computing, it has been necessary to ensure that they are simple to operate, for the user must also act as 'operator'.

Many of the micro-computers in current use employ an eight bit word. Typical of these machines is the North Star Horizon shown in fig. 3.4. The more recent sixteen bit machines, such as the ACT Sirius 1 shown in fig. 3.5, are now rapidly becoming widespread. Ultimately the acceptance of any

3.5 The ACT Sirius 1, a 16 bit micro-computer

machine depends on the availability of suitable software, and the entry of the larger computer manufacturers, including IBM, DEC and Wang, into the micro-computer market at this level has provided a strong stimulus to the software producers. It remains to be seen whether sixteen bit micro-computers will surpass the popularity of the smaller machines before thirty-two bit micros are readily available.

The major practical advantages held by sixteen and thirty-two bit machines over their eight bit predecessors lies in the greater amount of memory which they can directly access, and in their higher speed. In most eight bit machines memory size is limited to 64KB, whereas 1 to 16MB is not unusual in the more powerful machines. This larger capacity increases their ability to handle large amounts of data or more complex programs without excessive use of the backing store. The eight bit machine need not be any less precise in its arithmetic. Precision, as was pointed out in section 3.21, is a function of the software. However, all other things being equal, the greater the word length, the faster will be the execution of arithmetic functions at the same level of precision.

It is perhaps worth emphasising that many of the functions which archaeologists may require of computers can be performed quite adequately on a good eight bit micro-computer. For the preparation of reports using a

3.6 The Epson HX-20, a small portable 8 bit micro-computer (photo Epson UK Ltd)

word processing package such as WordStar (see section 7.4), or the manipulation of small data files, such a machine will normally prove quite adequate. The limitations of eight bit machines may, however, prove frustrating when attempting statistical analyses on large data matrices. Here, the increased storage and speed of the larger machines is advantageous. Similarly, for image processing applications, the power of the sixteen or thirty-two bit machine is essential. Until now, it has been necessary to employ mini-computers in such tasks. Wilcock (1982) describes a system of artefact profile capture using a television camera interfaced to an eight bit machine. This has demonstrated some of the possibilities for such work, but we anticipate that its full potential will only be realised on larger micro-computers.

The suitability of micro-computers for information storage and retrieval applications again depends on the amount of data to be stored and processed. Although less sophisticated and slower than similar applications run on larger machines, the ease of use and convenience of micro-computers makes them appropriate for use with smaller specialised data banks. Moffett and Webb (1982) describe such a system for storing and retrieving radiocarbon dates, and the use of micro-computers for excavation recording is discussed by several contributors in Stewart (1980).

Small hand-held micro-computers, such as that shown in fig. 3.6, are particularly suited to collecting data in the field. Data is stored either on cassette tape or in internal memory, and may be recalled and transferred to a larger machine for long term storage and processing.

3.23 Computer networks

A computer network consists of a number of processing units which are linked together by some means of communication. Historically, computers have been regarded as large centralised facilities. Remote access to such systems has been possible, but all storage and processing has usually been confined to a single site. The increasing use of computers in commercial applications has highlighted the need for local processing power and local data storage as an alternative, or an addition, to a large central installation. Such systems permit work to continue locally should the central machine fail. They allow local users to have immediate access to, and a large degree of control over, their own data. The decreasing cost of processors has contributed to the development of these network systems by removing the economic necessity of concentrating resources.

Networks exist, and are planned, in many shapes and sizes. Groups of small micro-computers may be linked together in order to share a number of more expensive peripherals such as printers, plotters or colour graphics displays. This approach is becoming popular for computer education in schools. The separate processing elements, or **nodes**, of these local networks are usually all located at the same site and are connected by wire or fibre-optic cables. Indeed, network processors may all be located in the same cabinet. Whilst this may at first seem contrary to the idea of distributed processors in networks, it can present a convenient means of providing separate micro-computer facilities for a number of people who need to share some data and peripherals. Thus a multi-user system may be developed without the degradation in performance which occurs when several users share a single processor.

At the other end of the scale, the recently inaugurated 'Project Universe' uses communications satellites to connect a number of large mainframes in educational and research establishments. This network is further extended by the inclusion of local networks in which a large number of linked processors share each satellite ground station. Communication between the computers of this system takes place at a rate one million bits per second which is about one hundred times faster than can be achieved over a telephone link (news article, *Wireless World*, April 1983, 55).

Between these extremes, networks have been established using the public telephone system or leased data links for communication. Private data networks have existed for some time, but the development of public data networks holds out the possibilities of standardisation and increased availability, together with far faster and more efficient communication than was possible using telephone or telex systems.

3.3 The Central Processing Unit

The CPU consists of three main elements: a **control unit**, an **Arithmetic and Logical Unit**, and a **memory** (fig. 3.1). Both program and data are normally held in the memory during program execution. The control unit takes program instructions in sequence from the memory and acts upon them. These instructions may involve moving data from one part of memory to another, branching to a different memory location before collecting the next instruction, or performing arithmetic or logical transformations on data.

The terms **Immediate Access Store** and **Random Access Memory** are also used for the CPU memory, the latter especially in connection with micro-computers. Both of these terms are frequently abbreviated to their initial letters, **IAS** and **RAM**. Whilst the name IAS clearly reflects the higher speed of access compared with that of backing store, the meaning of RAM is less apparent. The word 'random' implies that all memory elements may be accessed with equal speed, irrespective of the order in which they are selected. As will be seen in the next section, this is not necessarily the case with all storage systems.

Micro-computer users may also encounter the **ROM**. This is a **Read Only Memory**, the contents of which cannot normally be changed. Programs held in these devices are not lost when the machine is switched off. Their main purpose is to hold the instructions for the initial start up procedure of the machine, including the programs necessary to load the main operating programs, or operating system, from the backing store. A wide variety of such memory devices may be met, particularly in sales brochures, including the **PROM**, **EPROM**, **EEPROM** and **UVEPROM**. To the user, all are essentially similar.

A number of machines, particularly the small portables, are provided with **non-volatile RAM**. This has the advantage of retaining stored data when the machine is switched off. Re-chargeable batteries are used to ensure that the memory unit remains powered at all times.

3.4 Backing storage

The memory unit in the CPU is used only for storage of program and data during program execution. Longer term storage is provided by the backing store, invariably by recording data on magnetic media. Two principal methods exist, the first employing **magnetic tape** and the second, **magnetic discs**. Tapes and most types of discs can be removed from their respective I/O devices, thus allowing large libraries of data and programs to be built up. Only those actually needed at any time are mounted on the tape or disc drives and are accessible to the computer.

3.7 A magnetic tape unit (photo ICL)

3.41 **Magnetic tape**
A typical magnetic tape unit is shown in fig. 3.7. Outwardly they are similar in appearance to conventional audio tape recorders. The tape used is normally half an inch wide and is held on reels in lengths of up to 2400 feet. A typical tape format will employ nine parallel tracks allowing one character or byte to be recorded in a frame across the width of the tape. These character frames are recorded at a fixed interval giving typical recording densities of 800 or 1600 bits per inch. Magnetic tape is a **serial access medium**. Access to data on the tape is performed by reading through the tape until the required position

is reached, then reading or writing the data. It is not possible to search backwards through a tape. Instead, in order to read from an earlier part of the tape, it is necessary to rewind to the start.

Data is transferred between computer and tape unit in **blocks**. These are recorded on the tape with gaps between them to allow the drive space in which to start and stop. This ensures that the tape is travelling past the read/write head at the correct speed during data transfer. Each block has additional bytes to inform the machine when the end of a block has been reached. Each tape has a **header block** which contains such information as tape serial number, names, lengths and positions of data files held on the tape, etc. There is also usually a **trailer block** or label at the end of the tape to inform the system that the end of the tape has been reached.

Tape drives are relatively slow. This presents problems when access is required to data near the end of a tape, or if the order in which data is stored does not correspond with that in which it must be processed. For this reason, tape drives are suitable only where serial access is appropriate to the task in hand. A major use of tape is in **archiving**. The tape is used to make **back-up** copies of the data recorded on disc. This is normally done either daily or weekly on a three-tape basis, the tapes being rotated so that at any one time there are three previous generations available. The tape holding the oldest generation is re-used each time archiving is performed. In this way it is possible to recover data which might have been overwritten on the disc, whether by a user's mistake or as a result of some system error. Normally this process is under the control of the operating staff.

Many large computer installations have insufficient space available on magnetic discs to accommodate all of the programs and data for each of its users. To overcome this problem, each user will be allocated a tape. The required data will be copied from this tape onto a disc as requested by the user at the start of a session. If the data is modified, or new data is created, it will be written back to tape at the end of the session.

Whilst such a tape system is appropriate to mainframe and mini-computers, a much simpler system is found on many small micro-computers. This records data on conventional domestic cassette tapes. Although this system is extremely slow, and usually of little use on machines intended for serious tasks, it may be preferable to use such a method on micro-computers employed in on-site data recording. In such applications portability may be an asset and disc units may not be able to operate reliably under dusty conditions or where there are large variations in ambient temperature.

In the case of micro-computer systems using magnetic disc backing store, archiving is normally performed by making back-up copies on floppy discs rather than tape. Some machines, however, employ high speed tape cassettes similar to those used in domestic video recorders for making archive copies of large capacity disc units. On micro-computers archiving must normally be performed by the user. The importance of making back-up copies of all valuable programs and data on such machines cannot be over-emphasised, and is often only realised by an inexperienced user when it is too late. A single human error or machine malfunction can sometimes result in the loss of many hours of work.

3.42 **Magnetic discs**

The serial access method used with magnetic tape imposes severe restrictions on the speed at which data may be accessed by requiring that data must be read in the same order as that in which it was written. Whilst this method may be appropriate for many data processing applications, it would preclude any attempts to retrieve many small items of information from large files of data rapidly without prior knowledge of their location on the tape. Serial access would entail intolerable delays and extremely inefficient use of computer time. This problem can be overcome using the **direct access method** employed by magnetic disc units.

The surfaces of a disc are coated with a magnetic material similar to that used on tapes. This is divided into a number of concentric circles known as **tracks**, on which the data is recorded. Each track may be divided into several **sectors** each holding the same fixed number of characters. Any disc record will therefore have an address, which can be used to access it directly. The disc revolves at high speed and data is transferred by a read/write head mounted on an assembly which can be stepped in and out to select the required track. In this way, any sector may be accessed as required. The speed of such a direct access system is limited only by the speed of rotation of the disc and the rate at which the head can be stepped from track to track.

Magnetic discs come in a wide variety of types and storage capacities. The discs may be fixed or exchangeable, rigid or flexible, with capacities ranging between about 70KB and 1000MB, but in all cases the method of data storage is similar. A number of exchangeable disc units can be seen in fig. 3.2. These particular devices employ removeable disc packs each with a storage capacity of 200MB. The head assembly can be retracted in order to exchange disc packs. Similar, but frequently lower capacity, units are used on many mini-computers.

The separation between head and disc is extremely small. It is therefore essential that they are operated in a clean atmosphere; even a smoke particle could cause severe damage to a disc surface or head if trapped between them. Thus exchangeable packs are frequently impractical outside of an air con-ditioned computer room.

In micro-computer applications where a large capacity backing store is required, a similar device known as a **Winchester** disc is often used. These have several small diameter rigid discs. Unlike the exchangeable pack, Winchester discs are fixed within a sealed chamber. This permits their use in environments which might be hostile to exchangeable discs. Most Winchester discs in current use have a storage capacity between 5 and 40 MB, although this figure is constantly rising as new developments occur.

The **floppy disc** employed in many micro- and small mini-computers is less sensitive to such problems, as it employs a wider separation between head and disc. Nevertheless, this does not mean that they can be expected to operate reliably anywhere more dusty than a normal modern office environment. Floppy discs come in three different sizes. The first to be introduced was the eight inch disc; originally intended for loading operating systems and diagnostic programs into larger machines, it became popular on many early micro-computers. The smaller 5.25 inch mini-floppy as first introduced was limited to less than 100KB of data but subsequent advances have made capacities of 1MB or more available. Consequently the mini-floppy has become the most popular size and the number of new machines with eight inch discs has declined. The more recently introduced three inch micro-floppy may, in time, supplant the mini-floppy.

Several manufacturers have developed exchangeable hard discs for micro-computers. Most of these consist of small discs enclosed in a rigid envelope, which is inserted into a drive unit of similar appearance to the normal floppy drive. These offer the data storage capacity of a Winchester, combined with some of the advantages of the floppy disc.

The benefit of hindsight makes the draft standard recommendation of the MDA working party (Stewart 1980), which recommended archaeologists to adopt eight inch discs, now seem somewhat premature. We would, however, agree that discs with lower storage densities tend to be more reliable under adverse conditions. In practice, differences between the recording formats used on many machines mean that it is often impossible to exchange discs between different micro-computers. Indeed, individual variation in the alignment of heads frequently precludes exchange of discs between machines of the same model. For this reason it seems unneccessary to include a specification of disc format in such recommendations. Experience suggests that exchange of data using either direct connection between machines or a modem (see section 3.53) to communicate over telephone lines is quite adequate for most purposes.

An alternative to magnetic discs using the same optical technology as that developed for video discs has been introduced, but has yet to become widespread. This uses a laser to burn data into a plastic disc. Reading is also performed using laser light reflected from the burnt in data. Unlike the case of magnetic discs, it is not normally possible to record new data onto a previously used area of the disc. However, the low cost and enormous storage capacity of this medium mean that the disc may be used until full, writing to unused areas as necessary. When full, the latest generation of data could be transferred to a new disc. It would then only be necessary to retain the old disc for archival purposes, otherwise it could be thrown away.

An erasable form of optical disc is currently under development. Rather than burning the data into the surface of the disc, the writing laser is used to alter the reflective properties of the surface coating. If this technique can be perfected it is possible that the current dominance of magnetic storage media will be challenged.

3.5 **Input/Output devices**

The input and output devices form the interface between the human world and that of the machine. A wide variety of these are available, some catering only for input, some only for output, and others fulfilling both functions. In all but the smallest computer systems the transfer of data to and from the input and output units is usually controlled by a separate control unit dedicated to this purpose. The rate of data transmission between CPU and peripherals is normally very slow in comparison with that at which data is processed. Thus direct connection would entail the CPU control unit spending much of its time waiting for input to arrive, or for an output device to be ready to accept more data. The function of the peripheral controller is therefore to act as both a **buffer** and a **multiplexor** between CPU and peripherals. As a buffer, it provides a temporary store for transmitted data, passing it character by character to and from the peripherals. As a multiplexor, it deals with the routing of data between devices. An entire line of input data or instructions may be assembled until it can be transmitted at high speed to the CPU. Similarly the CPU need only be concerned with passing output a line at a time to the buffer, irrespective of whether the peripheral for which they are destined is ready to accept characters. The multiplexing function of the peripheral controller allows a large number of I/O devices to be connected to the CPU. Again, making use of the large speed differential between processor and peripherals, the multiplexor switches rapidly between the various I/O units checking for incoming characters and readiness to accept output.

Most remotely located I/O devices are linked to the computer via a **serial** connection. These should normally be configured according to either the RS232-C or the V24 standard specification, although the more recent RS423 may also be encountered. Whilst there are a number of technical differences, the user can usually regard these specifications as identical. Data is sent one bit at a time along a single wire in each direction. Extra control wires may be used to indicate that a device is busy, etc, but in their simplest form the RS232 and V24 serial communication links require only three wires; one data line in each direction plus a common return wire. The speed at which data is passed over such a link is known as the **Baud rate**. A speed of 300 Baud represents 300 bits per second, which is equivalent to about 30 bytes or characters per

3.8 A typical video terminal (VDU)

second. Most serial communication is performed at speeds between 300 and 9600 Baud, but both lower and higher speeds are sometimes used.

Parallel interfaces may also be encountered, especially by users of micro-computers. These pass an entire byte or word in parallel over a number of wires, using one wire for each bit. Additional wires are used to signal when a device is ready or busy. Parallel communication can be much faster than serial, but is only practicable for short distance communication in view of the complexity and expense of the required cables. Parallel connections are for this reason usually only employed inside the machine for communication between, for example, the CPU and memory. The term **bus** is frequently applied to such connections. The popular S100 bus for micro-computers uses 100 separate lines for communication between separate parts of the machine. The advantage of such a standardised system is that separate plug-in units may be obtained from many different manufacturers, enabling a computer to be expanded to suit the user's requirements.

3.51 **Terminals**

The user's normal means of communication with the computer is by means of a **terminal**. These usually consist of a **Visual Display Unit (VDU)**, which is similar to a television screen, and a keyboard unit like that found on an electric typewriter.

Fig. 3.8 shows a typical modern terminal of this type, and fig. 3.9 shows the

3.9 A keyboard

layout of a keyboard. Whilst the basic alphanumeric keys are in the same position as on most typewriters, it will be seen that there are a number of extra keys to cover the full range of available characters. Many keyboards include a separate numeric key pad similar to those on some telephones and pocket calculators. Unfortunately, there is no agreed standard for keyboard layout other than for the basic alphanumerics. As with typewriters, the position of the various punctuation marks etc. varies widely. Where the user has to make use of whichever terminal is available, this can prove very frustrating. The major difference between a terminal keyboard and that of a typewriter is that the former provides three levels of shift rather than two. As on a typewriter, there is a shift key for obtaining upper case characters, but there is also a control key which allows the unprintable characters to be sent. On the keyboard shown in fig 3.9 the control key is labelled 'ALT'. Certain control characters such as the line feed, backspace and carriage return are available on separate keys, but the remainder are obtained by pressing the control key and a letter key together. Thus, for instance, the function of a typewriter tab key can be obtained on many terminals by the combination of the control and 'I' keys.

Characters on the VDU are built up from a rectangular matrix of illuminated dots, usually ranging in size from 5×7 to 10×12 dots. Most VDUs provide about 24 lines each holding 80 characters. The characters to be displayed are stored in a small memory unit, each location of which corresponds to one character position on the screen. The screen is scanned by an electron beam, just as in a television, which is turned on only when an illuminated dot is required. In this way a monochrome picture, usually of white, green or amber according to the type of tube, is built up against a dark background. Fig. 3.10 shows a magnified view of part of a VDU screen in which the individual dots are clearly visible. Some VDUs will also display characters at two or more different intensities, and full colour displays are frequently found on micro-computers. Whilst most VDUs are designed

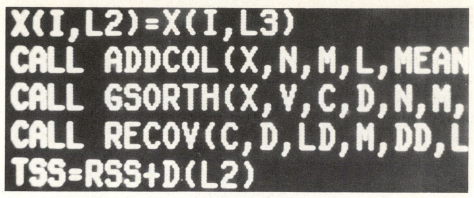

```
X(I,L2)=X(I,L3)
CALL ADDCOL(X,N,M,L,MEAN
CALL GSORTH(X,V,C,D,N,M,
CALL RECOV(C,D,LD,M,DD,L
TSS=RSS+D(L2)
```

3.10 Close-up of VDU screen showing how characters are composed of a number of individual dots

simply to display characters, others are available on which graphical information, ranging from line drawings to pictures using multiple intensities or colours, may be produced. These will be described more fully in section 3.74.

Whilst many micro-computers use video terminals connected to the processor via a serial link, some use a parallel connected keyboard together with a **memory-mapped** VDU. The memory unit of such a display forms part of the immediate access store of the processor. Thus the CPU has direct access to the screen, and the characters displayed on the screen correspond directly to the bytes held in a part of the memory. This permits far more rapid updating of screen contents by the CPU, but is not suited to applications requiring remote terminals. The major use of memory-mapped displays is in systems which make extensive use of the VDU to display graphics. On many of the smaller micro-computers, this system may use up a large proportion of the available memory, leaving little room for programs and data. More sophisticated machines provide additional memory for the display, thus overcoming this problem.

3.52 Tele-typewriter

The term **tele-typewriter**, or frequently just **teletype**, refers to a type of terminal in which some form of printer is used rather than a VDU. Before the widespread introduction of the VDU these devices were the standard means of communicating with the computer; nowadays they are less common. The older generation of tele-typewriters were extremely noisy machines, and their printing speed was very slow. The devices used today tend to be far more sophisticated, usually incorporating a relatively quiet dot-matrix or high quality daisy-wheel printer (see section 3.73). They are most useful when a small quantity of printed output is required urgently, especially when the alternative may be a long wait for output from a central line printer. A

3.11 'DecWriter' terminal

typical modern terminal of this type, incorporating a dot-matrix printer, is shown in fig. 3.11.

3.53 **Modem**
Whereas most I/O devices are connected directly to a CPU housed in the same or an adjacent building, the need frequently arises for them to be located at a **remote site**. In a commercial environment, a central computer system may be accessed by terminals located in branch offices. Similarly, in a university, terminals may be located in buildings away from the immediate confines of a campus. Where the distances involved are relatively short, direct connection may be feasible, but in many cases it is necessary to make use of the public telephone network.

Telephone systems cannot transmit data in the form normally used between computers and peripherals; firstly because they designed primarily for speech communication, and secondly because the high level of spurious noise would lead to an unacceptable number of errors. To overcome these problems, a device known as a **modem** is employed. This device is connected between the terminal or computer and the telephone line. The modem converts the stream of data into an audio signal (MOdulation) for transmission and decodes the sounds into binary values (DEModulation) at the receiving end. This is simply achieved by using separate tones to represent the 0s and 1s of the binary data. To avoid confusion between the data being passed in opposite directions, four tones may be used, two for each of the communicating devices.

This technique may also be used to pass data directly between two computers. Most modems currently in use, however, operate at quite low speeds between 300 and 1200 Baud (about 30 to 120 characters per second), which is convenient for on-line access from remote terminals, although telephone charges for transmitting large quantities of data may make this approach uneconomical.

More sophisticated modems capable of much higher transmission speeds are available, but these are not provided at all installations. Special data carrying **land-lines**, usually owned and administered by the telephone authorities, are used for high speed communication. In the absence of such equipment, exchange of tapes or discs remains a more economical means of getting large quantities of data from one machine to another.

Developments in computer **networks**, in which many machines at different locations may communicate with each other, are making high speed communication between machines more commonplace. These networks operate much faster than is possible using conventional telephone lines.

A less expensive alternative to the modem is provided by the **acoustic coupler**. Rather than being directly wired to the telephone line, these devices have a pair of rubber or plastic cups into which a conventional telephone handset may be inserted. The cups serve to exclude extraneous noise, and the signals are transmitted and received by a small loudspeaker and microphone inside the unit. Most acoustic couplers are limited to a maximum transmission speed of 300 Baud.

3.6 Input devices

The user normally communicates with the computer by means of a video terminal or tele-typewriter, which can deal with both input and output. In addition there are a number of devices with specialised input or output functions. Most of these will usually be attached to a large computer and be under the control of the operating staff, although some, particularly printers and graphics devices, will often be used in conjunction with a micro-computer, and therefore be under the user's control. This section deals with input devices. Output devices are covered in section 3.7.

3.61 Card reader

Despite the now widespread availability of terminals at most large computer installations, the use of **punched cards** remains popular, especially when the user can call upon the services of a data preparation team to punch the cards from hand-written coding sheets. The usual form of punched card is shown in

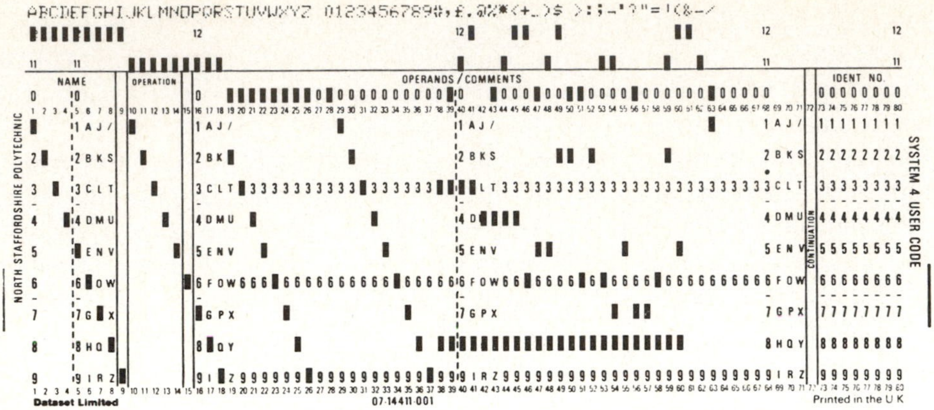

3.12 A punched card showing a typical character set

fig. 3.12. Any one of the set of 64 characters may be punched in each of the 80 available columns. They are represented by the presence of holes in one, two or three of the 12 rows.

The card is read by passing the cards rapidly over photo-electric devices which detect the holes for each column in turn. The line of characters thus assembled is passed to the computer. Cards can be read at speeds of up to about 2000 cards per minute. A typical high speed card reader is shown in fig. 3.13.

At installations where cards are frequently used, off-line card punching machines may be available for users to prepare their cards.

3.62 **Paper tape reader**
Although many machines in current use have this facility, it is most unlikely that many archaeologists will find a need for this largely outmoded input medium, unless they have access to one of the older generation of mini-computers.

Data is stored on paper tape by means of punched holes, the presence of which is sensed in the reader by optical devices. The holes are usually arranged in eight rows across the tape, a row of smaller holes being used by a toothed wheel to drive the tape through the reader. Other formats with five, six or seven holes may be encountered.

3.63 **Magnetic tape reader**
The magnetic tape reading facility is usually a function of the tape units otherwise used as backing store. We mention them again here as they may be called upon to act as input devices by reading tapes produced by other computers or prepared on off-line devices.

3.13 An ICL card reader

3.64 Optical and magnetic character readers

A number of different devices are available for recognising alphanumeric characters. These range from the magnetic character reader, which senses magnetic material in the special ink, recognising a special set of characters designed for this purpose, to devices capable of reading entire pages of printed, or even hand-written, characters. We will consider another method of hand-written input in the next section. Optical and magnetic character recognition find their widest applications in processing cheques, postal orders, and so on, and have yet to be usefully employed by archaeologists.

3.65 Digitising table

Computers are frequently used in archaeology to process graphical information. Plans, distribution maps, histograms, etc, may be produced automatically, but how do we get the graphical data into the machine? The conventional approach entails typing in large numbers of coordinates at a terminal. The **digitising table** or **tablet** provides a convenient alternative to such onerous tasks. Coordinates are generated automatically from the position of a moveable cursor or stylus. The locations of artefacts on a site plan, for instance, could be input to the computer by laying the plan on the digitising table and locating the artefacts using cursor or stylus. Similarly, line drawings may be produced by specifying that the digitised points be joined together. The cursor device may have a number of buttons which, under program control, may be allocated such functions as joining points by a straight line, or moving to a new position without drawing.

Digitising can also be applied to recognition of hand-written information. Sections of a pre-printed form laid on the table may be filled in by hand, with the computer recognising the characters. The position of the various sections to be filled in must be known to the computer, and a quite complex program is required to distinguish hand-written characters. A less complex application using a pre-printed form, but without the need for complex pattern recognition, may be used. Where the data to be entered consists of simple presence/absence information, or where multiple choice answers to questions can be used, then the digitising table may be used simply by placing the stylus in the appropriate boxes on a pre-printed form. In this case, the computer need only know the position of the possible entries on the form in order to recognise the answers. This technique can prove a very rapid method of input for repetitive types of data, especially for people who are not highly skilled in the use of a keyboard.

Digitising tables come in a wide range of sizes, with an active area ranging from the size of a sheet of A4 paper up to several square metres. The term digitising tablet is often applied to the smaller examples. Fig. 3.14 shows a

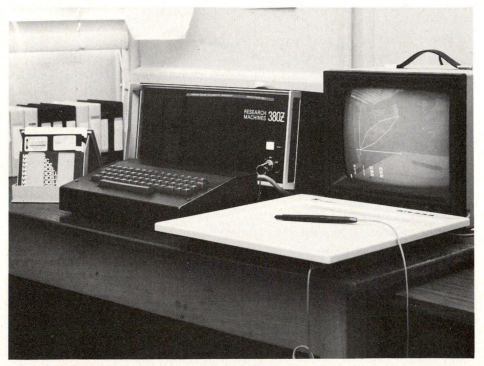

3.14 A digitising tablet in use with an RML 380Z micro-computer

small example being used for input to a micro-computer. More detailed descriptions of the wide range of digitising devices are to be found in Scott (1982) and Yoeli (1982).

3.66 Other graphics input devices

A range of other devices is available for entering graphical data into a computer. Many of these rely on the principle of scanning a picture with some form of light-sensitive detector and converting the received light level into digital information. Pictures captured in this way may be manipulated using a variety of image-processing techniques.

For many applications the scanning may be performed electronically using a normal television camera. Recent advances in small portable solid-state cameras which may be easily interfaced to a computer may help to make image-processing less expensive, and more widely available to archaeologists.

3.7 Output devices

Computers can produce output on a variety of different media. In many cases it may only be necessary to view results on a VDU terminal, but it is frequently necessary to produce hard-copy output which may be taken away from the machine and studied at leisure. The need also arises from time to time for output which is machine readable so that data may be transferred to other computers.

3.71 Card punch

Most punched cards are prepared on off-line card punches, but some machines have the facility to produce output on cards. This is really only of use in transferring data between machines with incompatible tape readers.

3.72 Paper tape punch

Paper tape may also be prepared by computer. The most frequent use of this method is in producing input data for other machines such as computer driven machine tools. Again, paper tape may be used as a last-ditch method of transferring data between machines.

3.73 Printers

In most computer systems the most frequently used hard-copy output device is the printer. These come in a wide variety of sizes, speeds and quality of print. In many cases, quality of output and speed are inversely related, and the choice of printer type will depend upon the application. Large mainframe computers servicing many users require high speed devices in order to produce a great volume of output without unnecessary delays. In this case quality has a low priority. On the other hand, an office word processing system will normally require very high quality, but the volume produced will be lower and speed will therefore be less important.

Characters are produced on paper by one of several methods. **Impact printers** impress a character via an inked ribbon in a similar manner to that of a normal typewriter. Variations on this theme are used in the majority of printers in use today. Other methods include ink jets, thermal printing using hot wire electrodes, a spark or laser to burn an image lightly onto paper, and electrostatic printing which operates in a similar way to many photocopying machines. The more recently introduced ink jet and laser devices are less common, but show some promise in combining high speed with high quality. Thermal printers, other than the laser variety, are normally only used in small devices such as printing calculators. The special paper is expensive but the printing mechanism is cheap to produce. It seems unlikely that these will ever find a use in data processing applications. The electrostatic device also requires quite expensive paper but is capable of reasonable quality output. These devices work in a manner analogous to that employed in producing microfilm output (see below, section 3.76). In the following sections we will consider in detail the three most common types of impact printer.

3.731 **Line printer**

The main type of printer employed in large mainframe installations is the **line printer**. These machines differ from other types of impact printer in that they print an entire line of characters virtually simultaneously. A typical line printer is shown in fig. 3.15. Line printers use continuous stationery, usually up to about fifteen inches wide, on which between 120 and 160 characters are printed per line. Speeds are typically in the range of 500 to 1500 lines per minute, it taking no longer to produce a full line of characters than it does a blank line.

3.732 **Dot-matrix printer**

The high speed and cost of line printers is not normally justifiable with smaller computer systems. For most of these, character printers are quite adequate. These produce their output character by character. This also applies to the printing mechanisms employed in tele-typewriter terminals attached to mainframe computers.

The most widespread type of printer used with micro- and small mini-computers and in modern tele-typewriters is the dot-matrix type. We have already met the idea of representing a character by means of a matrix of dots in our discussion of VDUs (above, section 3.52). Most dot-matrix printers are equipped with a print head consisting of a vertical column of small needles which may be fired against the paper, producing dots via the intermediate ribbon. Thus if a character is to be generated within a nine by nine matrix, a column of nine needles will be fired nine times as the print head moves over

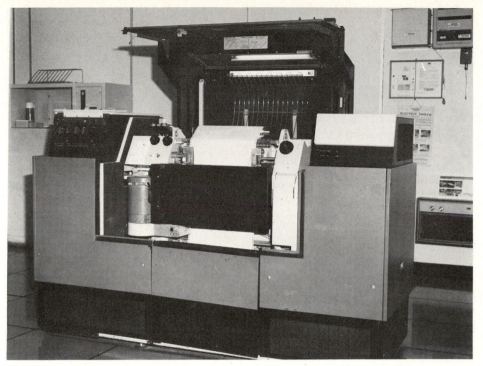

3.15 An ICL line printer

the paper. In each position, only those needles corresponding to the required dots are fired.

Typical dot-matrix printers produce their output at a rate between 60 and 300 characters per second. Many modern devices of this type are capable of printing in either direction and will seek the shortest route over the paper in order to optimise printing speed. Such functions are normally under the control of an internal dedicated microprocessor. The simplest dot-matrix printers produce only one type font. A number of more sophisticated devices allow the user to select from a number of different types of character, including emphasised, double width and condensed. The ability to produce superscripts and subscripts as well as limited graphics is also included in many of the printers now available. Fig. 3.16 shows a typical dot-matrix printer intended for micro-computer applications, the Epson FX-80. This particular example prints at up to 160 characters per second and can use either continuous or individual sheet stationery. Fig. 3.18 includes several examples of the wide range of character fonts and simple graphics which this machine can produce entirely under program control.

3.733 Daisy-wheel printer

Daisy-wheel printers employ a metal or plastic print wheel with the type mounted on long flexible fingers or 'petals' (fig. 3.17). A single print hammer

3.16 An Epson FX-80 dot-matrix printer

is used to impress the characters upon the paper, the wheel being rotated to the required position for each character. Such a system is also found on a number of modern electric typewriters, where it has largely supplanted the older 'golf ball' print head. Both types have been used for high quality computer printed output. The low mass of the print wheel allows the daisy-wheel printer to operate faster than the maximum of 12 to 15 characters per second typical of the older golf ball device. Daisy-wheel printers usually print between 20 and 60 characters per second. A wide range of type faces is available simply by changing the print wheel. Unlike a dot-matrix printer, this cannot normally be performed during a print run without manual intervention. As with dot-matrix devices, most daisy-wheel printers will accept continuous or separate sheet paper. Sheet feeding attachments are available for many daisy-wheel printers which allow printing on separate sheets without the need to insert fresh sheets manually.

Some daisy-wheel printers are capable of producing graphical output. This is achieved by using the full stop character to print dots. In this mode, the resolution can be as high as 120 dots per inch. The most advanced of such machines can operate in a vector plotting mode whereby lines may be drawn in any direction, with the paper being moved backwards or forwards as necessary.

3.17 A daisy-wheel

a   Most modern line printers can produce both UPPER and lower
   case characters, although some earlier models which only
   use UPPER CASE are still in use. Line printers are used
   where high speed is more important than quality.

b   The simplest dot-matrix printers produce only one type font.
   A number of the more sophisticated devices allow the user to
   select from a number of different types of character,
   inluding **emphasised**, double width and condensed,
   as well as superscripts and subscripts.

c   The daisy-wheel printer is designed to produce high-quality
   output similar to that of a typewriter. A wide range of
   print wheels is available for most of these printers.

     3.18 Examples of (a) line printer, (b) dot-matrix and (c) daisy-wheel output

3.19 Examples of graphics produced on (a) line printer. More elaborate pictures may be built up using the variations in shading made possible by successively over-printing characters on the same line without advancing the paper. Illustrated is a trend suface map produced by a program by P.M. Mather, Dept of Geography, University of Nottingham (Mather 1976).

(b) Dot-matrix printer. The ability to address the individual print needles on many of this type of printer makes them especially suitable for reproducing the type of graphics which may be displayed by some micro-computers. The example shown here was produced on an Epson MX-80 printer, and shows the same trend surface reproduced as a dot density map.

   Many daisy-wheel printers can produce similar results by repeatedly printing the full stop character with small intermediate movements of the paper.

   Figs. 3.18 and 3.19 show comparative examples of the type of printed and graphical output possible with line, dot-matrix and daisy-wheel printers. The range of quality is easily seen.

3.74 **Graphics displays**

The display of graphics on a VDU screen is a facility provided by a number of video terminals; the Hewlett Packard HP2648A shown in fig. 3.20 is a typical example. These devices work in similar manner to the character VDU, forming pictures from an array of illuminated dots, except that in this case each dot on the screen may be individually accessed. Data sent by the host computer to such a display unit is usually in the form of instructions to either move to, or draw a line to a specified position. This technique is known as **vector plotting**. The device usually incorporates a microprocessor control unit which calculates which dots need to be illuminated in order to draw any specified line. More sophisticated displays incorporate such facilities as automatic drawing of circles and ellipses, rotation of pictures about any axis and the ability to zoom in and out on parts of a drawing. The simpler displays rely upon the host computer, to which the terminal is connected, to provide such facilities.

Many micro-computers incorporate similar facilities into **memory-mapped graphics displays**. Fig. 3.14 shows an RML 380Z micro-computer being used in this manner. The existence of graphics displays on micro-computers opens up the possibility of their use not only as **stand-alone** graphics machines, but also as intelligent graphics terminals, with a capacity to perform some proces-

3.20 A Hewlett-Packard graphics terminal

sing locally, linked to larger machines. Colour and variable intensity monochrome displays are frequently provided by micro-computer graphics systems. The resolution of a typical micro-computer display ranges from about 80×40 to 800×500 dots, or **pixels**. Typical graphics terminals have a resolution in, or greater than, the upper end of this range.

In the memory-mapped or **raster** display, pixels cover the entire usable area of the screen, thus allowing block filling of part or all of a picture. This can often be done using a variety of colours or intensities. Another type of graphics display, which employs only vector plotting, may be encountered in some mini- and mainframe computer installation. This is the **vector** or **stroke-writing** display. Such devices are limited to producing line drawings, but their resolution is often far better than that of the memory-mapped display. They are usually only found in systems whose primary application is in producing high quality graphics. A detailed description of the operation of the different types of graphics displays is given by Scott (1982).

Graphics terminals normally provide the user with a means of moving a cursor around the screen and hence drawing or modifying pictures. Although this can be achieved using the keyboard, a number of other methods are available. A pair of **thumb wheels** can be used; one giving control over movement in the x-axis, the other in the y-axis. Simultaneous control over movement in both axes can be provided by a **joystick** or a **trackball**. The joystick uses a vertical shaft which can be pushed in any direction to generate movement. The trackball is a sphere, usually of about 75mm diameter, mounted such that only part of its surface is exposed. The ball may be rotated by hand in any direction.

Many graphics display terminals are equipped with a device known as a **light pen**. This can be used as an input device in a similar manner to the stylus or cursor of a digitising table (section 3.65, above). Applications include the interactive production of graphics and selection of options from a list, or menu, displayed on the screen. The light pen resembles an ordinary writing pen and is attached to the terminal by a length of cable. It contains a light sensitive element which, when pointed at the screen, allows the terminal to calculate the coordinates of the selected point.

3.75 Plotters

Graph plotters are used to produce line drawings on paper. Two main types are available, the **flatbed** and the **drum plotter** (figs. 3.21 and 3.22). Both types have a pen carriage which can move in one axis over the paper. This may be fitted with a single or multiple pens which may be raised and lowered onto the paper. Movement in the other axis is provided on the flatbed plotter by moving the entire pen carriage and its support along the length of the paper. The drum plotter uses a continuous roll of paper which may be moved backwards and forwards under the pen carriage.

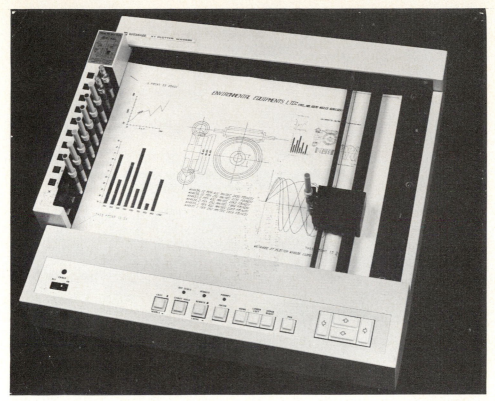

3.21 Watanabe flatbed plotter (photo Environmental Equipments (Northern) Ltd)

Plotters may be fitted with a variety of pens of different colours and line thickness, thus allowing appropriate pens to be selected for different parts of a drawing. All functions of such a device are normally under software control. Program packages such as GINO-F and Picaso (see section 7.3) are frequently used to generate pictures plotted in this manner.

Flatbed and drum plotters are available in a wide range of sizes accommodating paper from A4 to A0 size. A variety of small flatbed machines for A3 or A4 paper are available for micro-computer applications.

3.76 Computer output on microfilm
Contrary to some popular expectations, using computers rarely leads to a decrease in paperwork. In practice, the rate at which data may be analysed and results printed, together with the freedom to present results in different ways, often leads to a vast increase in the amount of paper generated by a project. This, in turn, can cause storage problems.

The obvious answer to such problems is to reduce all printed output which needs to be retained onto microfilm. Normally, this is an expensive operation requiring many hours of work by photographic technicians. However, direct

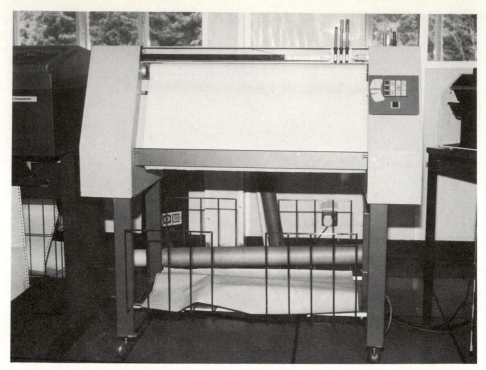

3.22 Benson drum plotter

output onto film from the computer may be achieved in a number of ways including **Computer Output on Microfilm**, or **COM**, devices. These devices can be extremely fast, operating at speeds of up to 500,000 characters per second, and can often prove far more economical than using paper. Output may be onto 16 mm or 35 mm film or, more efficiently, onto microfiche. In the latter case, one fiche may hold the equivalent of 200 sheets of listing paper. Some devices are also capable of producing graphical information in the same manner. COM represents an ideal solution to the problems of distribution and storage of archaeological reports and archive material. It is anticipated that its application in archaeology will grow rapidly as use of computers in the analysis of excavations and preparation of reports becomes more widespread.

Whilst such output devices can be very expensive and are not to be found at all large installations, a number of firms specialise in producing such output and will prepare fiches from tapes recorded on other machines.

3.8 **Other I/O methods**
Although generally beyond the scope of this book, the use of computers in process control and data logging cannot be neglected. These techniques have a wide range of potential applications in archaeological laboratories. In-

formation obtained from various sensors such as temperature or salinity transducers or scintillation counters may be directly input to a computer, enabling it to make decisions on control of the process or experiment. Wilcock, Short and Greaves (1983) refer to the use of computers as part of an integrated experimental system at the AERE radiocarbon laboratories at Harwell.

A system for recording dimensional data on bones from archaeological sites is described by Hardy (1982). This employs measuring calipers fitted with a linear displacement transducer as a direct means of data input.

3.9 Operating systems

The control of all of the different parts of the computer system is under the supervision of the **operating system**. This is a set of programs which permits the continuous operation of the computer and provides an interface between the user, the computer and the user's programs. Although the operating system is an item of software (chapter 4), rather than hardware, it is appropriate to introduce the topic here. We will consider the user's view of several operating systems in section 4.6.

In a small computer the operating system will enable communication between the terminal and computer, and allow the user to create, modify and delete files held on the backing store. The operating system also controls the passage of data between backing store, processor and peripherals, and allows programs to be loaded into memory for processing by the CPU. The Digital Research **CP/M**[1] system is an example of this type of simple operating system for micro-computers, which has become a world-wide standard for eight bit machines. As micro-computers become more powerful, more sophisticated operating systems are being developed for them and it it is not yet clear which will become the standards for sixteen and thirty-two bit machines. The adoption of **MS-DOS**[2] by IBM for their micro-computer has been instrumental in the rapid acceptance of this operating system on many similar sixteen bit machines. Versions of CP/M have been, or are being, developed for these machines, but operating systems, such as **Unix**,[3] which were originally developed for mini-computers are becoming more widespread.

The operating systems used on mainframe and mini-computers are invariably far more complex. These include facilities for scheduling the large numbers of jobs or tasks initiated by users and ensuring that all of the many peripheral devices are being used efficiently in order to maximise the overall efficiency of the system.

NOTES

(1) CP/M is a trademark of Digital Research Inc.

(2) MS-DOS is a trademark of Microsoft Corporation.

(3) Unix is a trademark of A.T. & T. Bell Laboratories.

4

SOFTWARE

4.1 Introduction

Software is defined as that part of the computer system which enables the hardware to operate. In other words, it is the series of instructions, or **programs**, which tell the computer what to do.

Several categories of program are covered by the term software:

> Operating systems
> Assemblers, compilers, and interpreters
> Utility programs
> Application packages
> Application programs

However, the first four of these categories are all programs normally written by professional programmers. The archaeologist will simply use them. Only in the last category may he or she become involved in writing software.

An operating system is a supervisory program which acts as an interface between the hardware, the processing program, and the user. The links with the hardware have been discussed in section 3.9. The interface with the user and the user's program will be described at the end of this chapter, in section 4.6.

Assemblers, compilers, and interpreters are programs which translate the instructions written by the user into instructions which the computer can understand. We will say a little more about the translation process in section 4.5.

Utility programs are those programs which perform standard procedures common to many applications. They will usually be supplied by the manufacturer together with the hardware and operating system, assemblers and compilers. Examples of utility programs include sorting and merging procedures, editors for writing and amending programs and data, and procedures for copying data and programs from one part of the computer to another, such as from disc to tape. Editors are considered further in section 5.421.

Applications packages may be defined as programs, or a suite of programs, designed to perform specific types of work. However, this needs qualification as they are also programs designed for use in more than one environment or organisation, but are generally written with the needs of a particular group of users in mind. Examples include payroll accounting systems, information storage and retrieval packages such as the GOS system maintained by the

Museum Documentation Association, and packages for data analysis such as SPSS (Nie *et al* 1975). Applications packages are not normally supplied with a computer system, and must be acquired separately. Therefore the packages that are available will be dependent upon the installation. They are the subject of chapter 7, where the benefits and drawbacks of their use will be discussed.

However, it is frequently the case that the archaeologist wishes to perform a specific task for which there is not an applications package available. In this case a program must be written. This is known as an application program, or user program. It is this fifth category of software which is the primary concern of this chapter. An application program is one which is written by, or for, the individual user, to perform a specific task. In a university computing centre, or in the computing services unit of a government department, there may be professional programmers whose job it is to deal with requests for programs for potential users.

4.2 **Programming: for and against**

Is it necessary for the archaeologist to learn how to program? There is no simple answer to this question. It is dependent upon the problem in hand, the facilities available, and, not least, the talents of the individual.

Many mainframe computer installations have a wide range of packages available. We believe that these are adequate for many of the computing needs of archaeologists. However, there are pitfalls in their use, which we will discuss in chapter 7, and there is a tendency that the problem will be fitted to the solution. There is a temptation to force the data through the programs available, rather than considering what analyses would actually be appropriate and rewarding. In some cases, the archaeologist may find that appropriate software is not available, or that the existing program would be an inefficient way of performing the task in hand. Often the archaeologist may find that the data format must be altered in order to submit it to a package. Rather than type it all in again in the new format it is far simpler to write a short program to read the data and write it out again in the new format. In our experience programs to alter and manipulate data files are one of the more frequent needs in archaeological data processing.

Similarly, the archaeologist may wish to amend an existing program; this may involve no more than altering the layout of the results. It may be accomplished by altering a few words or a few lines of the original program.

The level of programming knowledge required to perform such simple tasks is not great. Most people can acquire sufficient skill in programming to be able to write simple programs within two weeks. To achieve more complex tasks a fuller understanding, gained over several months, may be demanded. With a knowledge of one of the languages discussed in section 4.5 most of the computing needs of the archaeologist can be satisfied. Nevertheless, there will come a time when the programming contortions necessary to achieve a particular aim no longer outweigh the time required to learn a second language. Indeed, once a first language has been learnt then others will be acquired more easily. A reading knowledge of several programming languages can be useful.

Yet even if the archaeologist does not wish to write programs, a knowledge of programming principles may be desirable, if only to dispel some of the mystique associated with the 'black art'. This will also allow an understanding of what an existing program or package is doing, and may even help by encouraging logical thought about manual data processing. The discipline required by a computer orientated approach is often very valuable.

Even if the archaeologist intends to employ a professional programmer, it is important to be able to communicate requirements clearly to the programmer, who is likely to be more sympathetic to someone who has obviously taken the trouble to try to understand what needs to be done.

Yet, having said all this, learning a programming language is not something that should be undertaken lightly. Archaeologists can make profitable use of computers without ever having written a program. It should be stressed that programming can be a very time-consuming and frustrating business. Although a program may be written fairly rapidly, it can take much longer to actually get it to do what it was intended for. On the other hand, the feeling of accomplishment when a program finally works can be extremely rewarding.

This book makes no attempt to teach programming. Rather, it introduces some fundamental programming concepts, and compares and contrasts the most popular programming languages. Many adequate teaching books already exist for each of the programming languages and these will be referred to where appropriate. As with any language, the best way to learn is by experience. To learn to program one must sit at a terminal with one of these texts and actually attempt to get some of the program examples to work.

The rest of this chapter is in four parts. The first two are concerned with some general issues, which should be of interest to all readers, whether potential programmers or not. The third section is an overview of the more popular programming languages likely to be useful to archaeologists. It should be of help in choosing an appropriate language, if it has been decided that it is necessary to learn to program. The fourth section describes how the user might implement a program on a computer.

It will already be apparent that a program is a sequence of instructions. There are really three stages to writing a program:

    i)   Decide exactly what is to be done (section 4.3).
    ii)   Specify the sequence of operations necessary to bring about the desired result, i.e. the algorithm (section 4.4).
   iii)   Express the algorithm in a form which the computer can assimilate (section 4.5).

In professional data processing organisations the first two of these stages are commonly known as **systems analysis**; the third as **programming**. The archaeologist who intends to use a computer will frequently be both systems analyst and programmer. Furthermore, whilst the above three stages have been presented as distinct operations, it should be emphasised that in practice they are rarely so clearly distinguished. The process of problem definition, program preparation and programming are closely interrelated, with various feedback mechanisms operating between each category.

4.3 Defining the problem

Before starting to write a program it is essential that the problem is adequately defined. This requires knowledge of the objectives and scope of the intended program, the exact form of its input, and the form of output required.

Where the program is for an individual research project then it is the researcher's responsibility to be clear about what the desired objectives are. Where the program is intended for the use of other people, such as for excavation recording within an archaeological unit, then it is the duty of the analyst/programmer to discover what users require. They cannot be expected to know, for example, that the form in which data is being input may preclude a form of analysis which they assumed could be performed. A fact-finding stage is therefore necessary to establish what the system requirements are. The questions which must be asked include:

> What form is the input in when it enters the system?
> Where does it originate?
> What items are included in the input?
> What is the volume of input?
> Where is the input to be done?
> Who is responsible for data input?
> What is the accuracy and completeness of the data available?
> What form is the output in?
> What purpose is it put to?
> What are the security requirements?
> What are the financial constraints?

Where the program is being developed for other users, such as in an archaeological unit, then the techniques of professional systems analysts in commercial environments may be found to be useful. Lee (1979) and Millington (1981) provide full discussions of these.

4.4 Defining the operations

Having defined the nature of the problem, the next stage is to specify the sequence of operations required to solve it. The practice of sitting at a computer terminal and typing a program straight in is known as compulsive coding and should be avoided. Even the simplest algorithm usually requires careful thought about what is the best way of expressing it in a programming language. This section introduces two of the most popular tools used as aids to thinking about how one should tackle a problem with a computer: flow-charts and structure diagrams.

4.41 **Flowcharts**

A **flowchart** is a diagram showing how and in what order a series of operations are to be performed.

Occasionally, a problem may be so complex that a computer program to handle it might involve hundreds of operations, with complicated relationships between them. In these cases a program flowchart may be a useful aid to writing the program. It will also provide documentation. If the original programmer, or someone else, has to amend the program long after it was written then it may be easier to understand what the program is doing by examining a flowchart, rather than by wading through a program listing.

On the other hand, it may seem to be an unnecessary waste of time to draw up a flowchart for a simple program, which may be a 'one-off' for a specific purpose. In addition, if a program is properly furnished with 'comment' statements describing what it does, then further documentation of the program structure should be unnecessary. Furthermore, some programmers argue that the development of structured programming, as discussed in 4.42, has largely made flowcharting redundant. It has often become easier to follow a program listing than the flowchart.

Nevertheless, whether the archaeologist intends to become a proficient programmer or not, some knowledge of the principles of flowcharting may be valuable as they allow the logical definition of the various stages of a process, and aid understanding of how a computer handles the task. Therefore this section will outline the basic conventions of flowcharting. More detailed information on flowcharting techniques may be found in Fry (1981, 136–49) or Collin (1978, 89–122).

Consider the simple task of scanning a sequence of numbers, finding the smallest and the largest, and calculating the difference between the two. Let us suppose, for example, that these are measurements taken of the lengths of an assemblage of handaxes, and that we wish to know the difference in size between the longest and the shortest.

Now look at the simple flowchart in fig. 4.1. This flowchart represents an algorithm for the task. It has been drawn using certain symbols and according to certain conventions. These are used in order to represent the sequence as clearly and unambiguously as possible.

Each logical step in the procedure is shown in an appropriately shaped symbol. The operation to be carried out at each step is briefly described within the symbol. Although each logical step is written in a separate box it does not follow that each box will result in one program instruction. Flow-

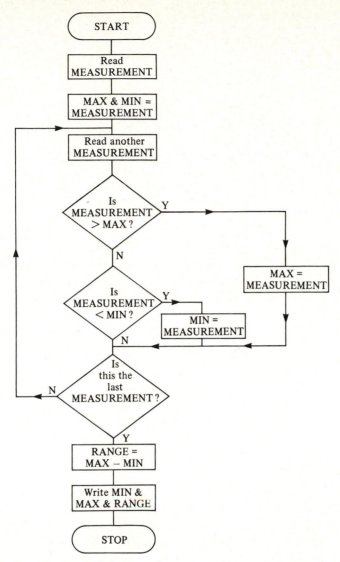

4.1 Handaxe flowchart

charts can be drawn at different levels of detail. Usually the best way to start is to draw the simplest possible flowchart first, and then to add more detail as required.

By convention flowcharts are read from top to bottom and from left to right, unless arrows on the flowlines indicate otherwise. Arrows should be used whenever they result in increased clarity. If necessary, flowlines may cross each other without implying any relationship. However, if there are two or more incoming flowlines to a symbol then they should not join another flowline at the same point.

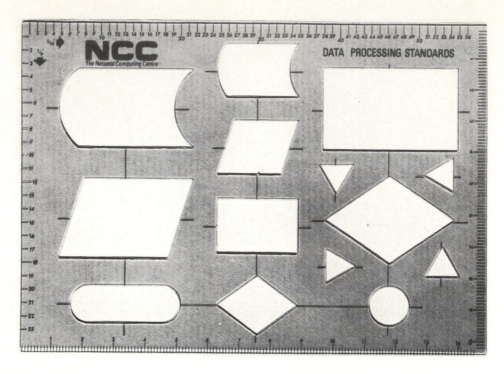

4.2 The NCC flowcharting template (National Computing Centre)

Many computer manufacturers specify their own set of symbols and produce their own template. The differences between each version can obviously lead to confusion and so the National Computer Centre has defined a set of standard flowcharting symbols (NCC 1977). Fig. 4.2 illustrates a template produced by the NCC. The four basic symbols which are used in a program flowchart are shown in fig. 4.3. The other symbols included in the template are largely concerned with the various possible forms of input to and output from the computer, and are used by systems analysts rather than programmers. We shall now look at the four basic symbols: operation, decision, connector and terminal.

The operation symbol is used seven times in the flowchart in fig. 4.1. The operations are:

Read MEASUREMENT
MAX & MIN = MEASUREMENT
Read another MEASUREMENT
MAX = MEASUREMENT
MIN = MEASUREMENT
RANGE = MAX − MIN.
Write MIN & MAX & RANGE

The decision symbol represents the process of executing a defined opera-

Operation

Decision

Connector

Terminal

4.3 The four basic flowcharting symbols

tion or group of operations which results in a change of value, location, or form of information. There are three decisions in fig. 4.1:

Is MEASUREMENT > MAX ?
Is MEASUREMENT < MIN ?
Is this the last MEASUREMENT ?

The decision symbol is used for an action which tests whether a statement is true or false, and depending on the answer, we do one thing or another.

Although there are no rules on the subject it is good practice to have the exits from a decision box arranged so that the most likely course of events leads us to continue a vertical, rather than a horizontal path. The decision and operation symbols are the most commonly used ones.

The use of the connector symbol should be avoided where possible, as it makes interpretation of the flowchart more difficult. It shows continuity between symbols where it is not possible to join them by flowlines, such as when they are on separate pages, or where a further flowline would make the diagram look untidy or clumsy.

The fourth symbol is the terminal symbol, which is used to show entry to, or exit from, a program or procedure. It normally contains either START or STOP.

The sequence of operations followed by a computer in order to solve our handaxe problem could be as follows:

To start, it reads in the first measurement and sets the maximum and minimum to this value.

Then it reads in another measurement and checks if this is greater than its stored maximum length.

If it is, then the maximum takes the value of the new measurement. The computer now no longer needs to check if the new measurement is smaller than the first. Logically, it cannot be and so the computer can jump to the next stage.

Alternatively, if the new measurement was found to be smaller than the maximum then it becomes necessary to check if it is smaller than the minimum.

If it is smaller then it becomes the new minimum length. If not, then the computer has to read the next measurement, and so follows a path which takes it back to an earlier instruction, thus forming a loop.

However, first it is important to check if this was the last measurement. If it was, then the minimum length must be subtracted from the maximum, and the result written out. Otherwise the program would attempt to read another measurement, and if it could not find one then it would fail.

Any loop in a flowchart must have some form of exit built into it; otherwise it would go on forever, or until something, such as input data, ran out. The exit is usually a test for the last item of data, or it may be built into the loop by a counter which says 'Go round this loop a specified number of times.'

This example has illustrated the algorithm required for a computer program to perform a simple task of scanning a sequence of numbers, retrieving two of them, and performing an arithmetic operation on them. But numbers are just one type of data which we may wish to process. Computers can also handle text, or **strings** of characters.

Consider a simple data file consisting of a bibliography. We shall see in chapter 6 that there are more effective ways of storing this information, but suppose for the present that all our references are listed sequentially, on one file. Each record (book or article) contains five fields which specify author, date, journal, volume, and title. They are followed by an unspecified number of further fields which contain keywords by which we may wish to retrieve references. A segment of the data file is shown in fig. 4.4. Of course, the records could be anything. For example, each record might be a grave from a cemetery. In this case the fields might be sex, age, and the various accompanying grave-goods. Suppose for the moment however that it is a bibliography and that we wish to retrieve all references to villas. We need to search by the keyword VILLA. The required algorithm is shown in the flowchart in fig. 4.5.

It will be apparent that there are two loops in this flowchart. The outer loop continues to fetch new records as long as there are still more to be fetched. The inner loop continues reading keywords whilst there are still more to be read. We jump out of the outer loop when there are no more records; and out of the inner one when there are no more keywords, or when we find a villa.

```
LETHBRIDGE,T.C.        1951       A CEMETERY AT LACKFORD, SUFFOLK
CAMBRIDGE ANTIQUARIAN SOCIETY. QUARTO PUBLICATIONS. NEW SERIES, NO. VI
CEMETERY     SUFFOLK      ANGLO-SAXON
RADFORD,C.A.R.         1936       THE ROMAN VILLA AT DITCHLEY, OXON
OXONIENSIA 1, 24-69
ROMAN        VILLA      OXON
JOHNSON,S.            1978       EXCAVATIONS AT HAYTON ROMAN FORT, 1975
BRITANNIA 9, 57-114
ROMAN        FORT        YORKSHIRE
JONES,M.U.           1968       CROP-MARK SITES AT MUCKING, ESSEX
ANTIQUARIES JOURNAL 48, 210-20
CROP-MARK    ESSEX       ANGLO-SAXON IRON AGE     SETTLEMENT   CEMETERY
WARD PERKINS,J.B.     1938       THE ROMAN VILLA AT LOCKLEYS, WELWYN
ANTIQUARIES JOURNAL 18, 339-76
ROMAN        VILLA      HERTS
WHEELER,R.E.M.        1943       MAIDEN CASTLE, DORSET
OXFORD
IRON AGE     HILL FORT    CEMETERY      DORSET
```

4.4 Bibliography data file

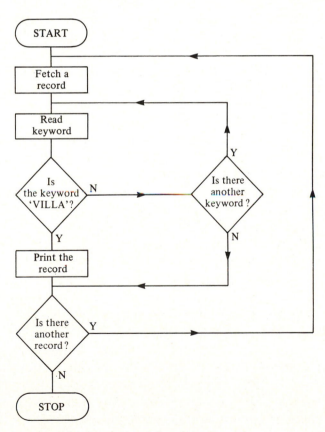

4.5 Bibliography retrieval flowchart

Having drawn up a rough flowchart it is advisable for the programmer to 'simulate' a computer by running through the instructions with test data, to check if there are any logical flaws. Care should be taken to ensure that sufficient variations of input data are tested to be representative of all the situations catered for by the program. Flowcharting should be seen as an interactive process. A flowchart should be drawn, tested with a dry run, then re-drawn, possibly several times over.

4.42 Structure diagrams

An alternative means of specifying the sequence of operations to be performed by a program is by structure diagram. A flowchart presents a program as a list of individual statements which are performed from top to bottom unless otherwise indicated. In fact, it is usually the case that groups of instructions are used to achieve particular tasks within the program. A structure diagram partitions a problem into independent modules, or blocks, of related instructions. Therefore it is suited to a method of programming known as **structured programming**. Ideally, all programming should be structured, but it is especially important for large programming tasks. In structured programming a problem is split into individual program modules which are manageably small. The advantages of a program consisting of blocks of about twenty lines over one of 1000 unstructured instructions are obvious. Firstly, each module may be written separately; secondly, it may be tested and corrected separately; thirdly, it may be modified separately. Thus program errors can be isolated to specific modules which can be corrected, or even scrapped and rewritten. If we wish to modify a module to perform a different function, or insert extra modules, we can be confident that changes there should not cause errors elsewhere within the program.

A structure diagram is a better way of representing a structured program than a flowchart. The examples we have used so far in this chapter are rather trivial ones to use a structure diagram for, but they will give an idea of what is involved. Both problems, to retrieve villas from a bibliography and to calculate the range of lengths in a handaxe assemblage, consist of three tasks. Firstly we have to read a record in; then perform a check, either for longest and shortest, or for villas; then finally output a result.

A structure diagram to represent this is shown in fig. 4.6. It consists of four modules, each of which is represented as a rectangular box with its name inside. The single module at the top may be regarded as the **control module**; it is the main program. It is linked by arrows to the three other modules. This indicates that it may **call** them, and that they are subordinate to it. Since we know what order they are called in, they have been drawn in that order from left to right, although they need not be. The smaller arrows beside the main arrow indicate the type of communication that is involved. The small arrow with an open circle on its tail is called a **data couple**. It indicates that data is

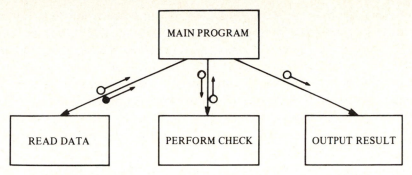

4.6 A structure diagram

passing between the modules, in the direction in which the arrow points. The other arrow, with a black circle on its tail, is a **flag**. In this case it is a flag to tell the control module when the end of the data file is reached. A flag should be distinguished from data; although it may be set and tested it is not processed. There is no point in adding another number to it, or writing it out.

Having partitioned the major tasks performed by the program, the modules at the base of the diagram can be further split into smaller sub-modules. For example, in the handaxe length example it can be seen that there are really two parts to producing the result, as first the minimum length has to be subtracted from the maximum, and then the answer written out. Therefore the third module calls two further modules (fig. 4.7).

In any real structure diagram there would be several levels of modules in a hierarchy. Each module description would be fairly vague, as the idea behind a structure diagram is to indicate the general nature of the task performed,

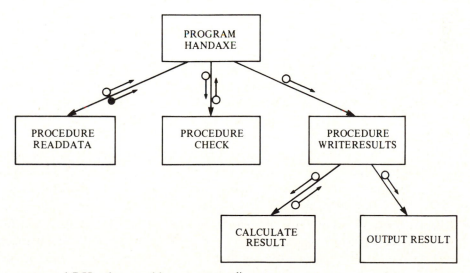

4.7 Handaxe problem structure diagram

rather than becoming entangled in the detailed program instructions. More information on structured program design, structure diagrams, and related tools, such as data flow diagrams, may be found in Yourdon and Constantine (1979) or Myers (1975). An alternative means of representing the structure of a program is by writing it in **pseudo-code**. Pseudo-code provides a narrative rather than a graphical representation of a program, and allows the programmer to use natural language to express the flow of a program unambiguously. The result is not dissimilar from the coding of a programming language, hence the term pseudo-code. The intention, however, is that it should be flexible enough to avoid including features of a programming language which would unduly influence the design. Two other terms, **top-down programming** and **stepwise refinement**, may be encountered describing an approach to structured programming. Both are used to refer to a design strategy which starts at the top with the most general elements of a problem, and breaks the task down into successively simpler modules.

4.5 **Programming languages**

We have seen that a computer program is a sequence of instructions. If these were fed into the machine in English it would not understand them. A computer operates on instructions written as binary numbers in **machine code**. Obviously programming in machine code is extremely tedious. For every instruction the computer performs only one task, and it is very inconvenient to have to write everything in binary.

To overcome some of the difficulties inherent in machine code programming, assembly languages were developed. An assembly language substitutes a meaningful word or mnemonic for a binary instruction. The program written in assembly language, called a **source** program, must be translated into a machine code program, called an **object** program, in order that the computer can understand it. Most computers have a special program called an **assembler** to do this.

Assembly languages are **low-level** languages. One instruction corresponds to one task performed by the computer. Therefore writing programs at this level results in a great many simple instructions, each of which is relatively easy. Yet there are so many of them that an assembly code program is likely to contain many errors, as well as taking a long time to write. Since an assembly language is closer to machine code than it is to everyday English it is fairly difficult to learn. Being **machine-orientated** it requires a good knowledge of the inner workings of the machine on the part of the programmer. Because assembly language instructions correspond to the machine code instructions of a particular computer it is also **machine-dependent**. Transfer of assembly language programs from one computer to another of different type is difficult. In short, the reader of this book should have no need for assembly languages.

To make computer programming easier a number of **high-level** languages have been developed, such as FORTRAN, PL/1, RPG, BCPL, BASIC, FORTH, APL, LISP, COBOL, ALGOL, Pascal, Modula-2 and C. These are high-level in that the individual instructions are much more powerful than instructions in low-level languages. One instruction in a high-level language may correspond to several operations in the computer. For example, an instruction may read:

$$A = B + C - D$$

This represents several operations at the machine or assembly language level.

Because high-level languages are so much more powerful a more complex program is generally required to convert source programs to object code. Two types of program are used. The first is called a **compiler**. It generates an equivalent object program in machine code, which can be executed directly by the hardware. FORTRAN, COBOL, and Pascal are compiled languages. The second type of translator is known as an **interpreter**. It scans the instructions, one by one, and performs each one directly. It does not produce an object code program. Instead, if the program is to be used more than once then it must be interpreted each time. Thus an interpreter is generally slower and less efficient than a compiler. Programs written in BASIC are generally interpreted, although compilers are available for this language.

The archaeologist who is contemplating learning a programming language would be wise to choose one of the high-level languages. Firstly, the program will be written more quickly, as each program instruction may tell the computer to do several things. Secondly, a program written in a high-level language will be more versatile. Recognised standards exist for each of the languages which are discussed in this chapter. A program written for one computer should work on another with a few modifications, depending upon the language. The programmer may often simply need to transfer a copy of the source program and re-compile or re-interpret it. The local compiler or interpreter is left to translate the high-level instructions into machine code instructions which the individual computer can use. Thirdly, a high-level language is easier to work with than a low-level one. As we shall see later, its instructions are written in words very close to everyday English. Therefore it is easier to understand one's own, or someone else's, programs.

It may be asked why a computer program may not be written in normal English, and the computer told to translate it. In fact the computer would need an enormous vocabulary, and the programmer would tend to assume it understood things which it did not, just as we do in everyday speech. Therefore all computing languages consist of a restricted number of precisely defined words, and a set of grammatical rules which allow instructions to be built up. The differences between programming languages consist of differences in vocabulary, and in acceptable grammatical constructions. This means that some languages are more appropriate for certain tasks than others. In the following sections we shall discuss four widely available high-level languages likely to be useful to archaeologists: BASIC, FORTRAN, COBOL, and Pascal. We shall attempt to indicate the sort of applications for which each is most suited. Nevertheless, it should be stressed at the outset that in practice, the choice of a programming language will largely be the result of local factors. Dictates of availability, personal preference, and especially of local expertise in the form of someone prepared to help and advise, are at least as important as questions of suitability to the problem in hand.

The potential programmer should also be aware of the questions of maintainability, intelligibility, and portability. **Maintainability** refers to the ease with which programs may be maintained; that is how easy it is to make them more efficient and amend them in accordance with the changing needs of the user. Programs written in some languages may be found to be easier to maintain than others, largely because sections may be removed and replaced without affecting the rest of the program.

Linked to this is the problem of **intelligibility**, by which is meant the ease with which one can understand what a program is doing. This is especially important where one may have to amend a program several years after it was written. If a program is intended for more than a one-off job adequate **documentation** is desirable. This should entail both extensive text with accompanying flowcharts or structure diagrams to act as a manual for using and amending the program, and comments embedded within the program describing the function of particular instructions and procedures.

Finally, the programmer should be aware of the need for **portability**, or the ease with which a program written on one computer may be used on another of different make. Like English, many programming languages have a number of distinct dialects. Computer manufacturers have each tended to produce different versions for their own machines. However, for most languages recognised standards exist and individual dialects will usually either be subsets or supersets of the standard. Subsets comprise a limited number of the features of the standard; whereas supersets should include all the features of the standard plus various additions. In order that a program may be portable it is advisable to follow the standard as closely as possible when programming, even if a particular task might be coded more conveniently using a non-standard feature. This should then mean that the program may be transferred to another computer of a different make without major alterations.

In the sections which follow considerably more space has been given to BASIC than to the other languages. This should not be taken to imply that we consider BASIC to be any more important than the others. Rather, we have chosen to introduce general programming concepts through actual examples in BASIC, instead of in an abstract form, such as pseudo-code. Some knowledge of these concepts is then assumed in the subsequent language sections, rather than being repeated. Consequently, the reader without programming experience who is specifically interested in Pascal, for example, might be advised to become familiar with the BASIC section first.

4.51 **BASIC**

BASIC (Beginners All-purpose Symbolic Instruction Code) was introduced in 1964 as a simple easily written language for beginners. It has now become a widely available and popular language, especially for use on micro-computers. It is also a powerful tool, particularly for using computers in a conversational mode, such as in question-and-answer data capture programs. BASIC was one of the languages recommended for the use of archaeologists in the Museum Documentation Association Draft Standard (Stewart 1980). For the archaeologist with access to a micro-computer it is indeed an obvious choice of language with which to learn programming. Since it is generally interpreted rather than compiled, program development is relatively rapid. A program can be written, executed, or **run**, edited, and run again, all from within the BASIC interpreter (cf. section 4.61).

For many simple problems a BASIC program may be perfectly adequate. On the other hand, many professional programmers tend to be scornful of BASIC. This is partly because they are used to large programs, and were trained on mainframe computers, for which BASIC is not so well suited. Using BASIC for permanent programs does become inefficient. If BASIC instructions must be interpreted each time the program is run a computer is obviously wasting time re-interpreting a fully developed program. Furthermore, BASIC is an unstructured language. We saw in section 4.42 that the best approach to large programs was to divide the problem into separate modules which could be developed independently. BASIC does not lend itself to this approach, although it can be done. Program control tends to shift back and forth abruptly within the program, increasing the likelihood of errors. Therefore if the archaeologist anticipates doing a lot of programming, then BASIC might be considered as a first language, and as a means of discovering if one has an aptitude for programming, but not as the only language to be mastered.

Many micro-computer manufacturers have produced their own versions of BASIC which only run on their machines. For example, there is BBC BASIC, Applesoft BASIC, RML BASIC, and so on. One of the most popular dialects which runs on many machines, and on which other dialects are based, is Microsoft BASIC. In the examples below we have used Microsoft BASIC, and have tried to use only those instructions which are standard.[1]

4.511 **Program format**

Let us consider a simple BASIC program:

```
10 REM     A PROGRAM TO CALCULATE THE AREA OF A BUILDING
20 LET AREA = 5.5 * 7.6
30 PRINT ''AREA IS''; AREA; ''SQ M''
40 END
```

When obeyed, this program would produce:

```
AREA IS 41.8 SQ M
```

It will be immediately apparent that some of the program instructions are similar to those in everyday English. However, rather than being in a continuous text, they are set out one per line. The program is obeyed one line at a time, working from top to bottom.

Each line is preceded by a line number. This is characteristic of the BASIC language. We could have numbered the lines 1 to 4, but by using an interval of 10 we shall be able to insert extra lines as we go along.

The first line is:

```
10 REM     A PROGRAM TO CALCULATE THE AREA OF A BUILDING
```

This line has no effect on the operation of the program. In fact the REM at the beginning tells the computer to ignore the rest of that line. It is a **comment** statement, inserted as a REMark to tell us what the program does. A lengthy program should always be sprinkled liberally with comments to provide documentation.

The second line is:

```
20 LET AREA = 5.5 * 7.6
```

This is an instruction to the computer to do something. The LET statement tells the computer that it is to assign the value of whatever follows the equals sign to the variable, in this case called AREA.[2] The instruction is known as an **assignment** statement. It should be noted that the equals sign does not perform the same function as in an arithmetic equation. Thus whatever is to the left of the equals sign does not equal what is to the right of it. Thus the equals sign is not used in the same way as it is in:

$$4 = 2 + 2$$

AREA is the name of a variable that the computer must create. It may be regarded as a box called AREA in which the computer stores a value, in this case the result of the calculation, i.e. 41.8. Of course, the box does not have to be called AREA; we have simply chosen that as it is the name by which we know this attribute. In this case the computer must perform a calculation in order to supply a value for AREA. The asterisk signifies that it must multiply the two numbers together. It has to be used because the normal multiplication sign is not part of the ASCII character set. In computer parlance the asterisk is used here as an **arithmetic operator**. The arithmetic operators encountered in BASIC programs are:

+   (addition)
−   (subtraction)
/   (division)
*   (multiplication)
^   (raise to the power of)

The third line of our simple program is:

```
30 PRINT "AREA IS"; AREA; "SQ M"
```

This instructs the computer to print out whatever it has stored in the box called AREA. The characters enclosed within quotation marks are printed literally. They are unnecessary to the operation of the program, but help us to interpret the result.

Finally, the fourth line is:

```
40 END
```

This simply tells the computer that it has now completed the sequence of operations for this program.

4.512 **Simple input and output**

An alternative way of writing the program would be:

```
10 REM    A PROGRAM TO CALCULATE THE AREA OF A BUILDING
12 DATA 5.5, 7.6
18 READ WDTH, LNGTH
20 LET AREA = WDTH * LNGTH
30 PRINT ''AREA IS''; AREA; ''SQ M''
40 END
```

The effect of this program is exactly the same, but the program is better as it sets up the boxes WDTH and LNGTH as two more variables. Consequently, several values could be placed in them, and be operated upon. The program uses two new BASIC instructions. The line numbered 12 is:

```
12 DATA 5.5, 7.6
```

The word DATA at the beginning of the line tells the interpreter that this is a DATA statement. The characters following are items of data that are to be used in the program. In this case they represent measurements of two attributes of a building, i.e. its length and width.

The second new line is:

```
18 READ WDTH, LNGTH
```

This tells the computer to read in some data from a DATA statement. The words following are the variable names given to the boxes in which the items of data should be stored.

Having set up width and length as variables we are now free to place any values in them and our program begins to be generally applicable. By re-writing the DATA statement any pairs of measurements could be inserted into the program and the area of other rectangular buildings calculated without additional alteration to the program. However, it would be better to make a further small modification to allow the program to accept values for WDTH and LNGTH provided interactively by the user. This improved version prompts the user for values for WDTH and LNGTH from the terminal keyboard. The area of any number of rectangular buildings may now be calculated without any alteration to the program:

```
10 REM     A PROGRAM TO CALCULATE THE AREA OF A BUILDING
12 INPUT ''WIDTH''; WDTH
18 INPUT ''LENGTH''; LNGTH
20 LET AREA = WDTH * LNGTH
30 PRINT ''AREA IS''; AREA; ''SQ M''
40 END
```

There are two new lines in this version, numbered 12 and 18. Their effect is to prompt the user with whatever is enclosed in the quotation marks, and store the number provided as the variable following.

When the program is run the sequence of events as appearing on the VDU screen or tele-typewriter would be:

WIDTH?5.5<cr>
LENGTH?7.6<cr>
AREA IS 41.8 SQ M

Those characters supplied by the computer are in bold type. The symbol <cr> stands for **carriage return**. It is provided by the RETURN key on the keyboard, and is necessary so that the computer knows we have finished typing our response and can continue with its next instruction. Thus the computer has initially printed '**WIDTH?**', to which the user has responded by typing 5.5 and pressing the RETURN key. The computer then prompts '**LENGTH?**', for which the user has entered 7.6 followed by RETURN. The computer has then performed the calculation at line 20 and printed out the result.

4.513 **The GOTO and IF statements**
In order to repeat this operation several times we can insert a loop into the program:

```
10 REM     A PROGRAM TO CALCULATE THE AREA OF A BUILDING
12 INPUT ''WIDTH''; WDTH
18 INPUT ''LENGTH''; LNGTH
20 LET AREA = WDTH * LNGTH
30 PRINT ''AREA IS''; AREA; ''SQ M''
35 GOTO 12
40 END
```

The effect of the extra statement, numbered line 35, is to **transfer control** to line 12. In other words, whenever line 35 is reached, the computer would go back to line 12 and repeat the instructions following. Every time new values are assigned to WDTH, LNGTH, and AREA, the previous values stored in the boxes are overwritten. Therefore we could use our simple seven line program to calculate the areas of hundreds of buildings. In fact, this program would carry on forever, (unless it was overridden), as there is no way out of the loop and line 40 would never be reached.

Therefore it would be better if we inserted a further line to allow the user to escape:

```
10 REM     A PROGRAM TO CALCULATE THE AREA OF A BUILDING
12 INPUT ''WIDTH''; WDTH
15 IF WDTH = 0 THEN GOTO 40
18 INPUT ''LENGTH''; LNGTH
20 LET AREA = WDTH * LNGTH
30 PRINT ''AREA IS''; AREA; ''SQ M''
35 GOTO 12
40 END
```

Line 15 introduces a new type of BASIC instruction known as a **conditional**. Conditional statements are in the form:

IF [statement is true] THEN [obey instruction]

In this case we test if the value of WDTH is zero, and if so, control is transferred to line 40, allowing the program to END. Thus the user can enter 0 for width in order to terminate the program. Otherwise, if WDTH is not zero, then we continue to the next instruction in sequence, i.e. line 18.

4.514 **File handling**

A more sophisticated version of this program might accept data on building widths and lengths from a file, rather than directly from the keyboard. In fact this would be a normal situation as it is better to store data in a permanent file that can be fed through various programs, rather than having to be typed in each time.

In this case the program might look like this:

```
10 REM     A PROGRAM TO CALCULATE THE AREA OF A BUILDING
12 OPEN ''I'', #1, ''DATAFILE''
15 IF EOF (1) THEN GOTO 38
18 INPUT #1, WDTH, LNGTH
20 LET AREA = WDTH * LNGTH
30 PRINT ''AREA IS''; AREA; ''SQ M''
35 GOTO 15
38 CLOSE #1
40 END
```

This introduces two instructions which are specific to file-handling in BASIC:

```
12 OPEN "I", #1, "DATAFILE"
38 CLOSE #1
```

The exact format of these lines need not concern us as it is peculiar to the Microsoft dialect of BASIC. However, most versions of BASIC will have commands which OPEN and CLOSE files. The name of the file in this example is DATAFILE, and it is assigned a **local name** of #1, by which the program knows it. If further files were required these might be assigned further local names consisting of the hash symbol '#' and successive numbers, such as #2, #3 and so on. The reader need not be concerned about such matters for the present; they will be discussed in chapter 6.

In addition, the format of the INPUT instruction has changed, to tell the computer to input from file #1. Furthermore, instead of checking for the input of a zero to exit, in this program we use a **special function** to detect the end of the input file:

```
15 IF EOF(1) THEN GOTO 38
```

This is another example of a conditional statement. It checks if EOF (End Of File) of file 1 is true, and if so, it transfers control to line 38 to close the file, and ends.

Programs which handle files might also write their results to an output file, rather than sending it to the terminal.

4.515 **More logical expressions**
We shall now consider a slightly more complex program which incorporates some of the BASIC instructions we have seen already. The reader may remember the flowchart we drew in section 4.11 in order to find the minimum and maximum value of a series of values for handaxe lengths, and calculate the range. The BASIC program to perform this task might be written as follows:

```
10 REM     HANDAXE PROGRAM
20 OPEN ''I'', #1, ''AXELGTHS''
30 IF EOF(1) THEN GOTO 140
40 INPUT #1, LNGTH
50 MIN = LNGTH
60 MAX = LNGTH
70 IF EOF(1) THEN GOTO 140
80 INPUT #1, LNGTH
90 IF LNGTH > MAX THEN GOTO 120
100 IF LNGTH < MIN THEN MIN = LNGTH
110 GOTO 70
120 MAX = LNGTH
130 GOTO 70
140 CLOSE #1
```

```
150 REM    CALCULATE RANGE
160 RANGE = MAX - MIN
170 PRINT ''MINIMUM LENGTH IS''; MIN; ''CM''
180 PRINT ''MAXIMUM LENGTH IS''; MAX; ''CM''
190 PRINT ''RANGE IS''; RANGE; ''CM''
200 END
```

This program reads data in from a file called AXELGTHS. It sets MAX and MIN to the value of the first length it reads; then checks these against subsequent values, incrementing them as necessary, according to the algorithm in fig. 4.1.

We are already familiar with most of the instructions in this program. However, it does introduce another type of logical expression that can be used with an IF statement:

```
 90 IF LNGTH > MAX THEN GOTO 120
100 IF LNGTH < MIN THEN MIN = LNGTH
```

The symbols > and < are **relational operators**. The effect of line 90 is that if LNGTH is greater then MAX then control is transferred to line 120. Line 100 says that if LNGTH is less then MIN then MIN is set to LNGTH. The relational operators available in BASIC are:

>   (greater than)
>=   (greater than or equal to)
=   (equal to)
<=   (less than or equal to)
<   (less than)
<>   (not equal to)

4.516 Subroutines

It may be observed that the program in section 4.515 is inefficient in at least one respect. Lines 30–40 are repeated exactly at 70–80. Such repeated sequences of instructions may be written as **subroutines** to the main program, which **calls** them. Therefore they need only be written once, but can be used as often as required. In this case a subroutine is hardly necessary because the it is so small, but the program could be written like this:

```
 10 REM    HANDAXE PROGRAM
 20 OPEN ''I'', #1, ''AXELGTHS''
 30 GOSUB 210
 50 MIN = LNGTH
 60 MAX = LNGTH
 70 GOSUB 210
 90 IF LNGTH > MAX THEN GOTO 120
100 IF LNGTH < MIN THEN MIN = LNGTH
110 GOTO 70
120 MAX = LNGTH
130 GOTO 70
140 CLOSE #1
```

```
150 REM     CALCULATE RANGE
160 RANGE = MAX - MIN
170 PRINT ''MINIMUM LENGTH IS''; MIN; ''CM''
180 PRINT ''MAXIMUM LENGTH IS''; MAX; ''CM''
190 PRINT ''RANGE IS''; RANGE; ''CM''
200 END
210 REM     INPUT SUBROUTINE
220 IF EOF(1) THEN GOTO 140
230 INPUT #1, LNGTH
240 RETURN
```

The subroutine begins at line 210. It is called by the instruction:

```
GOSUB 210
```

When line 240 is reached the program RETURNs to the point at which the call was made. Therefore a GOSUB differs from a GOTO as the transfer is only temporary in the former.

4.517 Arrays and more loops

Suppose that, instead of finding the largest and smallest handaxe, and calculating the range, we wish to sort all our handaxes into ascending order of length. We now encounter a different sort of problem, for instead of reading one length in at a time, checking it, and disposing of it (by overwriting the variable), we now need to hold all the handaxe lengths in memory at once. This may be achieved by using an **array** variable. We saw that LNGTH was one box, which could only hold one value at a time. By declaring an array called LNGTH(50), we can set up fifty boxes, or **elements**. The first box is LNGTH(1), the second LNGTH(2), and so on; the bracketed number is known as the array **subscript**.

This example is a one-dimensional array. It may be visualised as one column of fifty boxes. Other arrays, consisting of rows and columns, are known as two-dimensional arrays. LNGTH(4,5) is a two-dimensional array of four rows and five columns.

There are several different techniques for sorting lists of data into numeric or alphabetic sequence. This example program uses a **ripple sort** method (cf. Day 1972). Only five handaxe lengths will be sorted, but the program could be adapted to sort any number.

```
10 REM     RIPPLE SORT OF HANDAXE LENGTHS
20 DIM A(5)
30 DATA 5
40 DATA 8.9, 14.2, 11.5, 9.9, 13.1
50 READ NUMBER
60 FOR AXE = 1 TO NUMBER
70 READ A(AXE)
80 NEXT AXE
90 FOR SWEEP = 1 TO NUMBER - 1
```

```
100 LET M = 0
110 FOR AXE = 1 TO NUMBER − SWEEP
120 IF A(AXE) <= A(AXE + 1) THEN GOTO 170
130 LET X = A(AXE)
140 LET A(AXE) = A(AXE + 1)
150 LET A(AXE + 1) = X
160 LET M = 1
170 NEXT AXE
180 IF M = 0 THEN GOTO 200
190 NEXT SWEEP
200 FOR AXE = 1 TO NUMBER
210 PRINT A(AXE)
220 NEXT AXE
230 END
```

Line 20 is:

```
20 DIM A(5)
```

This is a DIMension statement which sets up an array A of five boxes.

The other new instruction in this example is the FOR-NEXT loop. One complete loop is:

```
60 FOR AXE = 1 TO NUMBER
70 READ A(AXE)
80 NEXT AXE
```

The effect of a loop is to make the computer obey a sequence of instructions again and again. In this case AXE is the loop counter. Since we have previously read 5 into NUMBER the computer executes this loop five times. We could have equally well have written:

```
60 FOR AXE = 1 TO 5
```

At each pass a number is read into an array element. At the first pass AXE is set at 1, so 8.9 is read into A(1). Then line 80 is reached and AXE is incremented by 1 and we return to line 60. At the next pass 14.2 is read into A(2). This continues until AXE is 5. There are three other loops in this program. There is one from lines 90 to 190, and an inner one from 110 to 170. Obviously, inner loops always increment more rapidly than outer loops. Finally, there is a loop from 200 to 220 which prints the sorted list.

4.518 String-handling

Finally, what about programs to deal with strings of characters other than numbers? We drew up a flowchart in fig. 4.5 to extract villas from a bibliography. How would this be implemented in BASIC? In fact it is quite simple, as BASIC has a special type of variable in which we can store strings. A string variable has a unique name like any other variable, except that the name must be terminated with a dollar sign. In effect this tells the computer that it must set up a bigger box to store this variable.

A simple program to retrieve villa references is listed below. This program might be used to extract references from the bibliography file shown in fig. 4.4.[3] We have assumed that no reference will have more than six keywords in all:

```
10 REM    BIBLIOGRAPHY RETRIEVAL BY KEYWORD
20 PRINT ''ENTER KEYWORD TO SEARCH ON ''
30 SEARCH$ = INPUT$(12)
40 OPEN ''I'',#1,''BIBLIO''
50 IF EOF(1) THEN GOTO 150
60 AUTHOR$ = INPUT$(20,#1)
70 DATE$ = INPUT$(10,#1)
80 TITLE$ = INPUT$(50,#1)
90 DETAILS$ = INPUT$(80,#1)
100 FOR I = 1 TO 6
110 KEY$ = INPUT$(12,#1)
120 IF KEY$ = SEARCH$ THEN PRINT AUTHOR$, DATE$, TITLE$
130 NEXT I
140 GOTO 50
150 CLOSE #1
160 END
```

The program makes use of a special Microsoft BASIC function which reads strings of a specified length. The third line is:

```
30 SEARCH$ = INPUT$(12)
```

This instructs the computer to read a string of twelve characters from the keyboard into a variable called SEARCH$.[4] The same function has been used in the lines numbered 60–90 and 110 to read each record from the bibliography into the variables AUTHOR$, DATE$, TITLE$, DETAILS$ AND KEY$.

The program operates around a major loop which uses a GOTO instruction to send it back to line 50 to fetch another record each time line 140 is reached. Only when the end of file #1 is encountered does it escape from the loop to line 150. There is also an inner loop from line 100 to 130 which reads in each of the keywords and checks them against the string that is being searched for. If a matching keyword is found then the record is printed to the terminal.

BASIC's string-handling capabilities make it an excellent language for interactive data capture programs. Words are readily accepted from the keyboard, stored as string variables, and written to disc.

We have dwelt upon several examples of BASIC programs in order to convey some fundamental programming concepts, common to all languages, and to give the reader some idea of what programming in BASIC in particular is like. This has by no means been an exhaustive survey of the BASIC language. To learn how to write BASIC programs the best introduction remains Alcock (1977). Monro (1978) can also be recommended.

4.52 **FORTRAN**

FORTRAN (FORmula TRANslating system) was the first of the high-level languages, and many would argue that it is now showing its age.[5] Nevertheless, the archaeologist who wishes to learn a programming language should give it serious consideration. FORTRAN is almost universally available on mainframe and mini-computers, but less common on micro-computers. The current version is FORTRAN IV, but this is so widely used that it is normally sufficient to refer to it simply as FORTRAN. In its standard form FORTRAN is not machine-dependent. Some manufacturers have extended their own versions to include non-standard extras, but a standard FORTRAN program should run on any machine supporting FORTRAN. The examples in this section are written in FORTRAN IV.

FORTRAN was devised mainly for use by engineers and scientists and it is ideal for programming mathematical formulae. It has a large number of built-in library functions for performing standard arithmetic operations. It has also been widely adopted by geographers and other social scientists for statistical purposes. Consequently, there are a large number of published programs written in FORTRAN (e.g. Mather 1976a) available to archaeologists. These include most of the techniques of spatial analysis and multivariate statistics which have been used in archaeology. Many of the applications packages, such as SPSS, BMDP, and GINO (see chapter 7), are also based upon FORTRAN, and a reading knowledge of the language may be beneficial for their use. On the other hand, because of what it was originally intended for, FORTRAN is not well suited to handling text and strings, beyond simply reading them in and printing them out. Nor is it ideal for nicely formatted output.

FORTRAN is very similar to BASIC. Indeed, the latter was based upon FORTRAN. Therefore a beginner who has learnt BASIC should experience little difficulty in switching to FORTRAN. However, like BASIC, FORTRAN is an unstructured language. Large FORTRAN programs, written for greatest efficiency, are not the easiest programs to understand. Indeed, it may be a horrific task to come cold to a large FORTRAN program and attempt to understand what each instruction is doing. However, a new version of FORTRAN known as FORTRAN 77 should be mentioned here. FORTRAN 77 attempts to incorporate all the old features of FORTRAN in a structured language. It is becoming increasingly popular, and where it is available may be found to be ideal for archaeological needs. Monro (1982) provides a good introduction.

4.521 **Program format**

Let us consider a FORTRAN version of the program written in BASIC in section 4.515 which read in the series of handaxe lengths from a file:

```
C HANDAXE PROGRAM
      REAL LNGTH, MIN, MAX
      READ (5,10) LNGTH
      MIN = LNGTH
      MAX = LNGTH
      DO 100 I=1,1000
      READ (5,10) LNGTH
      IF (LNGTH.EQ.0) GOTO 160
      IF (LNGTH.GT.MAX) MAX = LNGTH
      IF (LNGTH.LT.MIN) MIN = LNGTH
  100 CONTINUE
C CALCULATE RANGE
  160 RANGE = MAX - MIN
      WRITE (6,11) MIN
      WRITE (6,12) MAX
      WRITE (6,13) RANGE
      STOP
   10 FORMAT (F8.4)
   11 FORMAT (' MINIMUM LENGTH IS',F8.4,' CM')
   12 FORMAT (' MAXIMUM LENGTH IS',F8.4,' CM')
   13 FORMAT (' RANGE IS',F8.4,' CM')
      END
```

It will at once be apparent that although there is an overall similarity to the equivalent BASIC program, there are individual differences.

Firstly, not all the lines are numbered. In fact we could have numbered each line, but it is unnecessary in FORTRAN. Line numbers merely serve as labels, as in GOTO 160. Therefore any five-figure numbers can be used, and in any order.

Secondly, there are strict rules about the layout of a FORTRAN program, based historically on 80-character punched cards. Program instructions must be within columns 7–72; columns 1–6 have specific functions: a 'C' in column 1 tells the computer that this line is a comment (the equivalent of the BASIC REM statement). Any number in column 1–5 is regarded as a statement label. A character placed in column 6 is used to indicate the continuation of an instruction over more than one line.

A third difference is that the program needs a STOP statement as well as an END to terminate execution.

4.522 Variables

A further difference is the appearance of a new second line:

```
REAL LNGTH,MIN,MAX
```

In BASIC we met two types of variables: numbers and strings. In FORTRAN there are also several variable types, of which REAL for numbers written with decimal points, and INTEGER for whole numbers, are the most common. This enables each variable to be efficiently stored. Therefore, it may be necessary to declare all variables in FORTRAN, rather than just array variables as in BASIC, so that the appropriate sized box may be created. In practice, FORTRAN allows us to default to variables beginning with the letters I to N for integers, and with A to H or O to Z for real numbers. However, since our handaxe lengths are likely to be real numbers, and since we wish to retain intelligible names for these variables, in this program it is necessary to declare LNGTH, MIN and MAX as real variables. It should be noted that FORTRAN does not allow us to mix real and integer variables in the same arithmetic expression, without converting them to the same type.

4.523 Input and output

The third line of this FORTRAN program is:

```
READ (5,10) LNGTH
```

This replaces the BASIC line:

```
40 INPUT #1, LNGTH
```

In FORTRAN, READ serves to read data both from files and from the keyboard. It is the standard way of accepting data. In FORTRAN, DATA statements associate a variable with a character within the statement; though they are rarely used for getting data into a program. The following line stores 5 in the variable NUMBER:

```
DATA NUMBER /5/
```

The READ statement is followed by two numbers in brackets. The first tells the program which **channel** the data is to be read on, i.e. whether from a file, or the terminal, or another input device. By convention channel 5 usually indicates an input file. It will be remembered that in the BASIC program it was necessary to assign a file to the input channel, and open it:

```
20 OPEN "I", #1, "AXELGTHS"
```

In FORTRAN the assignment is normally done outside the program, and opening occurs when the file is first referenced (see section 4.62).

The second number associates the READ instruction with a FORMAT statement. The number 10 indicates the line labelled 10, which in this example is at the foot of the program, although it could have been placed anywhere:

```
10 FORMAT (F8.4)
```

The FORMAT statement tells the program what format the data is in, including the position of the decimal point. In this example the format is (F8.4). The F indicates that it is a real number; 8 gives the total number of character positions occupied, including the decimal point; and 4 indicates the number of characters following the decimal point. Thus the following numbers are in format F8.4 (in these examples stars are used to indicate spaces):

```
625.23**
*37.4***
105.205*
```

The other type of format instruction frequently encountered is for integer numbers. This begins with the letter I, and has just one number, indicating the total number of character positions. Thus the following numbers are in format I5:

```
*5625
***37
**105
```

FORMAT statements are a peculiarity of FORTRAN. They reflect (standard) FORTRAN's insistence that data must be in a fixed format, which can be a great handicap in many applications. On the other hand, the control over the exact form of the data can be useful. For example, the decimal point can be implied with a FORTRAN FORMAT statement. The following integer numbers could be read according to a F8.4 format:

```
62523**
*374***
105205*
```

If they were formatted exactly as above they would be stored as 625.23, 37.4, and 105.205.

It should also be noted that each time a FORTRAN READ statement is encountered the program will go to the beginning of the next line of data, irrespective of whether there are any values remaining to be read on the current line. Therefore some care is necessary in reading a data file.

FORTRAN has also forced us to amend our data file. It does not have a special function to test for end of file like BASIC. Therefore, if we do not know how many lines of data are to be read in, we must place our own flag which we can test for at the end of the data file. In this example we have placed a zero on the last line of data.

In addition, it will be seen that the statements controlling the output of results are also different in this FORTRAN program. FORTRAN does not have a PRINT statement. The equivalent is a WRITE instruction with an associated FORMAT statement, in a similar manner to the READ commands:

```
      WRITE (6,11) MIN
11 FORMAT (' MINIMUM LENGTH IS',F8.4,' CM')
```

The two numbers enclosed in brackets after WRITE are the channel number, and the label of the format statement. The conventional channel for an output file is 6. Again it must have been previously created and assigned, outside the program. The variables to be written are named after the closing bracket of the WRITE instruction; not as part of the FORMAT statement.

The FORMAT statement includes the characters to be written out literally, enclosed within quotation marks, and the format in which MIN is to be written.

4.524 **Loops**
The main block of the program is within a loop:

```
        DO 100 I=1,1000
        . . . . .
   100 CONTINUE
```

This is the equivalent of a BASIC FOR-NEXT loop, although in FORTRAN it is known as a DO loop. The first line may be read as:

DO what follows down to line 100 for I equals from 1 to 1000

In other words the instructions following are to be repeated until I has been incremented to 1000. When line 100 is reached for the thousandth time then the program CONTINUEs with the next instruction in sequence. Of course, in our example, 1000 has simply been chosen as a sufficiently large enough number so that all the handaxes are checked. In practice the program will jump out of the loop when the zero at the end of the data file is detected, and GOTO 160.

4.525 **Logical expressions**
It will be apparent that logical expressions are also written differently in FORTRAN. There are three examples in this program:

```
   IF (LNGTH.EQ.0) GOTO 160
   IF (LNGTH.GT.MAX) MAX = LNGTH
   IF (LNGTH.LT.MIN) MIN = LNGTH
```

The expression itself must be enclosed in brackets; and the symbols such as $>$ and $<$, for greater than and less than, are replaced by two letter codes bounded by decimal points. The full set of relational operators in FOR-TRAN is:

.GT.	(greater than)
.GE.	(greater than or equal to)
.EQ.	(equal to)
.LE.	(less than or equal to)
.LT.	(less then)
.NE.	(not equal to)

In addition, FORTRAN has three **logical operators** which allow more complicated logical expressions to be built up:

.NOT.	(logical inversion)
.AND.	(logical multiplication)
.OR.	(logical addition)

Thus a valid FORTRAN statement is:

```
IF (A.GT.C.AND.A.LT.B) GOTO 100
```

This causes transfer of control to statement 100 only if both A is greater than C and A is less than B. Alternatively, one could write:

```
IF (A.GT.C.OR.A.LT.B) GOTO 100
```

In this case control is transferred either if A is greater than C, or if A is less than B. Such simple expressions, which yield a result which is either .TRUE. or .FALSE. are also known by the rather off-putting description **boolean algebra**, after the nineteenth-century mathematician George Boole.

4.526 **Subroutines**

It should also be noted that a FORTRAN program can be written which calls a series of subroutines, as in BASIC. Thus a large FORTRAN program typically consists of a main program block, with calls to a number of modules, or subroutines. Where practicable it is preferable to use subroutines rather than GOTO statements. The GOTO statement is the principal reason why BASIC and FORTRAN listings are difficult to follow, and it is shunned by the adherents of structured programming.

4.527 **String-handling**

We shall not give a FORTRAN version of our string-handling program to retrieve references from a bibliography. This would not be impossible to write in FORTRAN, but since it does not have a simple equivalent of the BASIC string variable, it would be rather cumbersome. In order that they can be manipulated, text variables in FORTRAN have to be stored as arrays, with each character occupying one element in the array. Thus:

```
WORD(1)    V
WORD(2)    I
WORD(3)    L
WORD(4)    L
WORD(5)    A
```

In conclusion, if it is anticipated that a large amount of textual data is to be processed, then it is unwise to choose FORTRAN for the programming language, as it was never intended for such applications (although improved string-handling facilities are included in FORTRAN 77). If, on the other hand, one intends to perform a lot of number-crunching, then FORTRAN will prove a powerful tool. A FORTRAN program is also one of the most convenient means of changing data from one format to another, as this can be accomplished in a few lines. We have just provided a glimpse of the essential elements of the language here. For those wishing to learn FORTRAN there are a good selection of well-established teaching manuals available. These include Calderbank (1969), McCracken (1972), and Monro (1977). Alcock (1982) can also be strongly recommended. Mather (1976b) provides a short course in FORTRAN for geographers, which may also appeal to spatially minded archaeologists.

4.53 COBOL

COBOL is an acronym for COmmon Business Orientated Language. It was developed in 1960 under the auspices of the Conference on Data Systems Languages (CODASYL) to provide a business system orientated high-level language. FORTRAN was fairly widely used by then, but its file-handling facilities made it unsuitable and too restrictive for most commercial data processing applications.

As we have seen input/output in FORTRAN is in terms of simple streams of variables. Data processing required the capacity to describe record structured input/output, including the capability to give names to fields of data within records.

COBOL was developed, therefore, as a language more restricted in its computational ability, but with better file-handling, and structured records. COBOL is rather different from the languages we have looked at so far. As will be seen, it is a very 'wordy' language, and resembles English more closely than many other programming languages. However, rather than making a COBOL program any more comprehensible, this can just make COBOL programming rather tedious. Many programmers tend to write a shorthand version.

Nevertheless, COBOL is the most widely known and used language in the business world, and it has a lot to offer archaeologists, especially those more interested in routine data processing of large quantities of data, and less concerned with statistical applications. For example, the programs for the Danebury computing project, where it was necessary to process large amounts of data from the Iron Age hillfort, were written in COBOL (Lock forthcoming).

Unfortunately, despite the original fine intentions, COBOL is not standardised today. Hardware manufacturers have developed their own dialects and consequently COBOL programs are not fully portable. The example below is in ICL COBOL but we follow 'standard' COBOL as contained in the CODASYL specifications as closely as possible. For variations, consult the local manual.

4.531 Program format

COBOL programs comprise four divisions: **identification**, **environment**, **data**, and **procedure**. Each division may be further split into sections.

The identification division contains material to identify the program. It must include the program name, and it can also include other information such as the programmer's name, the date written and general comments.

The environment division lists the input and output files that the program will use, and assigns their internal name to an external name. Additional sections may specify the computer system being used.

The data division gives additional information about the files specified in the environment division. The arrangement of records within files and the arrangement of fields within records is described in this division. All variables or data names, as they are known in COBOL, are declared here. Therefore the same data division can be used for all programs using the same data, which can be an advantage in generating new programs.

The procedure division is where the actual computations are performed. All executable statements are found here. Thus execution is clearly separated from data in COBOL, allowing a program to be extended or amended by altering only the procedure division or the data division and leaving the others intact.

Sections may be further subdivided into paragraphs, which consist of sentences of one or more COBOL statements. Each sentence must be terminated with a full stop followed by a blank space.

It will be apparent that it is impossible to write a short program in COBOL. The language was designed for large programs which would be used for several years; not for quick one-off jobs. The identification and environment divisions, plus the facility to use long and hence meaningful variable names, means that a COBOL program is largely self-documenting. This may be useful in large establishments with many users and a high staff turnover; in other cases the extra programming investment required may be a handicap.

It would be possible to write a COBOL program to compute the problem of finding the shortest and longest handaxe. However, a more appropriate example to demonstrate the capabilities of COBOL is provided by the example where we wish to retrieve references to villas from a bibliography. The program might appear like this:

```
000010 IDENTIFICATION DIVISION.
000020 PROGRAM-ID. BIBLIOFILE.
000030 AUTHOR. J D RICHARDS.
000040 DATE-WRITTEN. 10/2/83.

000050 ENVIRONMENT DIVISION.
000060 CONFIGURATION SECTION.
000070 SOURCE-COMPUTER. ICL-2966.
000080 OBJECT-COMPUTER. ICL-2966.
000090 INPUT-OUTPUT SECTION.
000100 FILE-CONTROL.
000110      SELECT BIB-FILE ASSIGN TO DATAFILE.

000120 DATA DIVISION.
000130 FILE SECTION.
```

```
000140 FD   BIB-FILE.
000150 01   BOOK-RECORD.
000160      02  BOOK-AUTHOR            PIC A(20).
000170      02  BOOK-DATE             PIC 9(10).
000180      02  BOOK-TITLE            PIC X(50).
000190      02  BOOK-DETAILS          PIC X(80).
000200      02  BOOK-KEY OCCURS 6 TIMES  PIC A(12).
000210 WORKING-STORAGE SECTION.
000220 77   SEARCHKEY               PIC A(12) VALUE IS
                SPACES.
000230 77   MORE-DATA               PIC A(3) VALUE IS
                'YES'.
000240 77   I                       PIC 9 VALUE IS ZERO.

000250 PROCEDURE DIVISION.
000260 CONTROL ROUTINE.
000270      DISPLAY 'ENTER KEYWORD TO SEARCH ON'.
000280      ACCEPT SEARCHKEY.
000290      OPEN INPUT BIB-FILE.
000300      PERFORM RETRIEVAL UNTIL MORE-DATA IS EQUAL TO
                'NO'.
000310      CLOSE BIB-FILE.
000320      STOP RUN.
000330 RETRIEVAL.
000340      READ BIB-FILE AT END MOVE 'NO' TO MORE-DATA.
000350      MOVE 1 TO I.
000360      PERFORM CHECK 6 TIMES.
000370 CHECK.
000380      IF BOOK-KEY(I) IS EQUAL TO SEARCHKEY
                DISPLAY BOOK-RECORD.
000390      ADD 1 TO I.
```

The layout of a COBOL program, like that of one in FORTRAN, reflects the fact that the language was designed with punched cards in mind:

Columns 1–6 are reserved for line numbers, if desired, although these do not affect the execution of the program.

Column 7 is a continuation column. If a line is too long to be continued on a single card a minus sign may be placed in column 7, and the line continued on another card. Alternatively, an asterisk here indicates that the line is a comment and is to be disregarded by the computer.

Columns 8–11 are known as Area A. Certain COBOL statements must begin in the Area A columns. These include names of divisions, sections or paragraphs, as well as file descriptions.

Columns 12–72 are Area B. All other COBOL statements must begin somewhere in Area B.

Columns 73–80 are reserved for the programmer's own messages or comments. The computer ignores them.

For the sake of clarity each of the divisions in our program example is separated by a blank line. This is unnecessary for the operation of the program.

4.532 Identification division
In the identification division the program name is declared to be BIBLIOFILE, and the author and date written are noted. Other information on the organisation and so on could also be given.

4.533 Environment division
The environment division notes the class of computer the program was written on, and on which it is to be operated. In both cases it is an ICL 2966 in this example. A file called BIB-FILE is declared, and is assigned to the external file DATAFILE, which contains the bibliographic records.

4.534 Data division
The data division is frequently lengthy in a COBOL program as all the variables used within the program must be declared here, and their format specified. In this example the data division consists of two sections.

The first is the file section. COBOL programs are based upon the processing of files, from which data is read, and to which results are written. BIB-FILE is defined as consisting of BOOK-RECORDs, made up of four simple variables, and one array variable of six elements. Variable names in COBOL may be up to 30 characters in length, and as well as the standard alphanumeric characters they may contain hyphens, allowing one to define meaningful variable names. In this example the four simple variables are named BOOK-AUTHOR, BOOK-DATE, BOOK-TITLE, and BOOK-DETAILS. The array variable BOOK-KEY is declared as consisting of six elements, one for each possible keyword in BOOK-RECORD. Individual elements are referred to by a subscript number. Thus BOOK-KEY(1) indicates the first keyword, and so on. The record definition indicates that BOOK-RECORD is a continuous series of fields on one line, of 232 character positions in all, and with no line breaks.[6]

The second part of each variable declaration is the PICTURE clause, which defines the type and format of each of the variables. The most common COBOL data types are:

A	Alphabetic
X	Alphanumeric
9	Numeric
V	Numeric with implied decimal point
Z	Numeric with supression of leading zeros on output

A(20) indicates that BOOK-AUTHOR is an alphabetic variable of twenty characters; 9(10) defines BOOK-DATE as a numeric variable occupying 10 character positions. These definitions may alternatively be written in expanded form:

```
000170        02  BOOK-DATE        PICTURE 9999999999.
```

The second paragraph of the data division is the working storage section. All those variables which are not defined within files must be declared here. These are variables which are used internally by the program: loop counters, flags, etc. The number 77 preceding the names may strike the reader as rather odd. In the file section the variable names were alloted a level number (in this case 01 and 02), which indicated that they were members of a group or record structure. In the working storage section the level number 77 means that we are defining a simple field that contains a single data item.

The VALUE IS clause is used to assign values to variables and constants when the program is loaded into the computer. Thus SEARCHKEY is filled with 12 spaces, the flag MORE-DATA which is used to control the program when the end of the data file is reached is set to 'YES', and the loop-counter I is set to zero.

4.535 Procedure division

The procedure division comprises the instructions which control the execution of the program. The main paragraph is the CONTROL ROUTINE. Program execution starts here. The two following lines are:

```
000270      DISPLAY 'ENTER KEYWORD TO SEARCH ON'.
000280      ACCEPT SEARCHKEY.
```

This introduces simple input and output of small quantities of data at the terminal. The characters within single quotation marks are printed literally. The program then expects a value for SEARCHKEY to be entered, terminated by a carriage return. If we wished to retrieve references to villas then VILLA should be typed at this point. The computer is then instructed to open BIB-FILE for input with the command:

```
000290      OPEN INPUT BIB-FILE.
```

The next line introduces probably the most useful COBOL instruction, PERFORM:

```
000300      PERFORM RETRIEVAL UNTIL MORE-DATA IS EQUAL TO
            'NO'.
```

RETRIEVAL is the name of another paragraph in the procedure division. It may be regarded as equivalent to the BASIC or FORTRAN subroutine, or the Pascal procedure (cf. section 4.544). Its effect is to transfer program control to the paragraph headed RETRIEVAL. The commands listed under RETRIEVAL are then executed in sequence, and when the last one has been completed control returns to the next line in the control routine. There are several possible forms of the PERFORM instruction. The simplest is:

```
PERFORM RETRIEVAL.
```

In this case RETRIEVAL is executed once and then control returns to the calling routine. In the program example RETRIEVAL is repeatedly executed until the value of MORE-DATA is found to be 'NO'. Another example of the use of PERFORM may be found further down in our program:

```
000360      PERFORM CHECK 6 TIMES.
```

This specifies that the group of instructions contained in the paragraph headed CHECK must be executed six times.

Once MORE-DATA has been found to be equal to 'NO' then the program moves to the subsequent line of the control routine, which instructs it to close BIB-FILE:

```
000310      CLOSE BIB-FILE.
```

Finally, the control routine must be terminated by an instruction which tells the computer that it may cease execution of this program:

```
000320      STOP RUN.
```

We shall now examine the individual instructions which make up the RETRIEVAL routine. The first is:

```
000340      READ BIB-FILE AT END MOVE 'NO' TO MORE-DATA.
```

This introduces another type of input instruction, READ. READ reads a complete record at a time from a file; in this case, BIB-FILE. Therefore the computer fetches a complete book record, consisting of author, date, title, details, and keywords. We can also use WRITE in COBOL to output complete records at a time.

The second part of the instruction tells the computer that at the end of the file it is to move 'NO' into MORE-DATA. This is an example of a COBOL assignment. The next line is a further example:

```
000350      MOVE 1 TO I.
```

This tells the computer to place the value 1 in the variable I. It is equivalent to the BASIC or FORTRAN statement:

```
I = 1
```

The final instruction in RETRIEVAL is to execute CHECK six times; once for each of the possible keywords. CHECK consists of just two instructions. The first is:

```
000380      IF BOOK-KEY(I) IS EQUAL TO SEARCHKEY
                 DISPLAY BOOK-RECORD.
```

This checks if element I of array BOOK-KEY is equal to SEARCHKEY, and if so, then the complete BOOK-RECORD is displayed at the terminal. The second line is simple:

```
000390        ADD 1 TO I.
```

This increments the value of I by one each time CHECK is performed. Thus successive elements of the array BOOK-KEY may be referred to and checked. COBOL statements are often written out in full English-like expressions. Other arithmetic operations include:

```
DIVIDE 10 INTO I.
MULTIPLY 100 BY I.
```

We have seen that it is also possible to perform simple logical operations in COBOL, such as testing if two values are identical. We can also test if one is greater than or less than the other. However, it becomes difficult to perform more complicated arithmetic operations. COBOL does not have the range of arithmetic functions, for finding sines, tangents, logarithms, square roots, etc, that the other languages discussed in this chapter contain.

Therefore whilst COBOL may be an ideal language for programming information retrieval applications, and for manipulating and sorting data files, and can handle strings as readily as numeric data, it should not be used for statistical applications.

The structure of a COBOL program, allowing it to be split into individual paragraphs, does allow one to follow the operation of a COBOL program more easily than one written in FORTRAN for example. However, it cannot be regarded as a truly structured language in the same sense that, for instance, Pascal can be, for it lacks a block structure.

To find out more about COBOL the reader may consult McCracken (1976), Ashley (1980), or Lyons (1980).

4.54 Pascal

Unlike most names for programming languages, Pascal is not an acronym, but was named after the seventeenth-century French mathematician, Blaise Pascal. It also differs from the languages we have discussed so far by being a structured language. Pascal was derived from the ALGOL family of languages, and like ALGOL (which it has largely superseded), a Pascal program consists of procedures, and blocks of instructions, beginning with BEGIN and terminated by END. Each block is, in effect, an independent program. Therefore Pascal is an ideal language in which to write structured programs. In addition, unlike ALGOL, conventions for input/output were standardised in the original report (Jensen and Wirth 1978), rather than being left up to the individual implementation. Therefore a Pascal program is normally fairly portable.[7]

Pascal combines many of the best features of the languages we have examined so far. It has a record structure almost as good as that of COBOL, whilst maintaining most of the mathematical capabilities of FORTRAN. To this it adds some flexibility in string-handling, and simple presentation of output, plus all the benefits of structured programming. It is no surprise therefore that it is becoming increasingly popular on both mainframe and micro-computers. The Museum Documentation Association Draft Standard (Stewart 1980) recommends it as the first choice of programming language for archaeologists, and we would agree that for most applications it should probably be the first choice.

Our simple program examples cannot do justice to structured programming, but should convey some impression of how a Pascal program works.

4.541 **Program format**

Let us consider a Pascal version of the now familiar program to read in a series of handaxe lengths and find the shortest and longest:

```
PROGRAM HANDAXE (INPUT, OUTPUT) ;
 (* PROGRAM TO FIND THE SHORTEST AND LONGEST HANDAXE *)
VAR LENGTH, MINIMUM, MAXIMUM, RANGE: REAL;
BEGIN
   READLN (LENGTH) ;
   MINIMUM: =LENGTH;
   MAXIMUM: =LENGTH;
   WHILE NOT EOF DO
   BEGIN
      READLN (LENGTH) ;
      IF LENGTH > MAXIMUM THEN MAXIMUM: =LENGTH
      ELSE
      IF LENGTH < MINIMUM THEN MINIMUM: =LENGTH;
   END;
   RANGE: =MAXIMUM−MINIMUM;
   WRITELN ('MINIMUM LENGTH IS', MINIMUM: 8: 4, ' CM') ;
   WRITELN ('MAXIMUM LENGTH IS', MAXIMUM: 8: 4, ' CM') ;
   WRITELN ('RANGE IS', RANGE: 8: 4, ' CM') ;
END.
```

Pascal programs are normally set out as above, with one or a few instructions on a line, as in BASIC or FORTRAN. However, in Pascal this is purely for convenience, and the program could be written as a continuous piece of text. It is the semicolon which is recognised by the computer as terminating each instruction. In addition, it is usual to indent the instructions demarcated by each BEGIN and END, so that each program block can be readily distinguished.

The program flows logically from beginning to end, without the abrupt transfers of control that characterise BASIC and FORTRAN programs. Whilst Pascal does have the GOTO statement in its vocabulary, it rarely need be used.

The first statement in the example program is:

```
PROGRAM HANDAXE (INPUT, OUTPUT);
```

This simply declares the program name and lists the external files in parentheses. The instruction is terminated with a semicolon. In this case there are only two external files, which are predefined in Pascal: INPUT and OUTPUT. Other files may be established as required, but must be declared as variables within the program. INPUT and OUTPUT are automatically declared whenever used in the heading. All files must be associated with pre-existing files before the program is run (see section 4.6).

The second line is:

```
(* PROGRAM TO FIND SHORTEST AND LONGEST HANDAXE *)
```

This is a Pascal comment statement which has no effect on the execution of the program, and is solely for the convenience of the user. Comments in Pascal are enclosed within the symbols (*....*) or {....}. They may be placed anywhere in the program, including within executable statements.

The instruction BEGIN on line 4 marks the beginning of the main program block. Simple programs may have just one BEGIN-END, whilst complex programs may have several. The final END is followed by a full stop.

4.542 Variables
The third line is:

```
VAR LENGTH, MINIMUM, MAXIMUM, RANGE: REAL;
```

This is a variable declaration. All variables which occur in a Pascal program must be declared by a VAR statement. In this example LENGTH, MINIMUM, MAXIMUM, and RANGE, are declared as REAL variables. Pascal is fairly generous in allowing the use of long words as variable names, although only the first eight characters are significant in distinguishing between names in standard implementations. Thus sensible names which make the program easier to understand can be used. The standard variable types in Pascal include:

INTEGER	– values that are whole numbers
REAL	– values that are real numbers
BOOLEAN	– values that have the logic values of TRUE or FALSE
CHAR	– values that are one of the set of characters

However, one of the most powerful features of Pascal is the capability for users to define their own variable types. This can be done using a TYPE statement as follows:

```
TYPE WEEKDAY= (MON, TUES, WED, THUR, FRI);
```

The facility to define the possible range of values of a variable can prove valuable in data capture programs.

4.543 **Input and output**

The fifth line instructs the computer to read a value into the variable
LENGTH. A particular file could be specified, as in:

READ (DATAFILE2, LENGTH) ;

Otherwise the standard pre-declared INPUT and OUTPUT files are
assumed by READ and WRITE statements. Unlike COBOL and FOR-
TRAN, it is unnecessary to specify the format of the data to be read in.
Values simply need to be separated by a blank space. Pascal is therefore very
useful for dealing with free format records.

The subsequent lines assign the value of LENGTH to the variables MINI-
MUM and MAXIMUM. It should be noted that the assignment operator is a
colon followed by an equals sign (:=). This avoids the confusion, which exists
in BASIC, between the assignment operator:

20 LET X = 10

and the logical operator:

20 IF X = 10 THEN . . . .

The next statement introduces a form of loop in Pascal:

WHILE NOT EOF DO

EOF (End Of File) is a pre-declared boolean variable which may be true or
false. The statement indicates that whilst EOF is not true then the following
instruction should be repeated, until EOF becomes true. In this example, the
next instruction is a complete block of instructions marked by BEGIN and
END. Therefore the instructions enclosed within BEGIN and END are
repeated until EOF is true.

These instructions tell the computer to read the next value from the input
file into LENGTH; test if this is greater than MAXIMUM, or less than
MINIMUM; and adjust MINIMUM and MAXIMUM accordingly. The
construction of the conditional statement in Pascal allows the use of an
additional clause ELSE. The instruction following ELSE will be obeyed only
if LENGTH is not greater than MAXIMUM. The relational operators in
Pascal are identical to those in BASIC (cf. section 4.514).

Finally, the RANGE is calculated, and the results sent to the output file.
Since the instruction WRITELN has been used, rather than WRITE, each
result will be printed on a new line. The numbers ':8:4' incorporated in the
WRITELN instructions fulfil the same function as those in a FORTRAN
FORMAT statement. Thus the results are each printed in a field of eight
characters, with four characters after the decimal point. This allows Pascal
output to be easily formatted.

4.544 **Procedures**

The simple program described above merely had a main program block of instructions marked by BEGIN and END, and a further block of instructions which were obeyed in a loop, marked by a second BEGIN and END. More usually, a program written in Pascal will consist of several **procedures**, which may be regarded as the equivalent of the subroutine in BASIC or FOR-TRAN. The use of procedures allows a sequence of operations to be obeyed several times, but only written once. Furthermore, it allows the subdivision of a program into separate modules which may be developed and tested independently. In section 4.42 it was shown how, with structured design, the handaxe problem could be split into three modules, each called by a control module. One module read in the data; a second performed a check; and a third printed out the result. Although it is such a trivial example that in practice it would hardly be necessary, the Pascal handaxe program could be rewritten with three procedures, whose structure and relationship model the problem. For clarity a blank line has been inserted between each procedure. We shall also read the handaxe lengths into an array so that they are all held in memory, and assume that there are no more than 100 lengths in all:

```
PROGRAM HANDAXE (INPUT, OUTPUT);
(* PROGRAM TO FIND THE SHORTEST AND LONGEST HANDAXE *)
VAR I, AXENUMBER: INTEGER;
    MINIMUM, MAXIMUM, RANGE: REAL;
    LENGTH: ARRAY [1..100] OF REAL;

  PROCEDURE READDATA;
  BEGIN
    AXENUMBER: =0;
    WHILE NOT EOF DO
    BEGIN
      AXENUMBER: = AXENUMBER+1;
      READLN (LENGTH [AXENUMBER]);
    END;
  END;

  PROCEDURE CHECK;
  BEGIN
    MINIMUM: =LENGTH [1];
    MAXIMUM: =LENGTH [1];
    FOR I: =2 TO AXENUMBER DO
    BEGIN
      IF LENGTH [I] > MAXIMUM THEN MAXIMUM: =LENGTH [I]
      ELSE
      IF LENGTH [I] < MINIMUM THEN MINIMUM: =LENGTH [I];
    END;
  END;
```

```
PROCEDURE WRITERESULTS;
BEGIN
  RANGE: = MAXIMUM-MINIMUM;
  WRITELN('MINIMUM LENGTH IS', MINIMUM:8:4,' CM');
  WRITELN('MAXIMUM LENGTH IS', MAXIMUM:8:4,' CM');
  WRITELN('RANGE IS', RANGE:8:4,' CM');
END;

BEGIN (* MAIN PROGRAM BLOCK *)
  READDATA;
  CHECK;
  WRITERESULTS;
END.
```

Most of these instructions are already familiar, but note the form of array declarations in Pascal.

Each procedure is headed by its name in the form:

```
PROCEDURE READDATA;
```

The program instructions which form the procedure follow, marked by BEGIN and END. Each procedure is listed at the head of the program, following the variable declarations. Thus the first program instruction that is obeyed when the program is executed is now found almost at the end of the listing, following the line:

```
BEGIN (* MAIN PROGRAM BLOCK *)
```

Thus the first line to be obeyed on execution is:

```
READDATA;
```

This is the call to the procedure of that name.

Another new feature of this program is the introduction of a second form of Pascal loop:

```
FOR I: = 2 TO AXENUMBER DO
BEGIN
....
END;
```

This has the effect of repeating the instructions enclosed within BEGIN and END whilst I is incremented from 2 to the value of AXENUMBER.

It might be legitimately argued that the new version of the handaxe program, incorporating procedures, is longer than the original version, and would take longer to program. However, the real advantage comes when it becomes necessary to perform an extra operation on the handaxe lengths, such as sorting them into order of size. With the original program this would involve introducing new lines throughout the program, and amending existing instructions, with a possibility of the introduction of errors. With the second version, since we have read the lengths into an array, all that is necessary is the insertion of a new procedure, and a call to that procedure, to get the program to perform an extra task. If errors have been introduced then we can be reasonably sure that they are in the new procedure, as we know that the rest of the program works. In a long and complex programming problem, this might represent a considerable saving.

4.545 String-handling and records

Finally, it should be noted that Pascal is adequate for handling character strings as well as for dealing with numbers. Consider a Pascal program to retrieve records from a bibliography:

```
PROGRAM BIBLIOFILE (INPUT, OUTPUT, BIBFILE, RESFILE) ;
TYPE KEYWORD= PACKED ARRAY [1..12] OF CHAR;
     BOOKRECORD= RECORD
                       AUTHOR: PACKED ARRAY [1..20] OF CHAR;
                       DATE: PACKED ARRAY [1..10] OF CHAR;
                       TITLE: PACKED ARRAY [1..50] OF CHAR;
                       DETAILS: PACKED ARRAY [1..80] OF CHAR;
                       KEY: PACKED ARRAY [1..6] OF KEYWORD;
                 END;
VAR BIBFILE, RESFILE: FILE OF BOOKRECORD;
    SEARCHKEY: KEYWORD;
    I: INTEGER;
BEGIN
  WRITELN ('ENTER KEYWORD TO SEARCH ON') ;
  FOR I:=1 TO 12 DO
  READ (SEARCHKEY [I]) ;
  REWRITE (RESFILE) ;
  RESET (BIBFILE) ;
  WHILE NOT EOF (BIBFILE) DO
  BEGIN
    FOR I:=1 TO 6 DO
    IF BIBFILE^. KEY [I] = SEARCHKEY THEN
    BEGIN
       RESFILE^:= BIBFILE^;
       PUT (RESFILE) ;
    END;
    GET (BIBFILE) ;
  END;
END.
```

This program uses some of the more advanced features of Pascal, and the reader without previous experience of the language should not be concerned if it appears rather strange. The file-handling concepts involved will not be discussed until chapter 6.

The program uses the Pascal facility which allows users to define types of record. Each reference in the bibliography is regarded as an individual Pascal record. It can then be read, manipulated, and printed, by a single instruction each time, in a manner similar to that in which records were handled in the COBOL version of the program. Otherwise, each field within the record would have to be read, and dealt with, individually.

In the first line the program defines four channels for input and output: INPUT, OUTPUT, BIBFILE, and RESFILE. BIBFILE and RESFILE must normally be externally assigned to existing files. The first is the bibliography; extracted records will be printed to the second. If INPUT and OUTPUT are left unassigned when the program is executed then the terminal will be used for these channels, and data will be accepted from the keyboard.

The second line is:

```
TYPE KEYWORD= PACKED ARRAY [1..12] OF CHAR;
```

This instruction defines a type of variable to be used in the program called KEYWORD, which is a **packed array** of twelve characters. A packed array is a type of array in Pascal which saves storage space by packing characters closely together and is convenient for string-handling. The subsequent lines define a second type called BOOKRECORD which is declared as a **record** of five variables: AUTHOR, DATE, TITLE, DETAILS, and KEY. Note that the last variable, KEY, is itself an array of a user-defined type, KEYWORD.

The variable declarations follow. BIBFILE and RESFILE are declared as files of BOOKRECORD; and SEARCHKEY as a KEYWORD.[8] I is simply defined as an integer.

The remaining lines control the operation of the program. The user is first prompted to enter a keyword:

```
WRITELN('ENTER KEYWORD TO SEARCH ON');
```

SEARCHKEY is then accepted one character at a time from the keyboard:

```
FOR I:=1 TO 12 DO
READ(SEARCHKEY[I]);
```

If the desired keyword is less than twelve characters it must be padded out with spaces.[9] The next two lines may be unfamiliar:

```
REWRITE(RESFILE);
RESET(BIBFILE);
```

These commands are necessary to open the extra files that are to be used. REWRITE opens a file for output; RESET one for input, and fetches the first record from that file.

The program then enters a loop which continues to fetch records and checks them for the desired keyword until the end of BIBFILE is reached:

```
WHILE NOT EOF(BIBFILE) DO
```

This line introduces a special feature of record-handling in Pascal:

```
IF BIBFILE^.KEY [I] = SEARCHKEY THEN
```

BIBFILE^ is a variable which holds the current record from BIBFILE. To refer to a particular field of that record it is followed by a period and the field identifier. Thus BIBFILE^.KEY [1] refers to the first keyword held in the KEY array of the current BIBFILE record. If the keyword is found to be the same as the SEARCHKEY then the current record in BIBFILE is made the current RESFILE record with this statement:

```
RESFILE^: = BIBFILE^;
```

The next instruction writes the current RESFILE record to the file:

```
PUT (RESFILE) ;
```

Similarly, the following instruction fetches the next record from BIBFILE:

```
GET (BIBFILE) ;
```

When the program has fetched the final record EOF becomes TRUE and the program reaches the final END.

Although this has been an incomplete survey, we have discussed the most commonly used features of Pascal. It can be seen that it is a very elegant and powerful tool. Though not as easy as BASIC, Pascal is not a difficult language to learn from scratch, and will also teach the programmer good habits. There is a large number of adequate teaching books available. Amongst the best are Moore (1980), Findlay and Watt (1981), and Wilson and Addyman (1978).

Section 4.5 has not covered every high-level language, but it has dealt with enough of the more popular ones to give the reader a good idea of what programming is like. Although each of the languages has its own strengths and weaknesses, each should be applicable to most archaeological problems, within the limitations discussed above. Therefore whilst it will be apparent that some languages are better suited to certain types of application than others, it would be misleading to give firm recommendations on language choice. As already discussed, local factors such as availability and personal expertise are likely to dictate which language is used in practice.

However, mention should also be made of several other languages designed for specific purposes that may be useful to archaeologists. Some of these are in the form of applications packages and will be discussed in chapter 7. Others are programming languages such as SIMULA, SIMSCRIPT and GPSS, which are specifically intended for programming simulations. For more details of these, we would refer the reader to Moore (1978) and Aldenderfer (1981a).

4.6 **Program implementation**
Finally, it may be helpful to say a little about program implementation.

Having decided to write a program, how does one get it into a computer and how does one instruct the computer to compile/interpret and run it? This is the 'missing link' which is rarely dealt with in programming text books. The problem is that the particular form of the instructions is dependent upon the operating system of the chosen computer.

If one is using a mainframe computer then it may be possible to run a **job** (consisting of one or more program executions) in either batch or multi-access mode. On a large computer with more than one user one of the main functions of the operating system is to allocate resources between the people using the system at any one moment in time. This allocation should appear to be fair, or at least according to a set of priorities allotted to the various classes of user. Ideally it should appear to each user that he or she is the only person using the computer at that moment. One means of achieving this is to present each user with a **virtual machine**. In its general usage this implies that it should appear to users that they each have their own computer, with tapes and disc drives and various peripheral devices, such as printers, allocated to them.

Learning how to use an operating system is probably the area which presents the most problems to the archaeologist unfamiliar with computers. Yet it is impossible to offer much guidance because every operating system has its own unique set of instructions which just have to be learnt. If you are using a mainframe computer then the best plan is probably either to get an experienced user to show you, or to enrol on a 'basic users' course. Manufacturers' manuals are usually best left as a last resort. They are written by, and for, professionals and are frequently unintelligible to the rest of us. On the other hand, if you are using a micro-computer, then the operating system is more likely to be **user-friendly**, and the instruction manual adequate. We shall give examples from a mainframe, a mini-, and a micro-computer, just to show that it is not too difficult.

We would again stress that there has been no attempt to teach programming in this chapter. Nevertheless, if the reader has access to a computer he or she might like to key in one of the simple programs listed above, such as the sorting routine in section 4.517, or one of the programs to find the minimum and maximum of a sequence of numbers in sections 4.514, 4.521, and 4.541. All the program examples have been tested on a number of computers.

However, whether the reader experiments with one of these, or better, writes a program for him- or herself, it should not be expected to work first time. It is very easy to make a simple typing error, such as substituting a letter O for a zero, which can upset a program. Whilst some languages may be fairly tolerant in allowing variable spacing between instruction words, all are very strict about certain matters. For example, if a semicolon is omitted at the end of a Pascal statement, or if a COBOL or FORTRAN program starts in the wrong column, then the compiler will throw it out immediately, and will probably produce some apparently incomprehensible error message, such as:

LINE 19 ERROR 5043 SYNTAX ERROR

Do not be dismayed! Even professional programmers spend a substantial proportion of their time **debugging** programs. Three classes of program error may be distinguished:

1) Syntactic errors. Illegal statements which are grammatically incorrect.
2) Semantic errors. The grammar is correct but the programmer has written the wrong instruction if the computer is to do what was intended.
3) Logical errors. The algorithm itself is incorrect.

The first class of error is picked up by the compiler or interpreter, and is known as a **compile-time** error. The second and third groups may be detected only when the program is executed, and hence are known as **run-time** errors. These may be more difficult to detect. Indeed, a program may need to be run over several months before all the major bugs are identified. Finally, if program execution is actually brought to an unexpected halt by one of these errors, the program is said to have **crashed**.

4.61 **Micro-computers**

Let us assume we have a typical micro-computer system which supports a CP/M operating system and Microsoft BASIC and has dual floppy discs. We shall now look at a typical session. It should be emphasised that what follows is no substitute for reading the manual.

We are sitting at the terminal with the VDU screen and keyboard before us. The computer is plugged in and switched on. Before we can proceed a disc must be inserted in one of the rectangular slots, or **disc drives**, according to the manufacturer's instructions. Once this has been done the operating system must be **booted-up**, i.e. loaded into the computer. Some machines boot-up as soon as we close the disc drive door, or switch on with a disc already in place. Otherwise, it may be necessary to press a reset button, or hit a particular key on the keyboard. The disc drive should whirr once this happens, and a light on the drive may come on.

Once the operating system is ready we should receive the prompt:

    A>

This simply means that the A drive is the current **logged-on** drive (on which all programs requested will be assumed to reside, unless told otherwise) and that the computer is ready to receive an instruction.

Suppose we want to type in and run a BASIC program. We have a BASIC interpreter, and so we must first load that, probably by typing:

    A>BASIC

Assuming that the BASIC interpreter is resident on the current disc it will now be loaded into memory. We will probably receive another prompt when this process is complete, such as:

>**Ok**

We can now type in a BASIC program, line by line, including the line numbers. When finished, we simply type:

>RUN

to execute the program. When the computer has finished obeying our series of instructions it will again prompt:

>**Ok**

We can list our program on the screen again with the command:

>LIST

The BASIC interpreter will also have special instructions which allow us to edit our program. Once we are satisfied with it, the final version can be saved on disc (in this case as a file called MYPROG) by typing:

>SAVE "MYPROG"

The same file can be loaded back into memory again from disc with the command:

>LOAD "MYPROG"

4.62 Mini and mainframe computers

We shall assume that we have access to a terminal, and so do not have to submit everything, including programs and data, on punched cards for batch processing (see section 4.6).

We are sitting at the terminal. If this is a VDU and the screen is completely blank then it is probably not switched on. The on/off switch is frequently cunningly hidden at the back, towards the base. If we are using a decwriter or similar teletype-like device the on/off switch is probably somewhere to the side of the keyboard.

The first thing to be done is to **log on**. This makes us known to the system, which will allocate us some resources. We will probably have been issued with a user number or identifier to type in, and perhaps also a personal password as an added precaution to prevent others gaining access to our files. When the computer has acknowledged our presence, it will probably give a prompt, such as:

>**SESSION STARTS AT 14:24:15**

What happens from now on depends upon the specific type of operating system. Here we will use two different examples: the first, ICL VME2900, like many other mainframe operating systems, is found only on that manufacturer's machines. Our second example uses the Unix operating system, which has become popular on a range of mini-computers and, more recently, has appeared on some mainframes. It has also become increasingly widespread on the more powerful micro-computers.

4.621 **VME2900**

Under a ICL VME2900 system, a typical session might be as follows. Characters printed by the computer are again in bold type. The words in normal capitals are those supplied by the user. They are in the **job control language** specific to an ICL VME2900 series computer. A job control language is the language in which the user instructs the operating system what the requirements for the job are. Under most operating systems it is possible to group several job control instructions together in a short program or **macroinstruction**. These instructions can then be actuated collectively by giving the macro name. This may represent a considerable saving if a job is to be executed several times.

An explanation of the various file operations used below, such as opening and closing, and assigning local names, is to be found in chapter 6.

```
-BEGIN
-INPUTFILE(MYPROG)        Creates and opens a file called MYPROG.
/-                        Slash prompt indicates that we may type
/-                        in lines of program instructions.
/-
/-
/-****                    Four stars to close file.
-ASSIGNFILE(DATA,ICL9LP1) Assigns external file DATA to local name
                          ICL9LP1.
-CREATEFILE(RESULTS,ICL9LP2)  Creates file RESULTS and assigns to
                          ICL9LP2.
-PASCALCOMPILE(INPUT=MYPROG)  Instructs Pascal compiler to
                          compile MYPROG.
.........
```

COMPILATION COMPLETE - TERMINAL ERRORS

The compiler tells us there are errors in the program.

```
-ED(MYPROG)               Instructs editor to open file for editing.
-                         We type in edit instructions to amend
-                         program.
-
-PASCALCOMPILE(SOURCE=MYPROG) We try again.
.........
```

COMPILATION COMPLETE - NO DIAGNOSTICS

MYPROG has been compiled.
It will now be run.

FILE ICL9LP2 OPENED   MYPROG is executed.
FILE ICL9LP1 OPENED   Files are opened.
FILE ICL9LP1 CLOSED

FILE ICL9LP2 CLOSED	Files are closed.
-END	Execution complete. We
-LGT	close this session.

If all else fails a useful command which exists in all the better operating systems is HELP. HELP will normally contain information on all the system instructions.

4.622 **Unix**

When a user logs on to a machine running the Unix operating system, a program known as the shell is started automatically. This acts as a command interpreter, accepting commands from the user and executing the required system programs. The shell normally uses a '$' symbol as a prompt, although some systems will use '%' or perhaps another symbol.

The example below follows that in the previous section, although this time, a FORTRAN 77 program is entered, compiled and run. We begin, as before, after the user has logged on and received any outstanding messages from the system.

$ ed myprog.f **?myprog.f** .a	ed is the name of a standard Unix editor program. The extension '.f' to the file-name is a convention for FORTRAN 77 programs. ?myprog.f signifies that the file does not already exist. ed prompts with a dot, and the 'a' command is used to append lines to the file.
wq **256** $	Input is terminated by typing a dot on a new line. 'w' writes to the file, and 'q' quits the editor. ed then prints the number of characters written.
$ f77 myprog.f **myprog.f** **MAIN:myprog** $	The FORTRAN 77 compiler is started. The compiler replies with the name of the file, followed by the names of each section of the program. In this case there is only a main program called myprog. If compilation is successful then the shell prompt appears, otherwise error messages are given and finally a message such as: '**errors: no assembly**'. In the example shown here, the object program will be given the default name 'a.out'. If we wished the object program to be called 'myprog', then this could be specified on the command line thus: $ f77 -o myprog myprog.f
$myprog	To run the program, simply type its name. In this case any input or output will be from or to the terminal.
$myprog <datain >dataout	Unix allows these standard input and output streams to be redirected to files. The symbols < and > are used with the filenames to direct input and output respectively.

Finally, logging off is achieved by typing the system 'end-of-file' character in response to the shell prompt. This character is usually a Control-D, but varies between systems. Some systems also allow the user to type a command such as 'logoff' or simply 'off'.

NOTES

(1) Whilst we have generally used only standard BASIC in the program examples, we have utilised the facility that exists in most dialects to use variable names of at least six characters, in order to increase legibility. Standard BASIC only allows variable names to be one of the twenty-six letters of the alphabet, or a letter followed by a one-figure number, e.g. A1, A2. In addition, there are inevitably some differences in the input and output procedures in the examples, and those required in other dialects.

(2) In fact the LET is superfluous and most dialects of BASIC would allow one to write simply:

        20 AREA = 5 . 5 * 7 . 6

(3) The program demands that the data is in fixed length records in the exact form specified, and so each field must be padded out with the requisite number of spaces if it does not occupy all the character positions.

(4) The INPUT$ function has been used to keep this program example simple. However, it implies that if the desired keyword is less than twelve characters long it must be padded out with trailing spaces to make it up to the twelve characters. Therefore, in a real program it would be better to use a normal INPUT statement, with some of the special string-handling functions supplied in most dialects, in order to pad it out automatically.

(5) Although FORTRAN is frequently described as an acronym for FORmula TRANsla-tion, according to Sammet (1969, 143) the earliest document was entitled 'PRELIMINARY REPORT, Specifications for the IBM Mathematical FORmula TRANslating System, FOR-TRAN', dated 10 November 1954.

(6) The program will not work if a record is split over several lines.

(7) In practice there may be differences in the way individual implementations handle the input of non-printable characters, such as carriage returns.

(8) The program demands that BIBFILE has already been set up as a file of Pascal records in the form specified. The data should be in a continuous sequence without any line breaks. However, individual implementations frequently mark the end of each record with special markers. Therefore the file would have to have been written previously from within another Pascal program.

(9) In practice, a more sophisticated routine would be used to accept the keyword as typed, and would pad it out to the requisite length automatically, as in the COBOL version where SEARCHKEY was filled with spaces at the start of execution. The technique known as 'lazy i/o' is employed on input here to ensure sensible conversational use of the terminal. This does not follow the Jensen and Wirth (1978) standard.

5

DATA CAPTURE

5.1 Introduction

'Getting the data onto the machine' is a crucial aspect of any project which seeks the aid of computers. The method of recording and storing information determines the ease with which it may be retrieved and analysed. Therefore it is important that the potential computer user gives proper consideration to the data structure, the recording system, and the uses for which the data is intended.

We are concerned here with exploring the various means of recording archaeological data, and evaluate each in terms of ease of use, efficiency of storage, and ease of recovery of information. It will be seen that there is no ideal approach; rather that different methods are suitable for different types of data. It is the aim of this chapter to help researchers approaching computers for the first time to choose a method appropriate to their needs.

There are two aspects of data capture. Firstly we may need to code the data; then there is the actual method of getting it onto the machine. Sections 5.2 and 5.3 deal with coding problems; section 5.4 with entering data.

5.2 Coding systems

A coding system is a means of standardising the description of attributes. A system is necessary if artefacts are to be meaningfully compared.

There is very little literature describing coding systems for archaeological data. Oldenburg and Møllerop (1969) describe an attempt to code Late Nubian grave descriptions, and Forsström (1972) discusses a system of numeric codes used to describe pottery from excavations at Visby. Gardin (1958) outlines codes for four artefact types, and Chenhall (1967) describes a 'universal' coding system applied in the American South West. However, except for general purposes, such as Museum Documentation Association catalogue systems (Roberts 1980), standardised artefact coding systems are rarely possible. Gardin (1967, 27) admits that his codes are not universal and that other workers would produce different ones. However, he describes three rules which should lead to greater standardisation :

i) Orientation: to establish the position of the artefact in relation to the observer.
ii) Segmentation: to define attributes.
iii) Differentiation: to define attribute states.

Categorisation of data is necessary for analysis, although coding inevitably leads to some loss of information:

> The central dilemma when constructing descriptive codes for archaeological material is that the more objective and 'scientific' the code, the more cumbersome and impracticable it is. (Doran and Hodson 1975, 328)

Given that it is impossible to record a full scientific description of every artefact, each research project must define the attributes relevant to its aims. Rather than describing specific coding systems for various artefact types this section will therefore be concerned with the general aspects of coding.

The aim of a coding system must be to lose as little information as possible whilst reducing artefacts to their respective attributes for comparison. Measurements on a numeric scale may be recorded exactly as they are made (in centimetres etc). It may prove necessary to convert these values into proportions before analysis, or to broaden the intervals of measurement, but such transformations are best performed by the computer from the raw data.

Similarly, where attributes are present in varying quantities it is better to record their actual frequencies than either relative proportions or mere presence/absence. The presence of one animal bone in a pit fill is rarely of equal significance to the presence of one hundred bones. The aim must always be to record at the highest level of measurement possible (see section 2.3).

Measurements of qualitative (ordinal and nominal) data require codification of some sort. It is important that the possible attribute states be carefully defined. It is possible to add new attribute states to the list as research proceeds, but there is a temptation to invent a new word to describe the attribute state of every new artefact as it appears, often leading to duplication and redundancy of attribute states. Therefore, it is usually helpful to define a thesaurus of **keywords** (possible attribute states) for some attributes, from which the attribute state of the artefact must be chosen. For example, when coding the skeletal data from a cemetery it would be helpful to draw up a list of all possible attribute states at the start and to check for duplication:

> NEONATE
> INFANT
> CHILD
> ADOLESCENT
> ADULT

If we use ADOLESCENT and JUVENILE to describe the same age grouping there are problems in using the computer to find all graves of ADOLESCENTS. The computer will not know that a JUVENILE is the same as an ADOLESCENT unless we tell it. However, if another grave were to turn up with a new skeletal grouping, such as an ANIMAL, there is nothing to prevent this being added to the list.

We may define a code as a character, or series of characters, designed to provide unique identification of an attribute or attribute state. We shall now consider the possible types of coding system. There are three main approaches:

    i)   Full keyword (section 5.21);
    ii)   Abbreviated keyword (section 5.22);
    iii) Numeric code (section 5.23).

5.21 **Full keyword**
The first possibility is to use the full keyword as the code. Thus the word ADOLESCENT is entered into the computer. This reduces the chance that an incorrect code may be entered. It is more difficult to get a whole word wrong than a single arbitrary number. Errors are also reduced because the data input is intelligible to the coder. In addition it is easy to interpret raw data output from the computer as it is unnecessary to decode it in order to understand it.

On the other hand, data capture may be inordinately time-consuming and there is more chance of simple typing or spelling mistakes. If ADOLEC-SENT is entered, an automatic retrieval program searching for ADOLES-CENT graves will not identify this case unless it has a thesaurus listing ADOLECSENT as an equivalent of ADOLESCENT. Archaeologists frequently begin by wanting a system which is as close to English as possible, allowing the entry of codes in plain language. However, once they come to the chore of data entry, abbreviated codes are rapidly invented.

A further problem with using full keywords is that each code is likely to be of different length. Most graves may be ADULT, but with fixed format data we must allocate at least 10 character positions for this field to allow for ADOLESCENT graves. In most cases five of these spaces will be wasted. Finally, as we have seen in chapter 4, string-handling can be tricky in most programming languages, and can be extremely complex in some, such as FORTRAN.

5.22 **Abbreviated keyword**
The second approach of abbreviated keywords represents a compromise between storage space and intelligibility. Keywords are reduced to a fixed number of letters, usually three or four, which are entered in place of the full keyword. One method is to take the first letters of the word. Thus we have:

Neonate -	N E O N
Infant -	I N F A
Child -	C H I L
Adolescent -	A D O L
Adult -	A D U L

A superior method is to use mnemonics based upon the first letter and major consonants, as these are generally more recognisable as the original keyword, and hence are more memorable:

Neonate -	N N T E
Infant -	I N F T
Child -	C H L D
Adolescent -	A D L S
Adult -	A D L T

However, both methods demonstrate the major disadvantages of this approach. Confusion may easily arise between ADOL and ADUL, or between ADLS and ADLT, and it may be difficult to remember the actual letters which should be used.

The abbreviated keyword code really has little to recommend it. It loses in intelligibility, and gains little in storage space, or in processing time. Since letters are still being used, rather than numbers, programs to manipulate these attributes are likely to be more tricky to write. However, it is worth mentioning a particular variant, recommended by Gifford and Crader (1977) for coding archaeological faunal remains. Bones were coded according to a three or four letter abbreviated keyword, such as FEM for femur. Gifford and Crader then used a computer program to sort the raw data and translate the keywords into a hierarchical numeric code which could easily be used in sorting and further manipulation of the data. Although this approach has the advantages of both easily remembered code words and easily sorted code numbers it may require a large initial programming investment. This may become excessive if the user wishes to allocate numbers rather than let the computer automatically allot them.

5.23 Numeric codes

Several years ago it was conventional that all attribute states should be stored as numeric codes. In the case of nominal-level measurement these would be arbitrary numbers assigned to each attribute state. Ordinal, ranked states would normally be recorded by their assigned rank. The first rank as 1, the second as 2, and so on:

Neonate -	1
Infant -	2
Child -	3
Adolescent -	4
Adult -	5

The major purpose was to economise computer storage space when this was expensive. A two or three digit integer number can be stored far more efficiently than a multi-character word. Efficiency of storage is of continually decreasing importance with each hardware development, although it is still a virtue which should be aimed for. The approach still has a lot to recommend it. Firstly, computers can usually sort and process numbers more quickly than they can strings of alphabetic characters. Secondly, with large amounts of data to code it is quicker to type or write a two or three digit number than a full word. Thirdly, the use of a numeric code allows one to take advantage of properties of the number system.

However, a numeric coding system inevitably has several disadvantages. Firstly, it may be difficult initially to remember the codes, and it will be necessary to consult the **coding book** continually. Secondly, it is easy to mis-code an attribute state. For example, the coder might forget about neonates, and assuming infants are the first group, enter an infant as 1. Where there is no ranked relationship between attribute states:

Iron	1
Bone	2
Bronze	3
Flint	4
Limestone	5

such errors are even more likely. Thirdly, it may be impossible to scan the raw data and correctly interpret the rows of digits. In order to retrieve information a decoding program may be necessary.

Nevertheless, the numeric code remains a most efficient and commonly used coding method. It is worth considering a few varieties of it.

5.231 Sequential codes

With a sequential, or progressive code, numbers are allocated to attribute states in a straightforward numerical sequence. There is no logical connection between an attribute state and its code. For example:

Adult female	1
Adolescent	2
Infant	3
Adult male	4
......	.

As further skeletal classes come to light they are allocated the next number in sequence.

Most excavation context numbering systems use a sequential code, although this is a special case as each attribute state, or context number, is unique. As each context is dug it is given the next number in sequence. Some excavations use a special type of sequential code known as block code. Areas within the site are allocated blocks of numbers:

Area I	1-999
Area II	1000-1999
Area III	2000-2999
....	......

New contexts from a given area are allocated the next available number from within the sequence for that area. The system allows expansion at the expense of a large number of code numbers.

The context number also has some significance in this case. It might allow the director to identify immediately which part of the site a particular find was from. It would also allow a computer to identify and process the contexts from particular areas.

5.232 **Faceted codes**

A faceted code represents an improvement on the simple codes described above, as each character contains some information about the item.

For example, we should recognise that our skeletal data really comprises two attributes: AGE and SEX. We shall use two digits to represent this information. The first shall represent AGE, the second SEX. Furthermore, we can use a matrix to define a procedure for producing logical codes (fig. 5.1). Obviously, in practice it is unlikely that we shall be able to sex our neonates, infants, or even children. In these cases we might use a 0 to represent missing data. Thus an infant would be coded 20.

	SEX	
AGE	Male	Female
Neonate	11	12
Infant	21	22
Child	31	32
Adolescent	41	42
Adult	51	52

5.1 A coding matrix

This faceted code is capable of unlimited expansion. For example, we might have a third digit which was 1 or 2 according to whether the burial was flexed or extended. It would also be a good idea to have a fourth representing our confidence in the skeletal identification. Therefore we could have a number from 1 to 5 in the fourth column according to how certain our analysis was.

It should be noted that the value of most archaeological data may be increased by adding this further attribute, representing degree of certainty. It would allow one, for example, to select only those attribute measurements of which one was certain for a particular analysis.

Finally then, the complete code for an inhumation burial might be 5124. According to the coding system devised above this represents an extended burial of a probable adult male. It must be remembered that although this might appear to be just one number, it is really four independent attributes in four separate fields. The fact that there are no spaces between the fields is irrelevant. A faceted code may just be regarded as a string of characters. This particular example has the advantage that it can be read as a number if required, but it could equally well be made up of letters.

5.233 **Hierarchical codes**

A hierarchical code is a type of faceted code where each artefact is again represented by a single multi-digit number. The first digits indicate broad class, with succeeding digits giving a more and more detailed classification, in the same way in which the Dewey Decimal library system works. The section numbers in this book are organised according to a hierarchical system. Sorting data coded hierarchically is very efficient as it is merely a matter of sorting the code numbers into order of size. Chenhall (1967; 1971a) describes five ten-digit codes used to classify various artefact attributes:

> A - Apparent function or Use
> B - Form
> C - Material
> D - Technique of Manufacture
> E - Surface treatment and Design

Within the A code, for instance, A41 refers to tools and appliances, and A411 is a subdivision refering to weapons. Striking and thrusting weapons come under A4111, within which clubs are A41111 and spears A41112. Such a system is easy to use, but it is fairly rigid and it is difficult to change, apart from adding further subdivisions on at the base. Therefore the user must be clear about the hierarchy of the data from the outset. Fig. 5.2 shows a sample printout of Roman coin data, classified according to a hierarchical numeric coding system.

Finally, there are two commonly made errors in the use of numeric code. Neither is fatal, but both are inefficient. Firstly, each attribute state may be treated as an independent attribute and scored on a presence/absence basis. Thus each attribute state is given a separate field. For example, the skeletal data could be coded thus:

FIELD	1	2	3	4	5	6	7
	Neonate	Infant	Child	Adoles.	Adult	Male	Female
GRAVE n	0	0	0	0	1	0	1

It has taken seven fields to represent an adult female burial. Apart from the sheer waste of space, there are statistical problems in using presence/absence data in this way, with the implication that absence is of the same importance as presence. These are discussed by Doran and Hodson (1975, 104). In addition, if it is assumed that all attributes have equal significance, or

Site	Ruler	Catalogue	Volume	Mint	Reference number	Status	No of Coins	Provenance	Note
1656044		4			980	1	1	R2	
1656332		4			127	2	1	NWR8	
165706						8	1	R1	759
1658072			6	1	59B3		1	R4	
4268313			2	2	25	4	1	B1	
4268173			1	3	51	4	1	B1	795
4268313			2	2	25	4	1	DS	
449599						8	1		769
4498042			7	1	170D1		1		
4498102			7	1	291	3	1		
8368313			2	2	25	4	2		
838707						9	1		768

5.2 Roman coin data hierarchically coded

weighting, then by breaking down what is essentially one attribute into several in this way one may be giving it undue stress. Unless a weighting system is used it may bias the results of any sort of multivariate analysis.

Secondly, a related problem is the frequent misconception that a code number must be unique throughout an entire record. This is not normally true (see exception in section 5.33). When it reads data the computer will be given a set of instructions which will tell it which attribute it is reading in a particular field so that it can place it in the correct box, or pigeon hole. Either it will be given a format instruction if the data is in fixed format, or it will use a program to calculate its position by sorting through the data, or it will read an identifying assignment tag which will tell it which attribute it is dealing with. (These techniques will be discussed more fully in section 5.3.) Therefore an attribute code need be unique only to its own field. For example, the faceted code developed in section 5.232 to describe the skeletal data used a 2 in the first column to indicate an infant. It also used a 2 in the second column to indicate a female. Yet there could be no confusion because the position of the 2 indicated whether it referred to age or sex. The same codes may be used for attribute states of several attributes because each attribute is held in a different field.

5.24 **Principles of code design**

Whilst numeric coding is generally most appropriate, the coding method adopted must depend upon individual circumstances. The decision must be made with reference to the complexity and volume of the data, the importance of being able to read raw data, who is to do the coding, and so on. Frequently a combination of numeric and alphabetic code may be found to be the most appropriate.

However, there are several general points which can be made about code design. Lee (1979, 388-90) distinguishes ten features of a good code. In practice any code will be a compromise between these characteristics. We summarise them below:

1)   Uniqueness. Only one code must be applied to a given attribute state, although that state may be described in English in several ways.

2)   Expansibility. The code must allow for the growth of its set of attribute states.

3)   Conciseness. The code should require the smallest possible number of characters to define an attribute state.

4)   Uniform size and format. The code may be more easily processed if it is of uniform size and format.

5)   Simplicity. The code must be simple to apply and easily understood.

6)   Versatility. The code should be easily modified to reflect changes in artefact descriptions.

7)   Sortability. The code should be easily sorted, or convertible into a form that may be sorted.

8)   Stability. Codes which do not require frequent up-dating promote user efficiency.

9)   Meaningfulness. As far as possible codes should be meaningful, and should reflect the characteristics of the attributes they represent.

10)   Operability. The code should be adequate for present and anticipated data processing needs.

In addition, it is worth restricting codes to the familiar alphanumeric characters, i.e. twenty-six letters of the alphabet and ten digits. The use of symbols, such as hyphens, asterisks, periods, etc, should be avoided.

Finally, it is advisable to split codes of five or more characters into smaller segments. Thus:

AC12131498

is better divided as:

AC 121 31498

for example. Although the second case is slightly longer it gains in ease of manual inspection and use.

Having designed a coding system it is good practice to go away and attempt to code fifty or so records in order to test it. Invariably amendments will be found to be necessary. Nevertheless, by the end of the project a coding system will probably appear imperfect. But as Shorter (1971, 48) wrote for historians: '... if his codebook doesn't seem inadequate by the end of the project, he probably hasn't learned anything'. It is also wise to keep referring back to the coding system, even when one feels familiar with it. In particular, one should review decisions taken in earlier cases, so that almost imperceptible interpretative drifts are halted.

5.3 **Fixed** *versus* **variable format**

It is frequently found that there are several **conditional attributes** in the data set. These are attributes whose existence is conditional upon another attribute being present, at a lower level of complexity. For example, an attribute of a grave is the presence/absence of grave-goods. However, if grave-goods are present we may want to know which particular types are there. Several conditional levels may be involved, producing a hierarchical tree (fig. 5.3). For example, a pot may be either plain or decorated; it cannot be both. However, a pot with decoration may then be described by a whole series of further attributes, such as whether the decoration is incised, painted, stamped, or moulded. A pot may be decorated by one or more of these decorative styles. For each of these classes there are then further attributes, such as the type of incised patterns, their position, the number of lines, and so forth.

If records are of **fixed length**, that is, each record occupies a fixed number of character positions, then a field must be reserved for every possible

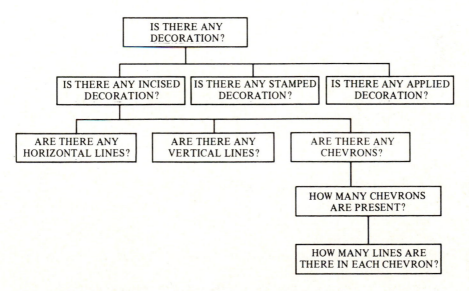

5.3 Hierarchical tree for Anglo-Saxon pottery data

attribute. Each field must occupy the same position within each record, and if an attribute state takes up less characters than are reserved for that field, then it must be padded out to fill the requisite number of characters, perhaps with spaces. This might be no problem in the first example. If no grave had more than five grave-goods then one only need leave five fields. Where five were present then each would be occupied; where less than five then the other fields would be blank. Whenever possible we recommend that fixed record length be adhered to. The wastage of storage space is easily made up for by the ease of reading and processing data. For presence/absence data however, care should be taken that for those records where conditional attributes do not apply these attributes are coded with a special symbol meaning 'not-applicable' rather than just as absent.

In the second example, where there are clearly several hundred possible decorative attributes of a pot, then a record might stretch over many lines, with most fields remaining blank for most pots. This large amount of wastage is becoming less worrying with cheaper storage, but the amount of space available to the individual user may still be limited. If several hundred complex artefacts are being coded this may be a problem. There are three main solutions: flags, field identifiers, and unique codes.

5.31 Flags
The first solution employs flags embedded in the data to tell the retrieval program where it is as it reads through the data. For example, processing the cemetery data set, the computer comes to the field for grave-goods. The first element read is a flag. If this is zero then there are no grave-goods present and the computer goes on to read the next field as the next attribute. However, if there are grave-goods present then the flag will indicate how many. If it is 5 then the computer will enter a loop, with the flag as a counter. It will read the next five entries as grave-goods and decode them appropriately. It will then proceed to read the next attribute. The data is stored sequentially with no blank fields. The technique is very efficient and uses minimal storage space. Fig. 5.4 shows data for early Anglo-Saxon pottery compressed in this way. However, unless one has some experience in programming it can be problematical as it is easy to get lost in the data.

5.32 Field identifiers
The second solution uses identifiers to indicate the contents of each field to the program. Each attribute type is allocated a unique code which is entered immediately before the attribute state. The computer reads the identifier, goes away to search its list to discover what the attribute is, then returns, reads the attribute state and decodes it accordingly. Thus we might allocate the identifier 12 to grave-goods. Each grave-good would then be preceded by the number 12 to tell the computer to read the following value as a grave-

```
SINGLE RECORD - DECORATIVE ATTRIBUTES OF ONE URN

  4 1820  1  1  2  1  4  2  3  2  6  2  2  3  3  2  2  0  0  9999

  4            SITE NUMBER
  1820         URN RECORD NUMBER
  1            P/A DECORATION [ '1' PRESENCE: '0' ABSENCE]
  1            P/A INCISED DECORATION [ '1' PRESENCE: '0' ABSENCE]
  2            NUMBER OF CLASSES OF INCISED DECORATION PRESENT: 2
  1            CLASS 1: HORIZONTAL   '1' HORIZONTAL:    '2' VERTICAL
  4            CLASS 2: CHEVRON      '3' CURVILINEAR: '4' CHEVRON
  2            NUMBER OF GROUPS OF HORIZONTAL LINES: 2
  3            GROUP 1: 3 LINES
  2            GROUP 2: 2 LINES
  6            NUMBER OF CHEVRONS: 6
  2            CHEVRON 1: 2 LINES
  2            CHEVRON 2: 2 LINES
  3            CHEVRON 3: 3 LINES
  3            CHEVRON 4: 3 LINES
  2            CHEVRON 5: 2 LINES
  2            CHEVRON 6: 2 LINES
  0            P/A APPLIED DECORATION [ '1' PRESENCE: '0' ABSENCE]
  0            P/A STAMPED DECORATION [ '1' PRESENCE: '0' ABSENCE]
  9999         END OF RECORD
```

5.4 Anglo-Saxon pottery data in compressed format

```
SINGLE RECORD - DECORATIVE ATTRIBUTES OF ONE URN

  1  4  2  1820  31  2  311  3  311  2  34  6  341  2  341  2  341  3  341  3  341  2  341  2

                    SUBSET OF FIELD IDENTIFIER CODES:

  1  4            1   SITE NUMBER
  2 1820          2   URN RECORD NUMBER
 31  2           31   HORIZONTAL INCISED DECORATION (NUMBER OF GROUPS)
311  3          311   NUMBER OF LINES IN HORIZONTAL GROUP
311  2
 34  6           34   CHEVRON INCISED DECORATION (NUMBER OF CHEVRONS)
341  2          341   NUMBER OF LINES IN CHEVRON
341  2
341  3
341  3
341  2
341  2
```

5.5 Anglo-Saxon pottery data in expanded form with field identifiers

good. Fig. 5.5 shows the same data for Anglo-Saxon pottery from fig. 5.4 coded with field identifiers.

The sites and monuments index for Fife, described by Kenworthy, Stapleton, and Thurston (1975), uses two or three character alphabetic field identifiers for each attribute. Thus NGR indicates the field containing grid reference, PH, that containing parish, SN, the sitename, and so on. Wilcock (1970b) describes a system used to catalogue prehistoric carvings which combines variable length records, using field identifiers, with fixed length

```
 10      RS S  A   H1    D1    C7        M1        SH174266  JDW 700104      300
 20      ABERDARON CHURCH              ABERDARON                            300
 30      LOWE                 HNW      2         125-126                    300
130      LOWE                 AC       (SER.7)4  362                        300


 10      RS S  A   H1    D2    C3        M1        SH584269  JDW 700104      301
 20      LLANBEDR CHURCH               LLANBEDR                             301
 30      BARNWELL             AC       (SER.3)13 154                        301
130      SIMPSON (1867)       ASCC     55                                  301
230      MORRIS               AC       (SER.6)12 252,255                   301
330      RCAHMW               MERIONETH          54                        301


 10      RI SM A   H1    D2    C6        M1        SH588288  JDW 700104      302
 20      DYFFRYN ARDUDWY              DYFFRYN ARDUDWY                       302
 30      LUKIS                ARCH     25        250                        302
130      LUKIS                ARC J    9         92                         302
230      SIMPSON (1867)       ASCC     28                                  302


 10      RS S  A   H2    D5    C36       M2        SN959558  JDW 700104      303
 20      LLANAFAN FAWR CHURCH         LLANAFAN FAWR                         303
 30      MORRIS               AC       (SER.6)12 255-256                    303


 10      RI SM A   H2    D5    C4        M1        SO101265  JDW 700104      304
 20      TY ILLTYD                    LLANHAMLACH                           304
 30      WESTWOOD             AC       3         273                        304
130      WESTWOOD             AC       (SER.3)13 353-354                    304
230      SIMPSON (1867)       ASCC     25                                  304
330      CRAWFORD (1921)      LONG BARROWS OF COTSWOLDS    64               304
430      DANIEL (1950)        PREHISTORIC CHAMBER TOMBS    118-120          304


 10      RI SM A   H1    D1    C1        M1        SN083426  JDW 700104      305
 20      TRELLYFFAINT                 BAYVIL                                305
 30      WHEELER (1925)       PREHISTORIC & ROMAN WALES    82               305
130      DANIEL (1950)        PREHISTORIC CHAMBER TOMBS    117              305
230      RCAHMW               PEMBROKE        760  256                      305


 10      RI SM A   H1    D1    C1        M2        SN094389  JDW 700104      306
 20      TREFAEL                      NEVERN                                306
 30      GRIMES               BBCS     5         277                        306
130      RCAHMW (1925)        PEMBROKE           255                        306
230      DANIEL (1950)        PREHISTORIC CHAMBER TOMBS    117              306


 10      RS S  A   H1    D2    C5        M1        SM999359  JDW 700104      307
 20      PARC Y MARW                  LLANLAWER /                           307
 30      BARNWELL             AC       (SER.3)14 177-178                    307


 10      RS S8 AB  H1    D2    C1        M1        SS927810  JDW 700105      308
 20      SIMONDSTON                   COITY HIGHER                          308
 30      FOX                  ARCH     87        133                        308
```

5.6 Petroglyph data from Wilcock (1970) with field identifiers
(*Science and Archaeology*)

sub-records. Each line of data is prefixed by a number which uniquely identifies the attributes recorded on that line (fig. 5.6). For example, 10 in columns 9–10 indicates SITE DETAILS; 20 indicates SITE NAME; and 30 indicates BIBLIOGRAPHY. If the sub-record is SITE NAME then columns 11–40 will contain NAME OF SITE, columns 41–70 NAME OF PARISH, and so on. Alternatively, if the sub-record is identified as BIBLIOGRAPHY, then columns 11–30 contain AUTHOR AND DATE, columns 31–60 contain TITLE etc. In Wilcock's system, where several references are required, successive lines are numbered 30, 130, 230 and so on. This is not required by the computer, which can count how many sub-records there are for itself, but it may be helpful for manual inspection of the data. In all cases columns 71–80 are reserved for the unique record number.

5.33 Unique codes

Another approach which has been used is to allocate to every attribute state a unique alphanumeric code. This method differs from the previous two in that the computer does not 'know' where it is. Instead, it reads in the coded attribute state, and then searches through its list of all attribute states of all attributes to find what it is. The method is not recommended as it involves a cumbersome coding system and often means that the computer must make a time-consuming search through an enormous coding list for each attribute it reads in.

5.4 Entering data

We are almost ready to enter data on the computer. Two methods of data capture exist. The first uses punched cards; in the second data is entered directly at a terminal. If one is using a micro-computer then the latter method will almost always be the one adopted, but if a mainframe is being used then one may have a choice. Punched cards are generally considered obsolete today, but still appear to be widely used by archaeologists. However, facilities for reading punched cards may be expected to disappear gradually from most computer installations, where they will be superseded by the second method of data entry, in which data is entered directly at a terminal. If one has easy access to a terminal then this method will normally be most convenient, although for large quantities of repetitive data, punched cards may still be preferable. They also have the advantage that as long as a card reader is available then one's data is completely portable between machines.

5.41 Punched cards

If a mainframe computer is being used it will normally be possible to feed the data in on punched cards. If so, then it is usual first to write it out on **coding sheets** (fig. 5.7). These are forms which have been preprinted with a grid of boxes in order to ensure a regular spacing of characters, and each character should normally be written in an individual box. The data is then transferred onto punched cards for direct input to the computer, either by data preparation staff, or by the user. Each line on a coding sheet corresponds to one punched card. Each line has eighty boxes, reflecting that one is limited to eighty columns, or character positions, on a punched card. Of course, a record may extend over several lines if required. There is generally space for about twenty lines of data on a coding sheet. Fig. 5.8 shows a punched card

North Staffordshire Polytechnic Computing Services

Name J.D RICHARDS	Username CDRES05
2960/29044082–	Job Name ASP

Filename/Title POTFILE 1

Date 12/4/83
Sheet 1 of 1 sheets

DATA

D

```
1 2 3 4 5 6 7 8 9 10 ... 80

TF981195 SHOULDERED URN          29.5   NOW IN NORWICH CASTLE MUSEUM
TQ673803 STORAGE JAR             27.0
TL774715 FLAGON                  32.0
         0 BOWL                   9.5   PROVENANCE UNKNOWN
TG235032 STORAGE JAR             33.5
TF981195 JAR                     18.0
TF110137 DISH                     4.5
TA046125 BOWL                   111.5   MISSING
SU490963 HEMISPHERICAL BOWL      15.0
```

5.7 A coding sheet

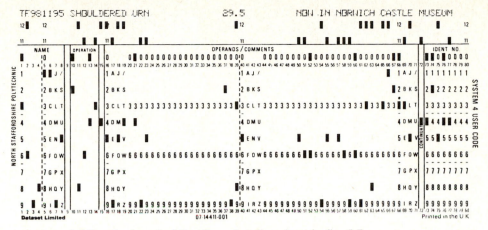

5.8 Punched card of first line of coding sheet in fig. 5.7

prepared from the data in line 1 of the coding sheet in fig. 5.7. Columns 1–8 give the grid reference, columns 10–30 the pottery type, columns 35–40 the height, and columns 50 onwards are reserved for free comment in this example.

Although this approach involves an extra stage it has the added benefit that the user has a permanent machine-readable, and generally machine-independent, record of the data in the form of punched cards. On the other hand, careful checking of the data is necessary as the method is notoriously prone to errors. Firstly, errors are often made in the preparation of the coding sheets. We have seen how the choice of coding system can help to reduce these, but it cannot stop them. Secondly, **punching errors** will be made in transferring the data to punched cards. These can be reduced if the cards are **verified**; in effect, put through the punch a second time. Nevertheless, some will slip through onto the computer. Therefore it is important to devise a systematic procedure of error checking. For example, one may thoroughly check one record in fifty, or one in one hundred. If only a few random errors are found then it is probably not worth worrying about. If the errors fall into a pattern , such as the shifting of one field by a column to left or right, then it may be corrected. Amendments must be made either by repunching the incorrect cards, or by using an editor to correct the stored data.

Frequently the most efficient technique is to collect data using standardised recording forms, with prepared spaces for each field or attribute (fig. 5.9). These should present the data in the same order in which it is to be entered on the coding sheets, and the layout should ensure that data is only entered once. It may also save time if data that is to be coded numerically is coded at this stage. All forms should be clearly identified with a form number, and as much data as possible should be preprinted on the form to speed up the coding process.

SITE [ ][ ][ ][ ][ ][ ][ ][ ][ ][ ][ ] URN NUMBER [ ][ ][ ] GRID: East [ ][ ][ ] North [ ][ ][ ]

RECONSTRUCTED Y/N [ ]   DELIB. HOLED Y/N [ ]   SHAPE [ ][ ][ ][ ][ ][ ][ ][ ][ ][ ][ ]

DIMENSIONS:

Height [ ][ ][·][ ]   Max.Diam. [ ][ ][·][ ]   H.of Max.Diam. [ ][ ][·][ ]   Base Diam. [ ][ ][·][ ]

Rim Diam. [ ][ ][·][ ]   Pedestal Diam. [ ][ ][·][ ]

INCISED DECORATION:

Field

Horiz.cont. 1 [ ][ ] 2 [ ][ ] 3 [ ][ ] 4 [ ][ ] 5 [ ][ ] 6 [ ][ ] 7 [ ][ ] 8 [ ][ ] 9 [ ][ ] 10 [ ][ ]

Vertical 1 [ ][ ] 2 [ ][ ] 3 [ ][ ] 4 [ ][ ] 5 [ ][ ] 6 [ ][ ] 7 [ ][ ] 8 [ ][ ] 9 [ ][ ] 10 [ ][ ]

Diagonal

Curvilinear

Other

STAMPED DECORATION:

Form Design   Urns with identical stamps :

1 [ ] [ ][ ]

2 [ ] [ ][ ]

3 [ ] [ ][ ]

4 [ ] [ ][ ]

PLASTIC DECORATION:

Bosses 1 [ ][ ] 2 [ ][ ] 3 [ ][ ] 4 [ ][ ] 5 [ ][ ]   Cordons 1 [ ][ ] 2 [ ][ ] 3 [ ][ ] 4 [ ][ ] 5 [ ][ ]

6 [ ][ ] Other

GRAVEGOODS:

ASSOCIATED URNS:

COMMENTS:

J.D.R.
20/3/8

5.9 Pro-forma recording form for Anglo-Saxon pottery data

Alternatively, it may be possible to design coding sheets for a particular data set. Data can then be immediately entered for punching, cutting out the recording form stage (fig. 5.10). If professional data preparation staff are involved then it is wise to consult with the punch supervisor on the design of the coding sheets for ease of use by the punch operators. A sensible layout allows the operator to read from left to right and from top to bottom. The most frequently used fields should be at the left of the form, so that the operator does not have to skip over the many blank characters that will appear in little used fields.

Careful thought is necessary when designing the layout of a record on the coding sheet. If fixed length records are used, a given field must always occupy the same character positions on the coding sheet. The first prerequisite then is to leave enough space for every possible attribute state within each field. For example, if only three character positions are assigned to pot height then a height which requires four characters will necessitate awkward readjustment of all the data, and perhaps alteration of format instructions. Similarly, if a numeric code is being used then enough room should be left in case extra code numbers are added, causing the field to spill over into other columns. Some computing languages, such as BASIC, have difficulty reading each field as a separate variable unless they are separated by spaces.

There are also certain conventions to be followed in completing coding sheets to avoid confusion of interpretation.

i) Only upper case alphabetic characters may be used.
ii) All characters, including decimal points, occupy one column.
iii) Integer numbers should be **right-justified**; that is, they should not be written with trailing spaces which might be interpreted as zeros. Thus for numbers without decimal points:

```
3456123        3456123
   5611  NOT   5611
  96750        96750
```

iv) Where real numbers are being coded, some languages may require the decimal point to be in a specific column:

```
21.5           21.5
 7.8   NOT      7.80
 9.55           9.55
```

This is good practice in any case, as it makes manual checking easier.
v) Plus signs need not be included for positive numbers.
vi) Zeros are written Ø to avoid confusion with the letter O.
vii) Ones are written 1 to avoid confusion with the letter I.
viii) Strictly speaking, spaces should be represented by the special character: ␣. In practice, data preparation staff will normally regard any box left blank between characters as a space. One should be aware, however, that to a

5.10 Coding sheet for bone data from Danebury (Cunliffe and Lock) computer a space is a significant character, just like a letter or number. This may be of particular importance when comparing strings; to a computer POSTHOLE is not the same as POST HOLE.

Newell and Vroomans (1972) describe how coding sheets were used to record the finds from a mesolithic excavation in the Netherlands. They used fixed length records of seventy-six characters to describe each flint. Thus each artefact conveniently fits on one line of a coding sheet and corresponds to one punched card. They recorded period, culture, grid square number, soil type and horizon, two dimensional coordinates, orientation, relative elevation, date, absolute elevation, series number of artefact, artefact code and condition of artefact. A hierarchical code was used to record the soil and artefact types. The coding system attempts to be unnecessarily comprehensive; thus the first ten characters, recording period and culture and including a machine instruction code, appear to be repeated for every record from the site. These would have been better appended later by the computer. Nevertheless, by comparing the computerised method with their previous manual recording systems, Newell and Vroomans claim a total increase in 'production' of between 70% and 111%. They achieved a turn-round time of two weeks between site recording and receiving catalogues and analyses, which is probably about average for an approach based upon coding sheets.

Fasham and Hawkes (1980) discuss the use of coding sheets and a mainframe computer to record excavations by the M3 Archaeological Research Committee. Their cost-benefit analysis suggests a time saving by a factor of four on a manual system.

5.42 Terminal entry

An alternative method of data capture is to type in the data directly, at a terminal keyboard. This does away with the intermediate coding sheet stage, and does not use expensive punched cards. In addition, provided a method of data retrieval exists, it allows the user access to information as soon as it has been recorded. This might be of importance in excavation recording applications, for example, where if errors or inadequacies are detected later it could be too late. Graham (1976) discusses the advantages of using a terminal for excavation recording, and several writers have experimented with the use of a terminal on site. Buckland (1973) and Wilcock (1973b) describe the use of a remote terminal on the site of a Roman fort in Doncaster to record data directly from the excavation. Powlesland (1983) discusses the use of a handheld portable micro-computer for site recording. This allows the archaeologist to enter data at first hand on a pocket calculator style keyboard. The data must later be transferred to a larger machine for storage. In an investigation of the archaeology of a Navajo Indian reservation in northeastern Arizona, Gaines (1981b) has used a remote terminal linked by telephone line to a mainframe computer over 300 miles away. More frequently, terminals at the computer installation will be used for data entry.

Whether a mainframe computer has the facility for users to type in data at terminals will depend upon the installation. Although this is increasingly common it can be an inefficient use of machine time. In addition, the user may find it rather tedious for large amounts of repetitive data, and the method is particularly vulnerable to inevitable machine breakdown. If a micro-computer is being used then typing data in at the keyboard will be the standard procedure for data capture, as micro-computers are not normally equipped with card readers.

When entering data at a terminal the user is no longer limited to upper-case characters, or to 80-column width for each line of data. However, in practice it may be necessary to retain these rules. The first will mean that the data can be listed on any standard mainframe line printer if desired and the second that it can be displayed on the screen easily.

Micro-computers are being used increasingly for excavation recording. Pryor (1980) discusses aspects of using a micro-computer at Maxey. He concludes that apart from the higher standard of recording, there are extra benefits to be gained from involving all excavators in the computer recording, and the consequent breakdown of the distinction between excavation and post-excavation. Benson and Jefferies (1980) discuss the system in use by Dyfed Archaeological Trust, and also mention applications to sites and monuments records. Kenrick (1980) outlines the pottery cataloguing system used by Colchester Archaeological Unit, whereby a micro-computer is used for data capture and validation, with data files being transferred to a main-frame computer for processing and listing. This is frequently the optimal arrangement. Whilst archaeologists may be able to call upon the resources to purchase a small micro-computer, they may not be able to afford large amounts of on-line storage (as in a hard disc), although they will frequently have mainframe facilities available in county council or university depart-ments.

5.421 Editors

Editors were defined in chapter 4 as utility programs which are usually supplied with the computer. They were mentioned there in the context of typing in and amending programs, but where small or medium sized data sets are involved editors may equally well be used for data entry and correction. If operations are on a small scale then it may be unnecessary to develop a specialised data capture program. It is easier to learn how to use an editor than it is to learn to program, and they are widely available for all ranges of machine.

Two basic categories of editor may be distinguished: line-orientated or screen-orientated, depending upon how much of a file is visible on the screen at any given time. Where one is simply using the editor for data capture and typing in data a line at a time there may be no apparent difference between the two types, but when one comes to amend entries then a screen editor will usually be far more convenient to use.

The simplest line editors treat a file as a sequential group of records in which each line of data is regarded as one record (cf. section 6.3). The user must start at line one and advance sequentially through the file making corrections to the current line, and usually transcribing the corrected version to a new file. Thus one cannot go backwards, and if a mistake is missed then the user must continue until the end of the file is reached, save the new version, and then start from the top of the new file until the missed error is reached. The better line editors allow the user to go both backwards and forwards through a file.

If a screen editor is being used then one usually has access to a whole screenful of data at a time, and often to the whole file. Therefore, whilst it is still usual to have a current line, representing the line on which any editing instructions issued would be performed, one may choose that current line with total freedom, moving backwards or forwards through the file at will.

Most editors, whether line- or screen-orientated, have a fairly standard range of commands. Firstly, there will be commands to control the current line position. Secondly, the user is able to alter whole lines or sections of lines by replacing strings of characters, or inserting new characters before or after an existing string. Thirdly, the user will be able to insert new lines, or to delete old ones. Finally, the user may expect to be able to merge several files together from within the editor.

In addition most editors will allow many of the instructions discussed above to be used in a global fashion throughout the file. For example, it may be possible to replace all occurrences of the digit '1' with the word 'ONE'. Obviously, where a screen-editor is being used then this can be done both backwards and forwards from the current line position. Modern sophisticated editors will also allow the user to pre-define a set of operation sequences using a macro-instruction. This may be useful in data entry where data is in a regular format.

5.422 Data capture programs

Most micro-computer users prefer to use a data capture program for data entry (e.g. Crowther and Booth (1982); Catton, Jones and Moffett (1982)). The program prompts the user for the entry for a particular attribute; accepts the data from the keyboard; and automatically allocates it to the appropriate field for storage. The prompt may simply take the form of a question displayed on the screen. The computer will await a response before displaying the next question. A refined version, possibly useful for archaeologists familiar with context recording forms, displays a facsimile form on the screen

RECORD NO.   243

SITE NO. :   109:   CONTEXT NO. :   886 :
GRID CO-ORDINATES   EASTING :   0309:NORTHING :   7723:
HEIGHT O.D. TOP :█   . :BOTTOM :   . :
PLAN NO. :   :   :   :   :   :
PHOTO B/W :   :   :   :COLOUR :   :   :   :

UNDER :   :   :   :   :CUT BY :   :   :   :   :
ABOVE :   :   :   :   :CUT INTO :   :   :   :
SAME AS :   :   :   :

DESCRIPTION :

MUNSELL :   : COLOUR :   :   :   :
SAMPLES :   :   :   :   :   :
INTERPRETATIVE COMMENT :

COMPLETED BY :   : DATE : / / :

CORRECT (Y/N)?

5.11 VDU with fascimile form

and as each attribute is entered it is allocated to the appropriate box (fig. 5.11). Each completed form may be held for visual checking before being permanently stored. Commercially available software which incorporates many of these features is described in section 7.5.

In place of the keyboard an alternative input device, such as a digitising tablet, may be used (see chapter 3). In this case the recording form may be placed as an overlay to the tablet and each attribute presented as a series of multiple-choice boxes. A cursor or stylus is then used to indicate the appropriate box. A light pen may be used in conjunction with the terminal screen to achieve the same results. A digitising tablet is also a useful instrument for recording the dimensions, or even complete profiles, of artefacts (cf. Main 1981; 1982; Morris and Scarre 1982; Richards 1982; Wilcock and Shennan 1975). A profile drawing, or sometimes the object itself, may be placed upon the tablet and its profile or measurements recorded directly. Similarly, digital calipers (Hardy 1982) or a television camera (Wilcock and Coombes 1982) may be used for automatic artefact measurement.

One advantage of using a data capture program is that data may be automatically encoded inside the computer. Thus it preserves a friendly response to the user who types or indicates the full keyword, whilst storing the attribute efficiently in numeric code. In addition the computer may be programmed to carry out automatic checking of the data, also known as **validation**, and will prompt the user to try again if an error is detected. For example, it may be told to expect a quantitative variable to be within a certain range – all pots higher than one metre are rejected! It may also store in memory a list of the permitted keywords for qualitative variables and check the entry against its thesaurus. The permitted list may be displayed if requested, obviating the need to search through sheets of paper when using a code book. It may be helpful to provide a facility which allows new keywords to be added to the list as entry proceeds. However, care should be taken that the list is not needlessly extended with a series of synonyms, especially if a number of people are involved in the recording. A fully developed system may allow the user to enter any one of several synonymous words but will code them as one attribute state. It may even correct the user's spelling mistakes!

Clearly, in a situation such as excavation recording, where a large number of complex records are to be entered, often by many different users, then a friendly and foolproof interactive data capture program is invaluable. Ideally, the system should include full checking of entries, a facility for both optional and compulsory fields, so that the user may omit some entries whilst others are demanded, and the ability to edit and retrieve data interactively as well as to enter it. Where inexperienced users are expected to use the data capture program it is important that facilities are also built in for error recovery. Users inevitably make mistakes and the programmer must take care that the program itself traps such errors and responds in a friendly manner, perhaps by giving the user another chance, rather than by crashing and leaving them at the mercy of the operating system. For example, if the user is requested to enter a numeric attribute which is to be stored in a real variable then many systems would crash if a letter was typed in error. The computer would be unable to place an alphabetic character in a storage box set up for a real number and would probably jump out of the data entry program. On the other hand, if the expected variable were initially declared as a character variable then any character would be acceptable. In this case perhaps the ideal solution might be to declare the variable as a character but to check in the program whether it was a number. If it passed this test it could then be transferred into a real variable box and manipulated arithmetically as required. If a letter had been entered in error then program control might jump to an error recovery routine which displayed a message to the effect that an invalid character had been entered and gave the user a chance to correct it.

Similarly, where the user is requested to respond to a question by typing in 'yes' or 'no' then a friendly program will allow the user to type in lower or upper case, and to enter simply 'y' or 'n' instead of the complete word. Alternatively it should actually state the exact characters required. Whenever the result of a response is to delete something then it is worth inserting a double-check to confirm that the user really wants to do this. Otherwise, a miss-hit key can lead to the frustation of seeing whole records, or even whole files, lost forever.

If the user intends to record several different data sets it is worth considering acquiring or developing a generalised data capture program which is not specific to a particular artefact type. The list of questions and possible answers and the data structure are held separately the basic program and are read in at the start of a session. Graham (1980) describes the basis of such a system, used at Mucking, Essex, and at Hartfield Kiln, Sussex. Even if the user is interested only in recording one data type a generalised program will be easier to modify according to developments in the coding system as only the **question source file** and not the program itself need be altered.

6

FILES AND FILE MANAGEMENT

6.1 Introduction

In chapter 2 we introduced the concept of a hierarchical structure for data storage and described how this may be related to the structure of archaeological data. We discussed the recording of attributes in fields, within records, within files of data. In chapter 4 some basic techniques of manipulating data using high-level programming languages were discussed. This chapter is concerned with the higher levels of the hierarchy and, in particular, with the organisation and manipulation of various types of data files.

Many archaeological applications of computers are limited to the performance of statistical analyses of artefactual data, whereas information retrieval techniques have yet to be fully exploited. Much of this chapter is devoted to the file management techniques which are used in information retrieval, and the reader who is primarily interested in statistical analysis may wish to ignore sections 6.4 onwards at a first reading. However, it should be emphasised that information retrieval systems are often suited to extracting data from large multi-purpose data sets for input to statistical programs.

6.2 Files

A **file** is an organised set of data, which should be structured in a manner which aids recovery of information.[1] Normally, it will contain a group of similar or related records which can be treated functionally as a unit. This definition applies equally to manual card indexes containing bibliographical references or a regional sites and monuments record, a ring binder with excavation context record sheets, or a computer-stored file of measurements of flint tools.

Whilst we are principally concerned here with files which contain records describing archaeological entities, it is worth noting that all information available to the computer user is normally stored in files. This includes not only data, but also the programs which are used to process it; the results obtained from the running of such programs; and any files of text which may be generated through the use of a word-processor or text editor program. In terms of the hierarchical model of data storage, program source listings and text files may be regarded as a special case where the file consists of one record, containing one field of many characters.[2]

Most operating systems provide a means for distinguishing different types of files and checking whether or not a file is of the appropriate type for the task in hand. This is normally achieved by means of a file description specified at the time the file is created.

6.21 Filenames

In order that both the user and the machine may distinguish between different files, each must be given a unique **filename**. This usually consists of a short string of characters, of which the first must be alphabetic, and the remainder alphanumeric. Spaces and punctuation characters are not normally permitted. Within these constraints filenames are normally chosen to give some indication of the content and purpose of the file. This filename is normally employed in all of the commands used to instruct the machine to perform operations on the file.[3]

6.22 File operations

There are six basic operations which may be performed on files: **creation**, **deletion**, **opening**, **closing**, **reading** and **writing**. A number of these were used in chapter 4, but more formal definitions are now required.

Creation and deletion are used once only during the lifetime of a file, whereas opening and closing are necessary each time the file is used. Reading and writing may be performed whenever the file is open for use. Creating a file consists of specifying to the computer such information as the filename and type. The file type determines the manner in which the file will be accessed, and the form in which data is recorded. The operating system will then make space available for the file and record its existence in a **file directory**, or **catalogue**. On multi-user systems, this directory will usually hold information on the files associated with each user, whereas on single-user micro-computers there will normally be a directory associated with each disc.[4] The directory also holds information used by the operating system to determine the file size and type, and which disc sectors are used to store the file.

File deletion is used when the file is no longer needed. In practice, a file held on re-usable media is not immediately erased; deletion merely removes the relevant information from the file directory, and the old data is overwritten when the space is required by another file. Whilst it may be possible to recover an accidentally deleted file by reconstructing the directory entry, it is normal practice to keep an archive of back-up copies of all files on a separate storage medium. In most large installations, this archiving is carried out at regular intervals (e.g. weekly), when the contents of all disc files are copied onto magnetic tape. These archive tapes are then kept for two to three weeks before re-use, so that in the event of accidental deletion or system failures it is possible to reconstruct a user's disc files.

When using a micro-computer, it is usually the user's responsibility to make back-up copies. These could be held on duplicate floppy discs, or perhaps on tape cartridges if the system includes hard discs. A file which already exists must be opened before it can be used. In opening a file, the computer will associate a given file on backing store with the file operations specified within a program. Files may be opened for either read access, which allows data only to be read from the file, or read/write access, which permits both reading from and writing to the file. This can give a measure of security to the data held in the file; opening the wrong file for read access can do little harm, but valuable data could be over written if write access was specified.

Once created, a file may have data written into it. When operations on the file have been completed, it is necessary to close it. This instructs the computer to calculate the length of the file and update the directory information accordingly. Some systems will also write a special code after the last record, which can later be recognised as signifying the end of the file.

6.23 File access methods

The manner in which reading from and writing to a file are performed within a program will depend on the access method of the file. In chapter 3 we discussed the serial and direct access storage devices on which the files are normally stored. Access to files held on serial media must always be **sequential**, whereas direct access devices can support both sequential and **direct access** files.

Sequential access files, whether held on serial or on direct access media, are always accessed as if they were held on a serial device. Reading or writing such a file always starts at the beginning, and is performed in the forward direction only. Direct access files allow access to any record within a file, with no restrictions on the order in which the records are selected.

The file access method chosen for a particular application will depend on the nature and scope of the project. Generally, sequential access will be used where the amount of data is relatively small, where a slow response is acceptable, or where all or most of the records in a file need to be accessed during each processing run. Direct access methods, on the other hand, are used where rapid access to individual records in a large data file is required.

6.3 Sequential access files

Sequential access files may be stored on either tape or disc, the only difference normally visible to the user being the greater access speed of the latter. Access to any given record is obtained by reading through from the beginning until the required record is reached. If it is subsequently found that information contained in a previous record is required, it is not possible to backtrack until that record is found. Rather, it is necessary to 'rewind' the file to the start before searching for the required record. For a file held on disc, this is operationally equivalent to closing and reopening the file.

To read the file one record at a time it is essential that the computer can recognise where one record ends and another begins. If the records are of fixed length, then each record may be fetched simply by reading the appropriate number of characters into memory. Variable length records need to contain either some information by which the computer may calculate the record length, or a distinctive character to mark the end of a record. The program will check for this character as the record is read and stop reading when it is found.

Consider an imaginary archaeological application: a research project concerned with the morphology and distribution of particular groups of flint tools. The archaeologist records values of a predetermined set of attributes for each tool. These might include such contextual attributes as the grid reference of the find spot or a code to identify the site, together with a number of specific attributes describing the size and shape of the artefact. The analysis of such data could include any number of statistical techniques, either using one of the packages of statistical programs discussed in chapter 7, or specially written programs. Such programs will usually read the entire file, storing the values contained in the appropriate fields in memory, before performing their analysis. The results are then written to an output file or to the printer. The use of such packages and the requirement to read all or most of the records each time the file is processed makes it appropriate to store this data in sequential form.

In a manual filing system, records are normally stored in a predetermined order, as, for instance, context records in order of context number. Similarly, each record within a sequential file would normally have one field which uniquely identifies that record, and would be used as a **key** on which to order the records within a file. In the case of the flint tool file, each tool would probably be given a unique reference number which would then be used to label the tool in the output from the statistical analysis programs. Where the file is used purely for such purposes, and is not intended for information retrieval, sorting the records into order on this key would aid cross-referencing with the archaeologist's notes, a manual card index, or other computer stored files of related data, but is otherwise optional. Where the application does not require records to be stored in order on a particular key field, strictly the file should be called a **serial** file. The word 'sequential' implies that records are stored in a predetermined and meaningful order.

The unique key need not necessarily be based solely on the value held in one particular field. The file holding data on Roman coin finds shown in fig. 5.2 contains fields for the site, issuing authority, reference catalogue, issuing mint, catalogue reference number, etc. All of these are coded in numeric form, and the file is ordered on all of these fields. Thus all coins from the same site are found together, and within each site those of the same issuing authority, and so on. Nor does the key need to be numeric; a bibliography might be stored in alphabetic order of author names as a primary key, date of publication being used as a secondary key to order references within each author.

In a file of context records held on the computer in sequential form, information on any given context could be found by reading each record in turn, then checking whether the context number field held the required value. When found, the contents of the record could be written to a new file for later use, printed on the line printer, or displayed on a terminal screen. As was seen in chapter 4, the record structures provided in languages such as Pascal and COBOL allow records to be read using a single command, rather than as a series of characters or numeric variables. This can greatly simplify the programmer's task in information retrieval applications.

The above example assumes that there is only one record to be found. Whilst this case may occur, if several records were required it would be

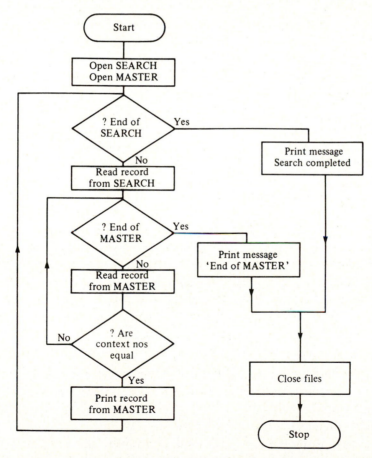

6.1 Flowchart for retrieval of context records from the sequential file MASTER. The required record keys (i.e. context numbers) are held in the file SEARCH.

extremely inefficient to have to repeat the entire process for each record. Any number of records could be found in one pass through the file if the required record keys were presented to the computer in the same order as the records were accessed. The simplest way to achieve this is to use a second file containing a list of the required keys, such as a list of the desired context numbers. This file could be produced by typing in the key values at a terminal, or it could be the output of another program. Fig. 6.1 shows a flowchart for the process of finding a number of context records, specified in the file 'SEARCHFILE', in the sequential context record file 'MASTER-FILE'.

Inserting new records into a sequential file is also usually performed using a second file which contains the new records sorted on the key field. However, in this case a third file is needed to contain the result of merging the new records with the old master file. Whilst this has the desirable effect of maintaining the old master file intact as a back-up copy, the new file is necessary as a result of the method used to read and write a sequential file. The computer maintains a pointer to the location of the next character to be accessed in the file. Thus, after a record has been read into memory, the pointer is set to the start of the next record. Any attempt to write the new record at this position would result in the next record in the old master file being overwritten before it could be read.

A flowchart showing the process of merging a file of new records held in 'UPDATEFILE' with those in 'MASTERFILE' to produce 'NEWMAS-TERFILE' is shown in fig. 6.2. This process could be extended to allow deletion and alteration of records by means of instructions embedded within the update file, or separate programs could be written for each function.

Virtually all computer installations have some form of editor program which may be used for updating files. Most of these work in a similar way to the sequential update described above, with editing commands supplied either in a file or direct from a terminal. Where the user is familiar with the format of the data records, it may be more convenient to use this program rather than to write a special program for updating the file. However, in cases where the data is coded rather than in an expanded form, where record structure is complex, or where the updating is to be performed by persons not fully conversant with the stored form of the data, an interactive data update program will usually be the best solution.

Clearly, the sorting and merging of data files are frequent requirements. Fortunately, most installations are equipped with flexible utility programs to perform these operations. A set of programs to perform the above functions could provide the basis of a simple information storage and retrieval system. Compared with a manual card index file containing the same information, such a system would offer certain advantages. There is no need physically to remove record cards in order to extract information, with the attendant risk

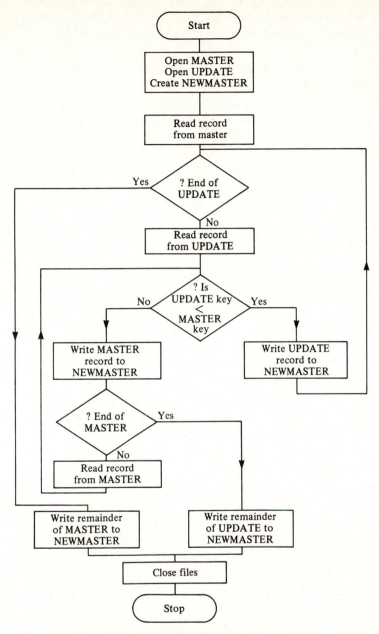

6.2 Flowchart for updating (inserting record) into a sequential file. The new records are held in file UPDATE, and are merged with the MASTER file into the NEWMASTER file. On completion, MASTER remains as a backup copy.

of loss or incorrect replacement; instead a copy of the required records can be printed and studied when and where convenient. If the file is large, there may be considerable savings in time and effort needed to extract the required information. Conversely it may be quicker to use a manual system for small files of relatively simple records, although this may be outweighed by the ability to produce permanent copies of the records. Further advantages may accrue in systems where a file of search keys is automatically generated by another program, thus introducing a degree of automation into, for instance, report preparation.

So far, it has been assumed that a unique key is sufficient to allow access to the required records. As is often the case with a manual card index, the utility of an information retrieval system will depend on the need for, and the extent and quality of, any cross-referencing which is incorporated. The major function of the unique key within a sequential file is in ordering records for updating purposes; for information retrieval purposes, greater flexibility is usually required. Whilst it is convenient to store bibliographic data in author-date sequence, it is likely that many *ad hoc* inquiries would wish to retrieve by subject. Hence in chapter 4, a field containing keywords was used for this purpose. Context number is a convenient key on which to order context records, but there are only a limited number of useful questions which we might ask of our data where this would be known in advance. However, if the objective was to study soils, post-holes or a particular class of artefact, the context number key would be of no use for retrieval purposes. Rather, we would need to be able to tell the machine to list, for instance, all contexts which were post-holes, or which contained pottery of a particular type. To do this, the program would read each record in turn and check for the appropriate value in the required field. Each context which fitted the requirement could then be displayed at a terminal or printed.

A more powerful retrieval program could be written so that rather than searching only on one field, the user may specify values to be found in any number of fields. The program could also allow for boolean relationships between field values. In this way, the user could specify logical combinations of values, or a range of values, between any fields as the search parameters. Thus the program could be instructed to find all those contexts which satisfy such logical criteria as, for instance:

> DATE >1949 AND SUBJECT=roman__villa.

This would provide a list of all recorded references published in 1950 or later which have been designated as concerning villas.

Or, using context records:

> (TYPE=posthole__cut OR TYPE=pit__cut) AND DIAMETER <1.00
> AND DEPTH >0.99

Here, the result would be a list in context number order of all those contexts which are described as pit or post-hole cuts with a diameter less than one metre and a depth of one metre or more. Further refinements which could usefully be added would include the ability to sort the output on any specified field, and to list only those fields which the user requires. In the above example, the data required might be limited to the dimensions, grid reference and context number, and these could be listed in order of, say, diameter. Where a reasonably large number of records need to be extracted, and there is no pressure for immediate output, then such a system running in a batch processing environment on a mainframe computer may be acceptable as a first stage in the automation of archaeological data processing. If, however, access to individual or small numbers of records is frequently required, then sequential files would prove extremely inefficient, with an average response time inversely proportional to the size of the file. In such a case it is necessary to turn to more direct techniques of accessing records.

6.4 **Direct access files**

Direct access to the records in a file depends upon knowing, or being able to calculate, the location or address of any record on the disc. A number of different methods of determining this address are possible. Some applications will use a simple algorithm to calculate it from the value of the primary key; others hold a separate index relating key values to addresses.

Direct access to records is extremely fast, making it suitable for direct inquiries from a terminal. Updating the file can also be performed directly as there is no need to sort new or replacement records into order; they may be keyed in as the information becomes available. Updating records is performed by directly overwriting the previous version; thus back-up copies must be made at regular intervals. Some systems incorporate **transaction logging** which keeps a record of all alterations performed on the file since the last back-up copy was made.

Whilst there are many techniques for performing direct access to files, many of them require an intimate knowledge of the low-level system control language used on the particular installation. A number of high-level language implementations provide facilities for simple use of such methods, but these are often additions to the agreed standard for the language. Some versions of Pascal used on micro-computers, for instance, permit direct access, whereas the language as originally defined (Jensen and Wirth 1978) allows only sequential files. For these reasons, the current discussion will be limited to the use of two commonly used methods: **Relative File Organisation**, which illustrates the essential features of direct access, and the **Index-Sequential Access Method (ISAM)**, which combines direct and sequential access techniques. We will first consider their application to fixed length records, and then discuss how variable length records may be accommodated.

6.41 Relative File Organisation

Relative File Organisation provides a simple means of direct access by using a counter to number the records in the file, and thus to provide a relative record address. Records are numbered from 1 to n, where n is the maximum number of records in the file. Once such a file has been declared the actual disc addressing is handled by the operating system, and the programmer needs only to refer to the relative number in order to access any record.

Relative files are normally defined within a program by specifying such parameters as the size of each (fixed length) record and the total number of records in the file. These are used by the operating system to reserve the appropriate amount of space on the disc, and to determine where each record starts. For instance, in FORTRAN 77, the following statement would introduce a file called 'RFILE' containing records of length 100 bytes:

OPEN(UNIT=5,FORM='FORMATTED',FILE='RFILE',
ACCESS='DIRECT',RECL=100)

Subsequent 'READ' or 'WRITE' statements would specify the required record number, e.g.

READ(UNIT=5,FMT=210,REC=RN,ERR=220,END=230) A,B,C,D

which would read record number 'RN' into variables A,B,C,D according to the FORMAT statement labelled 210. On detecting an error, control would pass to line 220, and, on reaching the end of the file, to line 230.

The record number might be derived directly from a primary key, such as the unique identifier used in a sites and monuments register, or the context number in the context record file. In the former case, the sequential allocation of numbers would ensure that each record in the file was eventually filled. Context numbers, however, are usually allocated in blocks, with the result that at the completion of the excavation, there may be a sizeable proportion of unused numbers. If the context number was used as the relative record address, this would mean that a proportion of the allocated file space remained unused. If the file was re-organised to remove unused record spaces, then the context numbers would no longer correspond to the relative record numbers. Renumbering contexts would probably lead to confusion, so it would be necessary to generate an index relating records to contexts.

6.42 Index-Sequential Access Method

ISAM uses a combination of direct and sequential access methods. Writing and updating is usually performed as for a normal sequential file, with the data stored in order on a predetermined key. The difference lies in the maintenance of an index file which holds the key values of the records together with their corresponding addresses on the disc. This index is updated each time the main file is written to, and is available to provide the address values necessary for direct access reading. Again, a number of indexes could be employed to order the records on different keys. Thus context records might be entered into the file in the order in which they were excavated (*arrival order*), although an index based on context number would allow them to be accessed as if they were stored in context number order.

It is possible to use the direct access capabilities of ISAM for insertion and deletion of, and alteration to, individual records, but this would normally be reserved for minor alterations to the data.

Whilst some commonly used programming languages, e.g. COBOL, support both relative files and ISAM, others, e.g. FORTRAN 77, provide only the former technique directly. However, from the description of relative files given above, it will be seen that it is possible to develop an ISAM system using the facilities offered by relative file organisation. In this case, it would be the programmer's responsibility to maintain the index, which would contain the relative record numbers associated with each record, rather than the direct disc address.

When using direct access facilities for updating ISAM files, gaps will result from deleted entries, and records may overflow their allocated space. Languages which provide the necessary facilities for handling ISAM will usually deal with such problems, but it may be necessary to build in appropriate 'housekeeping' routines when using other languages.

6.43 Direct access with variable length records

So far, we have considered only direct access with fixed length records, and it might appear that the only solution to the problem of variable length records would be to allow sufficient space for each record to be of the maximum possible length. Where the variation in length between records is small compared with the average length of the records, this would be the simplest solution. However, some applications may require greater flexibility in record lengths in order to avoid excessive waste of storage space. Whilst these problems may be dealt with automatically when using languages such as COBOL, there are a number of possible solutions which may be employed when using a language which supports only relative file organisation.

One approach is illustrated in fig. 6.3. Here, the relative record length is chosen to be smaller than the average stored data record. Each stored record begins at a relative record boundary and fills one or more relative records. The unused space is now only a fraction of the relative record length. If the restriction on starting a stored record at a relative record boundary were removed, then even this space need not be wasted. In this case the index would contain an extra field indicating the offset (number of character) from the start of the relative record at which the stored record begins.

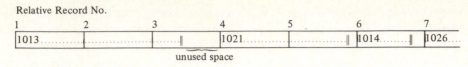

Relative Record No.

1	2	3	4	5	6	7
1013..........	....	....‖	1021..........	.........‖	1014......‖	1026....

unused space

Structure of Index

Key	No. of Records	Relative Record No.
1013	3	1
1014	1	6
1021	2	4
1026	2	7

6.3 Variation on ISAM used to accommodate variable length records. The index contains an entry for the key to the logical record, the number of records to read and the relative number of the first record.

6.44 **Limitations of the indexed approach**

The use of relative or indexed direct access files in information retrieval is superior to the sequential file approach only if key values on which searches are to be performed are known in advance. Searching on non-indexed fields will still entail reading the entire file as if it were in sequential form. The problem may be overcome simply by increasing the number of fields which are to be indexed, and some systems may allow for the creation of extra temporary or permanent indexes as the need arises. The indexes, however, have to be stored somewhere, and increasing the number of indexes will lead to greater time being spent reading and processing them.

A relatively simple application, such as a bibliography file, may need indexing on only a small number of fields, say, author name and subject (although, even in this example, it is possible that some requests may require retrieval by publication date, or name of journal). On the other hand, excavation context records or a sites and monuments register would contain so many fields on which indexing might be required that such a system would prove very inefficient. In these cases, it may be preferable to index only the most commonly used fields, and rely on sequential searching for less frequent types of request.

6.5 **Alternative data structures**

The flexibility of an information retrieval system depends upon its ability to present information in a form which suits the requirements of all potential users. With relatively simple data sets of limited application, such as a bibliography file, satisfactory results are usually obtained using a small number of indexed keys or multi-parameter searches. Where the applications of the data are more varied, these basic techniques may prove inadequate.

A number of archaeological applications require the ability to express relationships between individual entities, rather than simply regarding each occurrence as a discrete item. For instance, in a file of records describing objects recovered from a cemetery, we might hold two or more independent models of the relationships between objects. For one purpose, all objects from the same grave would be seen as a useful grouping; for another, we might wish to group all items of the same type from the entire cemetery. Similarly, we might wish to use the stratigraphic sequence of an excavated site as a structural model in order to aid retrieval.

Whilst related records could be accessed via indexes, the relative frequency of questions such as 'What else was in this grave?', 'Which other graves produced this type?', or 'Which context lies above this one?', together with the need to limit the proliferation of indexes in order to economise on storage, may make it desirable to utilise existing links between records.

6.51 **Linking records**

As we have seen, the order in which records are stored or indexed may be used to aid retrieval of records which describe entities with similar characteristics. Such entities are related by some similarity between certain field values. Many applications require stronger relationships between entities. For instance, many of the excavation recording systems in use in Britain today follow that developed by Harris (1979), and include the relationships ABOVE and BELOW or BEFORE and AFTER which may be used as **links** between individual contexts. Such links may be used to impose alternative structures to that implicit in the ordering of records. Thus context records may be stored in order of context number, but if the ABOVE/BELOW fields contain the key values (context numbers) of related contexts, then retrieval may be performed according to stratigraphic sequence. The system used by the Central Excavation Unit of the DOE makes use of several additional relationships, including CONTAINS and PART OF, which provide links in a hierarchical structure relating contexts to 'features' to 'structures' (Jefferies 1977). Opinion is divided on whether or not it is valid or necessary to record these latter relationships at the time of excavation. They may be derived using the above/below relationships, either manually or automatically (see, for example, Bishop and Wilcock 1976; Wilcock 1982), and may be used to provide a useful data structure for post-excavation analysis.[5]

Linear, hierarchic or network relationships (fig. 6.4) may be incorporated in a file by means of links. In any system which allows records to be accessed directly from a terminal, the user may then step through groups of related records at will. This ability to 'browse' can often prove more valuable than using a system which requires all retrieval parameters to be carefully defined in advance.

The use of links or **pointers** is not restricted to relating records of the same type within a single file. They may also be used to relate different entity types

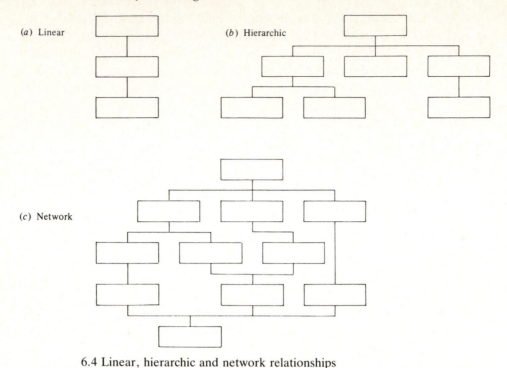

(a) Linear

(b) Hierarchic

(c) Network

6.4 Linear, hierarchic and network relationships

which are held in separate files. This is done frequently to avoid unnecessary repetition of data, and hence waste of storage space. It would be preferable in a sites and monuments file to maintain a set of pointers to the records of a bibliography file, rather than to store the entire bibliographic references as sub-records within each site record. This approach retains the ability to regard the related entities as distinct entity types, and thus to maintain flexibility in information retrieval. We will return to this topic when we consider the database approach in section 6.6.

6.52 **Inverted files**

So far, we have assumed that whereas different users of a data set may have differing concepts of the relationships between records, they share a single model of the structure of the record. This is often achieved by deciding on a single entity (artefact), and recording all those attributes which may be of use to each application in a single contiguous data record.

This approach has frequently been taken when assembling sites and monuments registers of the type kept by many local authority planning departments in Britain. Fig. 6.5 shows a typical recording form for such work, which might be used in either a manual or an automated storage and retrieval system. The primary function of such registers is usually to provide information about the archaeological consequences of any proposed planning de-

STAFFORDSHIRE HISTORICAL AND ARCHAEOLOGICAL DATA SYSTEM
STAFFORDSHIRE COUNTY COUNCIL
COUNTY PLANNING DEPARTMENT

DISTRICT		01 RECORD NUMBER
PARISH		
CARD OF	04 OWNER	06 DEFINITIVE RECORD AT

| 02 SITE ADDRESS | 03 TENANT ADDRESS | | 07 LAND USAGE - NAT - |
| | | 05 DATE ACQUIRED | W. MID. |

08 LEGAL STATUS								
NT	NP	SCHEDULED	LISTED	PRES. ORD.	SSSI	AONB	CONS. AREA	AAI	LNR
09 SITE STATUS								
NT		SCHEDULED	GUARD'SHP	REC. ROUTE	OPEN TO PUBLIC	CONS. AREA	PLAQUE	GUIDE	NR
10 LISTED BLDG. GRD.								
I	II ✱	II	III	A	B	C	UNCLASSED	PROPOSED

11 SPECIAL REFERENCES OS | | CA | | 13 L | H | SITE SIZE

| NGR | 12 | LB | AAI | W | D |
| S | | AM | | A | V |

14 SITE DESCRIPTION

TYPE						
FORM						
PERIOD						
DATE						
EPOCH						
DATING AUTHORITY						
DATE DATED						
METHOD						
DATING REF.						
BLDG. MAT.						
ROOF MAT.						
BLDG. TYPE						
WM TYPE						

| 15 GEOLOGY | 16 SOIL | 17 CLIMATIC PHASE | 18 CONDITION | 19 OTHER FEATURES |

20 FINANCIAL ASSISTANCE					
DATE	£	TYPE	DATE	£	TYPE
		ACCEPTED			ACCEPTED
		DECLINED			DECLINED
		PAID			PAID
		LAPSED			LAPSED

| 21 GUARDIANSHIP AUTHORITY | 22 SOURCE AND DATE OF LOCATION DATA |

| 23 SITE CHARACTERISATION |
| CONTINUED OVER |

24 MAIN PUBLICATION REF.

25 ARCHIVE DATA						
COLLECTION						
GEN. REF.						
SPEC. REF.						
MATERIAL TYPE						

6.5 A typical sites and monuments record form (Staffordshire County Council Planning Dept)

velopment, and whilst the data might be assembled and maintained by archaeologists, archaeological research requirements are invariably only a secondary consideration. The record contains an extensive collection of data, ranging from basic locational (contextual) attributes, through legal, geological, land usage, and more specifically archaeological data, to cross-references to other sources, including photographs, maps, and planning applications. It is highly unlikely that any one user would ever require access to all of this information, but many inquiries would be satisfied by the record structure which views the 'site' as the fundamental entity.

Consider now the problem of attempting to analyse such data in terms, say, of the distribution of sites of different types in relation to soil type. Using a select-and-sort approach, we might instruct the machine to select site records of the appropriate type, then sort firstly on soil type, and then on site type. This would provide the required information, but it would probably be more convenient to express the information in tabular form rather than as a long list (fig. 6.6). Indeed we might wish to write the data to a file in this form in order to perform a statistical analysis. In section 2.44, we observed that attributes may become artefacts when we change our frame of reference. Similarly, we have transformed part of the sites and monuments file such that the attribute 'soil type' of the original record is now an entity whose attributes are the identifiers of the sites of each type occurring on that soil type. In the tabular form, we have grouped sites of the same type together so that there are now a fixed number of attributes, each giving the total number of each type of site on each soil type.

In this case, only a small part of each of the original records has been transformed in this manner. In other applications we may wish to transform the entire record. The Roman coin finds file of fig. 5.2 could be transformed to show 'coin type' as the entity, and number of coins of each type on each site as the attribute. In this case, the unique coin type is derived from a combination of the issuing authority, mint, catalogue reference, etc, and is directly equivalent to the unique key derived from these fields in section 6.3. Fig. 6.7 shows the data in fig. 5.2 transformed in this manner.

This transformation process, which is known as **inversion**, is often necessary when preparing data for statistical analysis.[6] The sites and monuments example made use of **partial** inversion in order to derive the required information from the much larger data set. Any number of such partial inversions could be performed to suit different views of the same data set.

Files for information retrieval are sometimes stored in an inverted form from the outset. In such cases, the first entry in the file would contain each distinct attribute state associated with the first attribute, together with the identifying key of each record which held those values. Thus the file consists of all occurrences of the first attribute, followed by all occurrences of the second, and so on. Where the number of possible attribute states is small, this

(a)

Site	Soil Type			
Type	1	2	3	4
1	2	0	2	0
2	1	3	0	1
3	2	2	5	3

(b)

Site No	Site Type	Soil Type
1	1	1
2	1	1
3	1	3
4	3	4
5	1	3
6	2	4
7	2	1
8	3	1
9	3	1
10	3	4
.	.	.
.	.	.
.	.	.

6.6 A simple table (a) showing the number of sites of each type occurring on each soil type, provides a more convenient representation of the data than a file of site records (b) with site and soil types as attributes.

might be realised as a simple table, as in fig. 6.7, but where such a table might contain a large number of zero elements, it is preferable to record the identifiers of the records. Fig. 6.8 shows this strategy applied to coin data, where the identifiers of those sites on which the coin type occurs are recorded, together with the number of occurrences of the type.

It should be noted that, in this latter case, the records are of variable length, whereas the example in fig. 6.7 results in fixed length records. However, record length will change when record occurrences are added or deleted. We have already met multiple index systems in which the indexes contain pointers to those records which have particular values. These are sometimes referred to as **inverted indexes**, as they allow access to records stored in a normal manner as if they were inverted.

Coin	No of coins on site:							
Type	1	2	3	4	5	6	7	8
.	.	.	.	.	.	.	.	.
.	.	.	.	.	.	.	.	.
195	0	12	6	0	0	0	10	0
196	0	0	3	0	1	0	2	1
197	1	3	0	0	0	1	0	0
198	0	0	0	1	0	0	0	3
199	0	0	0	1	0	0	1	0
200	0	1	0	0	0	0	0	0
201	0	0	0	0	0	0	0	0
202	1	0	0	1	0	0	0	0
.	.	.	.	.	.	.	.	.
.	.	.	.	.	.	.	.	.

6.7 Roman coin finds in *Inverted* form. Data of the type shown in fig. 5.2 transformed so that each record refers to a single coin 'type', and contains the number found on each site as attributes.

Coin Type	Site No	No of Coins	Site No	No of Coins				
.								
.								
195	2	12	3	6	7	10		
196	3	3	5	1	7	2	8	1
197	1	1	2	3	6	1		
198	4	1	8	3				
199	4	1	7	1				
200	2	1						
202	1	1	4	1				
.								
.								

6.8 The inverted coin find data of fig. 6.7 in a potentially more compact form. The records contain the repeating sub-group of fields *Site No* and *No of Coins*, and are of variable length.

6.6 Data banks and databases

The terms **data bank** and **database** are frequently used as synonyms describing any system which stores a large body of data, which is available to a number of users via information retrieval programs.[7] Here, we use the terms in a more precise manner. A data bank is understood to be:

> A comprehensive file of data, usually stored on a direct access device. Data stored on a data bank is usually available to a large number of users by means of remote

terminals, and is often updated by means of a real-time system. (Chandor *et al* 1977)

Most of the applications discussed so far satisfy this definition. In each case, the structure of the file is determined by the major application. Thus each file consists of similar records referring to occurrences of the entity or artefact type under consideration. The records in a bibliographic file refer to published articles, those in a sites and monuments file refer to sites, and those in the excavation file refer to excavated contexts.

This approach is satisfactory as long as the data is required to serve only a single application, or where the different applications can co-exist within the same logical view of data structure. The first applications to be developed following a change from a manual to a computer-based information system should perform adequately, but as time passes and further applications are developed, the system becomes increasingly complex and difficult to maintain. More and more time is spent in writing programs to transform the data into the forms required by the separate applications. In the worst cases, the original advantages in using the computer are outweighed by the resulting effort required simply to maintain the system.

Such applications are said to be **data-dependent**. It is necessary for the programmer, and, to a lesser extent, the user, to understand how the entire data bank is organised and accessed in order to make use of any part of the system. If, at any time, it is necessary to alter the data storage structure or access methods, to accommodate either new data items or logical views of the data, then it follows that all of the applications software will require substantial alteration. We could not, for instance, change from normal to inverted file storage (which might better suit the application) without drastic re-organisation.

An alternative approach might be for each user, or group of users, to maintain separate files which reflect their local data models. The applications are still data-dependent, but the structure, and hence the task of programming, is simplified. Although this may prove adequate for short term or self-contained projects, in many cases it will merely delay the onset of problems. **Data-redundancy**, where the same data is stored separately in a number of different files, can lead to further problems. Firstly, whenever it is necessary to change an occurrence of a data item, every file in which that item occurs must be edited. This implies that every user who is permitted to amend data must be aware of the contents of each file and must either perform all necessary updates, or at least inform the other users that their data is no longer accurate. Secondly, the inefficient use of storage space may result in an unacceptably slow response on smaller machines.

Though not always fully achieved, it is a primary aim of the database approach to avoid these problems. Thus, in contrast to a data bank, a database may be defined as:

> ... a collection of interrelated data stored together without harmful or unneces-
> sary redundancy to serve multiple applications. The storage of data is done so as
> to achieve independence from the programs that use the data, and the structure of
> the data allows for future application development. (Elbra 1982)

The following sections provide a brief introduction to the major functions and facilities of database systems, and a description of the various data models employed. An in-depth discussion of the operation of database systems and the techniques which are used in establishing a database is beyond the scope of this book. For general discussions of these topics, the reader is referred to Elbra (1982) and Date (1975). Many of the techniques employed in the database approach are equally applicable to conventional file based systems. Maddison *et al* (1980) provide a thorough introduction to the topics of **data analysis**, **functional analysis**, and **normalisation**, which are used in establishing a database system.

6.61 **Database systems**

Database systems have their origins in the need to provide overall central control of the operational data of large organisations. Such organisations, be they government departments, university administrations or commercial enterprises, invariably consist of a number of smaller departments, each of which may have their own view or model of that part of the organisation's data set with which they are concerned. This is analogous to the archaeologic-al team, some of whom may be concerned with the day to day running of current excavations, whilst others are performing post-excavation analyses using data on contexts and finds from earlier excavations. Likewise, the planning officer and archaeologist have alternative views of the sites and monuments data.

Central control, usually by a **database administrator**, helps to reduce problems of data redundancy, where the same data items might otherwise be stored separately for a number of different applications. Similarly, inconsis-tencies which could result from the need to update all occurrences of the same data item in separate files are avoided. Data items need only be stored once in the database to be available to all users. Whilst this might be expected to cause security problems by allowing access to sensitive data by unauthorised users, most systems allow the database administrator to impose access res-trictions where necessary.

6.62 **Database architecture**

Fig. 6.9 shows a typical database system structure, or **architecture**. This is a four tier structure, with the users and applications programmers at the top and the physical database storage at the bottom. In between are those parts which remove considerations of physical storage from the user, and allow different groups to make use of their own local data models. Each **local logical**

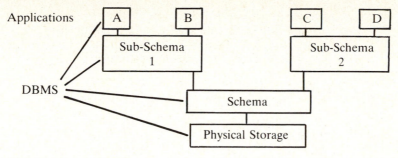

6.9 Database architecture

data model, or **sub-schema**, describes the data types required by a single user or group of users. This information is stored with the details necessary to map the local model to the **global logical data model**, or **schema**. The schema describes the entire database in terms of data types, and is held with details of how this is mapped to the data on the physical storage media.

All four levels are controlled by the **DataBase Management System (DBMS)**, which acts as an overall control program for the system. The schema and sub-schema are representations, in a form appropriate to the DBMS, of global and local conceptual data models. They are used to tell the DBMS which data item types (fields in a simple file; attributes in the conceptual model) are to be grouped together in each record type, and how the record types are to be related to each other. In most systems, **Schema** and **Sub-schema Data Description Languages (DDL)** are provided so that these models may be defined within the database.

A **Data Manipulation Language (DML)** is normally provided to aid the functions of data input, modification and retrieval. This frequently takes the form of a number of extensions to a conventional programming language, such as COBOL, which are used in writing the applications programs by which the user accesses the database. An alternative approach is to use a separate **Query Language**. In some systems this may be provided in addition to a normal DML and will allow only simple interactive inquiries originated by a user via a terminal. However, a number of systems employ a more advanced query language which may be used either interactively or for writing applications programs.

6.63 **Database models**
In section 6.51 we discussed how relationships between records may be expressed using links. In a database system there may be many different record types, each of which may be related to one or more other record types. Relationships may be of three types: **one-to-one (1:1)**, **one-to-many (1:n)**, and **many-to-many (m:n)**. In each case *one* implies none or one, and *many* implies none, one, or more. Fig. 6.10 shows a number of examples of such relationships between typical archaeological entities. Note that an m:n rela-

1:1 relationship

one POT *has* one MAXIMUM, DIAMETER

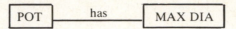

1:n relationships

one SITE *contains* many PITS

n:n relationships

many POTTERY TYPEs *are found in* many CONTEXTS

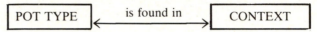

6.10 Examples of *one-to-one*, *one-to-many* and *many-to-many* relationships between archaeological entities

		Context				
		C1		C2		C3
Pottery Form	PF1	0 , 0		60 , 4		800 , 32
	PF2	80 , 5		0 , 0		25 , 2
	PF3	0 , 0		200 , 10		0 , 0

(each box contains weight and no. of sherds)

6.11 Imaginary data for the relationships linking the entities Pottery Form and Context

PF1, ...(attributes of PF)

    C2,   60,   4
    C3,   800,   32

PF2, ...

    C1,   80,   5
    C3,   25,   2

PF3, ...

    C2,   200,   10

6.12 Hierarchical model of 'Pottery Form *is found in* Context' relationship

tionship may be broken down into two distinct 1:n relationships which may be appropriate to two local data models. Thus, that between POTTERY TYPE and CONTEXT could appear in one local model as 'one POTTERY TYPE *is found in* many CONTEXTS', and in another as 'one CONTEXT *contains* many POTTERY TYPEs'. The 1:1 relationship implies that one of the related entities is wholly dependent on the other. That is, they both contain attributes of the same entity, and can therefore be amalgamated into a single logical record.

The type of relationship structure which may be used is dictated by the type of data model on which the DBMS is based. The three data models, and, hence, types of database system, which may be used are: the **hierarchical** model, the **network** model and the **relational** model.

Consider the relationship 'POTTERY TYPE *is found in* CONTEXT'. For each occurrence of this relationship, we might wish to record the weight and number of sherds found. Fig. 6.11 shows part of a imaginary data set containing this data in tabular form. The database will also contain records describing each pottery type and each context. Fig. 6.12 shows the model of the relationship under the hierarchical system. Note that this is the user's model of the data which need carry no implications for the internal storage of data items. The context number, weight and number of sherds may be visualised as repeating sub-records of the POTTERY TYPE record. In this model, the only access route to the weight and number of sherds data is through the pottery form. Similarly, if the 'CONTEXT *contains* POTTERY TYPE' relationship were to be used, the only access would be from the context. Starting from a given pottery form, the 'is—found—in' relationship might be used to extract those contexts in which it occurred. It would then be necessary to change to the model expressed by the 'contains' relationship to retrieve further information on any of the selected contexts, such as which other pottery forms were found. Data relating to the relationship is always found in the hierarchically inferior record. This is implicit in the hierarchical model.

Fig. 6.13 shows the same relationship in a network model. Here, the data

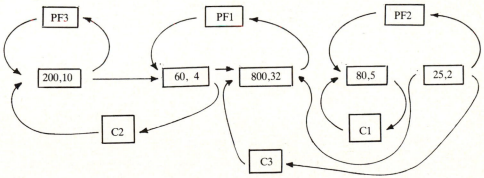

6.13 Network model of 'Pottery Form *is found in* Context' relationship

associated with the relationship is held separately from that associated directly with the entities, with pointers or links which direct flow around the
network. The entity records also hold pointers to the first relationship
occurrence. By following the connections between the **nodes** of the network
from any given entity, all related entities will be reached. The final pointer of
each route leads back to the start, thus indicating that all occurrences have
been found. In a network database any node may be used as the entry point of
an access route provided that it has a unique identifier. Note that this model
directly incorporates the m:n relationship between POTTERY TYPE and
CONTEXT, unlike the hierarchical case, which required two 1:n relationships. In practice, however, many network database systems will require
the m:n relationship to be expressed as two 1:n relationships in the schema.
The advantage of this approach lies in the ability to start at any entry point
and step through the nodes of the database, retrieving all related information.

The relational model does not distinguish between entities and relationships (Codd 1970; Date 1975). Rather, it regards each relationship as an
additional entity type. Thus, in a relational database, we would have POT-
TERY TYPE, CONTEXT, and POTTERY TYPE IS FOUND IN CON-
TEXT entities, as shown in fig. 6.14. Because there is no distinction between
them, the same operations may be performed on both entities and relationships. Both hierarchical and network data models must usually make use
of the relative positions of data, or of pointers, and therefore must always be
somewhat data-dependent. The relational model, on the other hand, is quite
free of any considerations of storage structure and is totally data-
independent.

Much of the attraction of the relational model lies in its apparent simplicity. Each entity type may be regarded as a simple sequential file containing
records describing occurrences of that entity. Records which fulfil any given

Pottery Form   Context

| PF1,.................. |
| PF2,.................. |
| PF3,.................. |

| C1, ... |
| C2, ... |
| C3, ... |

Pottery Form is Found in Context

PF1,	C2,	60,	4
PF1,	C3,	800,	32
PF2,	C1,	80,	5
PF2,	C3,	25,	2
PF3,	C2,	200,	10

6.14 The Relational model views a 'relationship' as a distinct entity type

criteria may be selected, just as in a simple information retrieval system. Similarly, the records may be re-ordered by selecting different indexes. The new ordering may be seen by the user as a different 'file' produced by sorting. Reports may be produced or **projected** in which the data from the 'file' is presented in summary form. The real power of the database approach is realised only when these facilities are combined with an ability to **join** records from two different 'files' to produce a third. This is done using a field common to both records; both 'files' are read sequentially, and every time the same value is found in the join field of both records then they are put together and written to the output. This is repeated until all joining combinations have been found. The new records which are produced may contain any combination of fields from the input records.

6.64 **Database on small computers**

Although the database approach has been traditionally associated with large organisations and mainframe computers, implementations of each of the three database models are now available for micro-computers. Clearly, these are not capable of dealing with such large data sets, or of the rapid response of the larger systems. Nevertheless, they can often prove adequate for the data sets of smaller research projects.

The task of establishing and maintaining these smaller databases frequently requires a level of programming expertise which is beyond the average user of a micro-computer. On the other hand, many simple file management packages provide basic facilities such as sorting, indexing and retrieval of information. Many of these may be used by people with no programming experience, and may be quite adequate for simpler applications.

In between these extremes there are a number of packages which allow multiple files containing records of related entities to be processed. Most of these employ a simple form of the relational database model, the apparent simplicity of which is often much easier for the non-specialist to understand. In section 7.5 we will discuss a number of these.

NOTES

(1) In practice, a file may (and occasionally does) contain nonsense. The definition given here is, however, adequate for any file which is to be of practical use.

(2) Whilst such files may be seen as a single **logical** record by the user, it will be apparent from the description of storage devices in chapter 3 that the computer will treat the long stream of text as a sequential series of fixed length **physical** records, each stored in a single disc record or sector. In practice, the logical records defined by the user will rarely be of the same length as the physical disc records, and the computer's operating system will automatically perform all necessary mapping between the two.

In a number of systems, only a simple line based editor program is available. In such cases each line of text would normally be regarded as a single record.

(3) In many cases a **local** filename will be used to refer to a file within the body of a program. The machine is made aware of the relationship between this local name and the external filename by some form of assignment statement executed prior to running the program.

(4) Throughout this chapter, files are normally considered to be resident on disc. Where a file is stored on a magnetic tape, each tape will normally start with a **header** record which identifies the tape and its contents in a similar manner to the disc directory or catalogue.

(5) We do not question Harris's assertion (1975) that the stratigraphic matrix diagram should be produced manually on site, but feel that the ability of the computer to do this task should be seen as a valid checking procedure.

(6) Readers familiar with the 'data cube' model employed by many geographers (see, for instance, Berry 1964; Johnston 1978, 5-6, 180-1) will appreciate that file inversion is analogous with rotation and transformation of the data cube in order to perform analyses in different modes.

(7) See, for example, Gaines (1981a), where 'data bank' is used as a general term to cover both data banks and database.

7

PACKAGES

7.1 Introduction
One of the categories of program introduced in chapter 4 was the applications package. It was defined as a program, or suite of programs, designed with a specific group of users in mind, but used in several environments or organisations. Applications packages are generally written by professional programmers, and come as optional extras to a computer system.

Since many of the tasks which the archaeologist may wish to perform on a computer may be accomplished by such packages it is appropriate that they should be considered in more detail. In this chapter we shall consider four areas in which existing applications packages are likely to prove useful to archaeologists: statistics, graphics, word processing and database management systems.

7.2 Statistics
A wide range of statistical packages are available. In this section we shall describe a selection of the most popular ones: **SPSS**, **BMDP**, **MINITAB**, **GENSTAT**, and **CLUSTAN**. All these packages are likely to be found on mainframe computers. MINITAB and a smaller version of SPSS, known as **SPSS-11**, are also available for mini-computers, and with increasing memory size, equivalent packages are becoming available for micro-computers. There are already packages such as **VisiCalc** available for micro-computers, which although not designed for this purpose, may be used to perform simple statistical routines.

There are several advantages to be gained from using an existing package rather than writing a program. Firstly there is obviously a considerable saving in time. One need not learn programming, and one's knowledge of computing may be limited to where to find the appropriate hardware, and familiarity with the operating system and with the use of the package. Generally, packages are designed so that those unfamiliar with computers should find them easy to use. Secondly, packages are usually well tried and tested. One can be reasonably confident that the results are correct. Thirdly, there is likely to be local experience of their use, and possibly expertise on how they should be applied to a particular problem.

On the other hand, there are considerable pitfalls in the use of statistical packages. Because a program is available there is a temptation to force one's data through the package, regardless of whether the technique is appropriate. Whilst the results will be correct, they may rest upon certain initial premises about the data. Most statistical packages have little ability to distinguish between proper and improper applications. For example, as long as it was coded numerically, one could perform a principal components analysis on nominal data. The results would almost always be nonsense, although this might not be immediately apparent from examining the output.

Furthermore, the power of packages such as SPSS means that a single instruction may produce output that is measured in terms of inches of thickness of listings paper. Whilst it may all be useful, one should bear in mind that it may take several days to look through and extract the relevant information. If one generates enough information there is a danger that 'significant' results may be produced simply by chance. For example, in 1000 cross tabulations of every attribute with every other attribute of an artefact, one would expect there to be ten results statistically significant at a 0.01 level, by the laws of probability.

It is essential, therefore, that statistical packages should be used with caution. The most sensible approach is to adopt a problem-solving methodology. Questions or hypotheses should be posed which statistical methods may be used to test. Generally, it is better to request only those statistics for which one has some theoretical expectations based upon the research hypotheses. There is extreme danger in adopting the alternative inductive method of 'hitting' a data set with every statistical technique available, in the hope that something significant may turn up.

Furthermore, statistical novices would be well advised to apply standard descriptive statistics (e.g. frequency distributions, means, standard deviations), before turning to more advanced multivariate techniques (e.g. principal components analysis, clustering, multi-dimensional scaling). Frequently, quantitative problems in archaeology may be solved by the application of simple statistics such as percentages or averages, rather than by heavy number-crunching. One should always have an understanding of a statistical technique, and particularly the assumptions it makes about the data, before seeking to apply it.

This book is not the place to discuss the application of quantitative techniques in archaeology. The rest of this section is devoted to a discussion of the facilities offered by several statistical packages. Doran and Hodson (1975) and Ihm (1978) provide a discussion of those techniques which have been applied in archaeology. Orton (1980) gives a useful guide to the role of mathematics in archaeology. The reader without a mathematical training may also find two texts written for geographers in a similar position very readable (Ebdon 1977; Hammond and McCullagh 1978). Despite a geographical bias to the examples, these books give a clear description of those techniques which are also likely to be used by archaeologists. Another geography text (Johnston 1978) provides a good introduction to multivariate statistics. For those with a mathematical background Green (1976) may also be useful for multivariate techniques.

7.21 **SPSS**

SPSS (Statistical Package for the Social Sciences) is probably the most widely used package in the social sciences.[1] Therefore we shall consider its capabilities in some detail. It consists of a set of related programs, or procedures, for the manipulation and statistical analysis of many types of data, with a particular emphasis on the needs of the social scientist. It has gained wide acceptance in archaeology. Plog (1981) describes its use as a file management system for a complete archaeological data bank. Once raw data has been entered in an SPSS compatible format, the computer can be instructed to carry out a variety of tasks in any order. It is unnecessary to re-enter the data at any time. It is also possible to retrieve data from the system for use with other programs.

SPSS is available on most mainframe computers in educational establishments, although the user may find that access is restricted to batch processing. The newcomer should not be deterred by the size of the user manual (Nie *et al* 1975; Nie and Hadlai Hull 1981). This describes all the procedures available, and attempts to introduce the statistical techniques as well. Initially, the user need only consult the first few chapters which cover the data organisation and description, and the chapter dealing with the particular procedure required. The most useful procedures for initial analysis frequently turn out to be CROSSTABS, FREQUENCIES, and SCATTERGRAM (see below). The essential information is contained within the SPSS Primer (Klecka, Nie and Hadlai Hull 1975), which is a far slimmer volume. Once the user is familiar with the workings of the system, occasional reference to the Pocket Guide, which is smaller still, may be all that is necessary.

7.211 **SPSS data organisation**

Data to be analysed by SPSS must be organised in records, or cases, as SPSS terms them. Hence, the level at which records are defined in the initial data coding determines the unit of analysis. Each record consists of several fields, containing measurements of attributes (cf. chapter 2). A record may occupy several physical lines if required. However, each record within an SPSS file must comprise the same number of fields. There is no programmed limit to the number of records which may be entered in a file, although in practice an upper limit is likely to be fixed by the amount of storage available to the user. Irrespective of the number of records, the user is limited to a maximum of 500 fields, or attributes, per record.

The data may be held in fixed-column or free-field format. If it is organised in fixed columns, the values of each attribute must be located in the same column for each record. For data organised in free-field format, there need be no correspondence between the columns occupied by the same attribute in successive records, as long as the sequence of the attributes remains the same from one record to the next. In practice the user is recommended to adhere to fixed-column data, so that errors in the data may be more easily detected.

One very useful feature of SPSS is a facility which permits the user to specify missing values for each of the attributes (see section 2.6). Frequently, in archaeology, it is impossible to take measurements on a particular attribute for some artefacts. If a code number is chosen to denote this condition, then SPSS allows the user to exclude the artefact from analyses as desired.

To use SPSS it is necessary to write a short program in the SPSS control language. This comprises several paragraphs which declare the headings which will be used to label the output, inform the computer of the data format, associate an attribute name with each field, and instruct the computer which SPSS procedures it is to perform, on which attributes.

The layout of an SPSS control program must obey certain rules, which reflect the package's ancestry on punched card implementations. Each paragraph has two segments:

i) A control field, which occupies columns 1–15, and contains the control word, or words, which identify the paragraph to the computer. The control words must be left-justified, i.e. begin in column 1, and must conform exactly to those given in the manual.

ii) A specification field, which occupies columns 16–80, and contains the parameters required by the particular control word. All specifications may be free format, as long as they are restricted to columns 16–80. The parameters may continue from one line to the next if necessary, as long as columns 1–15 of subsequent lines used to complete the specification are left blank.

The data may be organised at the end of the control program if required, or, more usually, it can be held as a separate file, which is assigned to the program when SPSS is run.

Fig. 7.1 presents a typical SPSS program, demonstrating several features of

```
RUN NAME        SITE DISTRIBUTION PLOT                   J.D.RICHARDS
FILE NAME       SPONG   DISTRIBUTION OF CREMATION BURIALS, SPONG HILL, 1972-8
VARIABLE LIST   EASTING,NORTHING,HEIGHT,MAXDIAM,HMAXDIAM,BASEDIAM,RIMDIAM
INPUT MEDIUM    DISK
INPUT FORMAT    FIXED(7X,2(F4.0,1X),5(F4.1,1X))
N OF CASES      482
VAR LABELS      MAXDIAM  MAXIMUM DIAMETER/HMAXDIAM  HEIGHT OF MAXIMUM DIAMETER
                BASEDIAM  BASE DIAMETER/RIMDIAM  RIM DIAMETER/
SCATTERGRAM     NORTHING(4297,4890) WITH EASTING(1520,2267)
OPTIONS         4
STATISTICS      ALL
*SELECT IF      (MAXDIAM/HEIGHT GE 1.3)
SCATTERGRAM     NORTHING(4297,4890) WITH EASTING(1520,2267)
OPTIONS         4
STATISTICS      ALL
READ INPUT DATA
FINISH
```

7.1 An SPSS control program (reproduced by permission of SPSS Inc.)

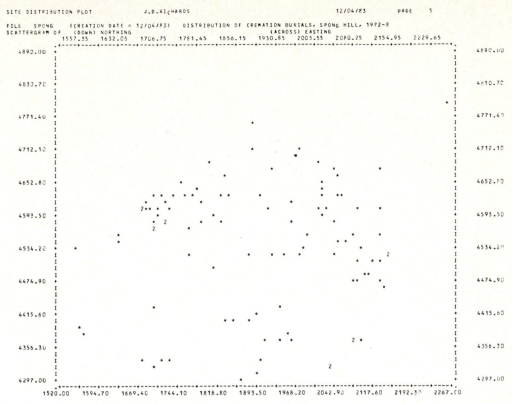

7.2 SPSS scattergram produced by the program in fig. 7.1 (reproduced by permission of SPSS Inc.)

the system. The program uses a file containing information on cremation urns in a cemetery. Each record is an individual urn. There are fields for the grid reference, and for measurements of the size of each urn. The program draws a scattergram of easting against northing, thereby producing a site plan. It then selects and draws just the wide urns (computed by dividing height by maximum diameter). This output is shown in fig. 7.2.

The ability to define and compute new variables within an SPSS program, and to select subsets of the data file to operate on, demonstrates the power of SPSS. Nevertheless, quite complex operations with the SELECT IF statement may be necessary in order to extract particular subsets of the data.

In this example we have used SPSS to produce some simple graphical output. Whilst the line printer site plan produced by this simple program would obviously be inadequate for publication purposes, the benefits of being able to generate automatically scattergrams of any desired attribute should be self-evident. Furthermore, a plotter routine might be linked to SPSS if quality plans were required. McNett (1981) demonstrates a similar application of the SELECT IF option with a SCATTERGRAM procedure, producing plots of horizontal slices through a site. The two disadvantages of this approach are the size of plot one is restricted to, and the fact that different artefact types or attributes may not be distinguished on the same plot, as there is no facility for defining symbols.

A major benefit of using SPSS is that having set up a program which defines a data format, declares variable names, and so on, it is a simple task to alter one or two lines in the program in order to perform a totally different operation on the same data. In fact the major labour investment in the use of SPSS is frequently in setting up the data definition statements, and ensuring that the data is in the correct format. It may take several attempts to get this right, especially if the user is unfamiliar with FORTRAN type FORMAT statements. Indeed, when a data file is first set up it is advisable to use the WRITE CASES facility to write a number of records out just as they have been read in. This frequently reveals that a crucial decimal point is in the wrong column.

7.212 SPSS procedures

The procedures offered by SPSS include those listed below. For full details the reader should consult the user manual (Nie *et al* 1975; Nie and Hadlai Hull 1981).

> **CONDESCRIPTIVE** calculates measures of central tendency and dispersion for attributes measured on an interval or ratio scale.
> **FREQUENCIES** calculates similar descriptive statistics for attributes measured on a nominal or ordinal scale and produces both tabular and histogram plots.
> **CROSSTABS** produces table displays of relationships between two attributes, measured on a nominal or ordinal scale, with assorted tests of significance.
> **SCATTERGRAM** produces a scatterplot diagram of the relationship between two attributes.
> **REGRESSION** accomplishes a variety of multiple regression calculations.
> **ANOVA** performs analysis of variance.
> **DISCRIMINANT** performs discriminant analysis.
> **CANCORR** performs canonical correlation.
> **FACTOR** provides several methods of factor analysis, including a principal components option.
> **REPORT** (SPSS Release 7/8 onwards) allows the user to generate tabulated reports for listing records, and aggregate statistics.
> **NONPAR CORR** and **NPAR TESTS** (SPSS Release 7/8 onwards) provide non-parametric tests.

In addition, SPSS Release 9 includes procedures for drawing line graphs, histograms, and pie charts, on a plotter.

At the time of writing a new system called **SPSS-X** is beginning to appear at some of the larger mainframe installations. This incorporates all the features of earlier versions and will eventually replace them. It also includes major changes in file handling, improving the file and data management facilities offered by SPSS. Many of the individual procedures have also been revised, and a new manual has been produced (SPSS Inc 1983).

7.22 **BMDP**

BMDP is an almost directly equivalent package to SPSS, again available on many mainframe computers in educational establishments. Despite its full name (Biomedical computer programs), it provides roughly the same choice of statistical techniques as SPSS, although it has a greater range of multivariate statistics, including some clustering procedures. The choice between the two packages must largely rest upon local availability, and individual preference. The BMDP manual (Dixon and Brown 1979) is possibly less comprehensible than the SPSS manual, and whilst it gives a greater range of examples, it provides less information on the statistical techniques involved.

Like SPSS, the BMDP package consists of a set of procedures, each performing a particular statistical technique. However, rather than calls to procedures being included in the control program (in the local operating system language), only the specific procedure required is called when the program is run. Therefore only one procedure may be performed per job. If further tasks are to be performed on data generated by an earlier job this must be saved in a file. Hence a BMDP control program consists only of the data description, which is standard to all procedures, and the parameters to the procedure required.

Otherwise, a BMDP control program follows a similar pattern to an SPSS one, although it appears more like a piece of the English language. Each instruction consists of a control word, which identifies the paragraph, followed by the parameters required by the control word, in a series of sentences. Although only eighty columns may be used in all, there are no internal restrictions on the layout of the commands, which may run as a piece of continuous text. In practice, however, it is advisable to follow a rigid format for the sake of clarity. In order that the computer may identify individual instructions, paragraphs must be separated by a slash, and sentences must be terminated with a full stop, which can be infuriatingly easy to omit.

As with SPSS, data to be processed by BMDP must be organised by record, and in addition must always be in fixed-field format. Hence each field within a record must occupy the same columns in each record. As the BMDP procedures are written in FORTRAN, a FORTRAN style FORMAT statement is again required to specify the data layout. Again, do not expect to get it right first time.

Missing values may also be declared, and in addition, BMDP includes a procedure which estimates values with which to replace a missing value code, based upon the other data present in that record. There are also extensive facilities for performing transformations of the data.

The other procedures offered by BMDP include:

> Data description.
> Scatter plots and histograms.
> Frequency tables.
> Linear and nonlinear regression.
> Analysis of variance and covariance.
> Nonparametric statistics.
> Cluster analysis, with a useful but limited range of clustering methods.
> Multivariate analyses, including procedures for factor analysis, discriminant analysis, and canonical correlation analysis.

7.23 MINITAB

MINITAB is an easy-to-use flexible and powerful statistical package which is designed for those with no previous experience of computing. It was originally intended to be used as an introductory statistics course but has become widely used as a research tool. It differs from the other packages described in section 7.2 in that it may be used in an interactive mode as well as in batch mode.

Under batch mode the user writes a program, types it in at a terminal (or punches it onto cards), then submits the entire program to the computer. The user must then wait a short while before getting all the answers back at once. This is the usual manner of running statistical packages.

Under interactive mode, on the other hand, the computer executes a command directly it is typed in, and before the next one is entered. This may be useful in exploratory data analysis, when the results of one command may determine what one wants to do next.

MINITAB is written in FORTRAN and has been implemented on mini-computers as well as mainframes. It is based on the concept of a worksheet in which data is stored. Columns, constants, or matrices may be defined and operated on by MINITAB commands. The commands themselves are presented in a logical order and may be written in full English-like sentences, or abbreviated to four-letter keywords. Whilst not providing the full range of facilities offered by its larger relatives such as SPSS and BMDP, MINITAB does offer the following:

> Descriptive statistics.
> Simulation and sampling experiments.
> Significance testing.
> Correlation and regression.
> Analysis of variance.
> Nonparametric statistics.

The package can operate very quickly, but there is usually a restriction on the maximum size of data set which can be accommodated. It was designed for moderate size data sets which can be held in the main memory of the computer.

The reference manual (Ryan, Joiner and Ryan 1981) is very clear, and there is also a student handbook (Ryan, Joiner and Ryan 1976) which may be used in conjunction with the package to provide an introductory statistics course.

7.24 GENSTAT

GENSTAT is a GENeral STATistical package which attempts to combine the flexibility of a high-level programming language with the convenience of a package. It includes many standard statistical procedures for routine analysis which may be used individually or may be integrated in such a way that the user is able to program more complex or unorthodox procedures. If such procedures are frequently required they can be stored and subsequently retrieved.

GENSTAT may therefore be regarded as a high-level programming language which allows the user to specify an algorithm more concisely than would be possible in FORTRAN, for instance. Since such programs are shorter, mistakes should, in theory, be fewer. Consequently, whilst a greater knowledge of computing is required than for SPSS or BMDP, the GENSTAT package may prove useful for more advanced statistical applications. In addition to the user reference manual (Alvey *et al* 1977), there is also an introductory guide (Alvey, Galwey and Lane 1982) which assumes no previous computing experience. The newcomer is gradually introduced to using GENSTAT through a series of simple exercises.

The data manipulation features offered by GENSTAT include:

> Free format program layout.
> Looping and conditional branching.
> Logical expressions.
> Free or fixed field input.
> Missing values allowed.
> Output of labelled tables, graphs, histograms and contour plots.

In addition, the standard procedures offered by GENSTAT which are likely to be useful to archaeologists include:

> Regression.
> Cluster analysis, with a selection of agglomerative and divisive methods.
> Multivariate analyses, including principal components analysis, with factor rotation, principal coordinates analysis and discriminant analysis.

7.25 CLUSTAN

Cluster analysis is an area where archaeologists have gained a reputation as heavy users of computer time. Whilst its relative importance will probably decline, as other applications increase, clustering is undoubtedly here to stay. Its principal application in archaeology has so far been in the generation of typologies from the clustering of attributes.

Cluster analysis should not be contemplated until an understanding of the theory has been gained. Hodson (1970) provides an archaeological introduction to the field, whilst Everitt (1974) probably remains the most popular general introduction.

Many of the statistical packages which we have considered include some clustering procedures, and lists of FORTRAN procedures which may be tailored to individual needs may be found in Mather (1976a). However, the most comprehensive clustering package available is probably CLUSTAN (Wishart 1978). The central version of CLUSTAN was developed for IBM 360 and 370 computers, but versions are available to run on many other mainframe computers. As statisticians invent new clustering algorithms, CLUSTAN has regularly been updated.

The CLUSTAN package consists of a number of modules, written in FORTRAN, which correspond to the various CLUSTAN procedures. Any number of procedures may be run in different sequences during a single job. Because of its high demands on computer time the package must normally be run under batch processing, although the job may be set up at a terminal. The user must provide a command sequence consisting of a series of keywords which call the CLUSTAN procedures, and procedure parameters which specify the tasks to be performed. The data to be analysed may be entered with the control file, or read from another file.

The procedures offered include:

> Reading of continuous or binary data, SPSS generated files, or distance and similarity matrices.
> Calculation of distance and similarity matrices.
> A wide range of clustering algorithms, including hierarchical agglomerative clustering, generalised partitioning methods, monothetic divisive clustering and the Jardine-Sibson B_k method.
> Many options for measuring the similarity between cases, the similarity between clusters, and the overall homogeneity of a classification.
> Printing of results and statistics.
> Output of dendrograms and division trees on line printer or plotter.
> Plotting of scatter and cluster diagrams.

Under the current control version of CLUSTAN the user is restricted to a maximum of 200 continuous attributes, or 400 binary attributes. There is a maximum limit of 1000 cases for most of the procedures.

A slight difficulty with using CLUSTAN in the past has been that writing the control statements largely consists of placing numbers (which are the procedure parameters) in fixed columns. This could be difficult to set up at a terminal. If it detects an error CLUSTAN attempts to complete those tasks which have valid inputs, but program crashes caused by a misplaced character can be frustrating for the user. The introduction of an extra program called CLUSCOM for some implementations overcomes this problem. CLUS-COM is a Pascal program which allows the user to enter the control file at a terminal. It issues a series of prompts, to which the user replies in his or her own language, and CLUSCOM then sets up the CLUSTAN control file. In addition it makes some checks on the consistency of the commands, and allows the user to change them before CLUSTAN is used.

7.3 Graphics

In a recent review of applications of computer graphics in archaeology (Arnold 1982), the following areas were cited as indicative of the range of current activity:

> Statistical graphics and tables.
> Artefact profiles.
> Artefact and site distributions.
> Cartographic illustrations.
> Contour plots.
> 3D perspective plots.

As we have seen in the preceding sections of this chapter, a number of statistical software packages provide facilities for graphics output. These range from simple scattergrams generated on a line printer to graphs, histograms and pie charts which may be drawn on a plotter or other graphics device. In the following sections we will discuss a number of packages designed specifically to simplify the process of generating graphics on a variety of output devices.

The basic requirement of any graphics package is to produce output in the form of instructions to a plotter which enable points and lines to be drawn. This involves nothing more than moving to specified positions with the pen either raised or in contact with the paper. On a display unit, the equivalent instructions would move a cursor (which need not necessarily be visible), illuminating the required pixels if the 'pen' were 'down'. Most graphics displays and plotters are provided with built-in instructions to perform these operations. Similarly, facilities for the production of text and simple geometric shapes such as triangles, rectangles and circles may be available. It is therefore possible to write programs to drive such devices directly. Unfortunately, each graphics device has its own set of instructions which are rarely compatible with any other device. Hence it is usually impossible to check whether a program written to drive a plotter is working properly by viewing its output on a display. If the program is complex it would be extremely tedious to have to write different versions for each of the devices with which it might be used. The advantages incurred in using graphics packages are therefore two-fold. Firstly, **device independent** programs may be written which allow results to be displayed on a range of different devices. This also implies that the software will be **portable**, that is, it may be used by others at different computer installations, provided that they have access to the appropriate combination of hardware, programming language and package. Secondly, many packages provide facilities for drawing complex shapes, such as 3D surfaces, using a single instruction. This frees the user from the need to generate such results from basic drawing commands.

Much of the available graphics software is supplied as a library of subroutines which must be called from within an applications program. It is therefore not in a form where it may be readily applied by a non-programmer. This initial disadvantage is, however, offset by the freedom to develop programs tailored to user's requirements.

Many of the packages are available at a large number of sites, such as GINO-F in the United Kingdom and others which are compatible with the Calcomp range of plotters in the United States. This permits a limited degree of portability between systems, but the recent ISO draft standard Graphics Kernel System, or **GKS**, holds some promise for international standardisation.

7.31 **GINO-F**

GINO-F (Graphical INput/Output - FORTRAN version) is one of the most widely used graphics software packages (CADC 1975). It consists of an extensive library of subroutines written in ANSI standard FORTRAN IV, and can therefore be used on a wide range of computers. GINO-F was originally developed for use on mainframes but has subsequently been widely implemented on mini-computers. Recently, it has been made available for use on the RML 380Z micro-computer.

The basic drawing routines provide for straight lines, circular arcs, and the plotting of dots, characters and a limited set of symbols. All lines may be drawn solid, dashed or chained, and drawing may be performed using either two- or three-dimensional coordinate data. No less than thirteen different routines are provided for plotting characters, allowing extensive control over their size, position and angle. Italic characters may also be plotted with any angle of slope. The characters to be plotted may be supplied in any form, routines being provided for the output of strings of text, integer and real numbers.

General purpose line drawing routines allow a line to be constructed from a number of coordinates held in an array. The resultant line may consist simply of straight segments joining the specified points, but a facility is included to fit a curved line to the data. This can be particularly useful when drawing graphs or reconstructing artefact profiles from point measurements.

Programs using the GINO-F library are device independent, that is to say, they will function with any graphics input/output device. This is achieved by use of a separate **device driver** routine for each different device employed.

7.3 Distribution map produced using GINO-F

These are integrated into the package when it is installed on a machine, thus allowing the selection of devices during the running of a program. Facilities are also provided for selecting different sizes and colours of pens, and selecting the size of paper used on a plotter. Any routines used by a program but which are meaningless on the nominated device are ignored. Thus, for instance, changing pen colour will have no effect on a monochrome display.

It is often desirable to set a boundary to a picture outside of which plotting is prevented. This is known as **windowing**. GINO-F provides facilities for setting a window anywhere in 2D or 3D space. Once set, the window may be disabled or enabled as required.

A wide range of facilities for transforming pictures is provided. A picture element may be **shifted** in space, **rotated** and **scaled**. In 3D pictures, rotation may be about any axis. Scaling may be performed equally on all axes, or, alternatively, each axis may have a different scale factor. Transformations may be turned on or off as required, and it is possible to save a number of different transformations to be recalled when needed. A useful feature of GINO-F is the range of functions which may be called to find out the current state of transformation, windowing, paper size and type, and pen colour and type.

Viewing of 3D pictures is catered for by a range of commands. These allow selection of either parallel or perspective projections, and give full control over the relative positions of the observer and the viewed object.

Although GINO-F is the one most frequently encountered, there are a number of other libraries in the GINO family. **GINO-2D** is a two dimensional subset of GINO-F commands which have been rewritten in order to reduce the large overheads in storage and execution time involved in generating 2D graphics using the full GINO-F system. **GINOGRAPH** is a set of routines for drawing graphs, histograms and pie charts with minimum effort. **GINO-ZONE** provides facilities for shading areas of drawings, and is intended for the production of thematic maps, etc. Finally, **GINOSURF** may be used to produce complex 3D surfaces.

The distribution map and graphs shown in figs. 7.3 and 7.4 were produced using only the basic drawing routines of GINO-F.

7.32 **MYLIB**

A major archaeological use of computer graphics is in the production of maps and plans. Satisfactory results can often be obtained using one of the general purpose graphics packages, but this will often involve much work in developing subroutines for drawing frequently used special symbols, lines and patterns. There are a number of commercial cartographic systems available, although these are normally offered as integrated packages containing both hardware and software. To the archaeologist, their sophistication is unnecessary and their cost unjustifiable.

The **MYLIB** system (Yoeli 1982) of subroutines and programs represents a useful compromise between the general purpose and the specialised packages. It is designed to be used with digitising and plotting equipment and provides a large number of routines for generating conventional map symbols. Additional subroutines may be added according to the user's requirements. An example of one type of map which can be produced with these routines is shown in fig. 7.5. The system is intended to be used with a Calcomp plotter, but modification for use with virtually any other graphics output device is a simple programming task involving no more than the three basic routines which perform the tasks of plotting lines, symbols and text, and numbers.

The MYLIB library of programs and subroutines is available in machine readable form at a nominal cost from the Department of Geography at Nottingham University. Although all of the required routines could be produced using a package such as GINO-F, the low cost of this library more than offsets that of developing even a small number of such routines.

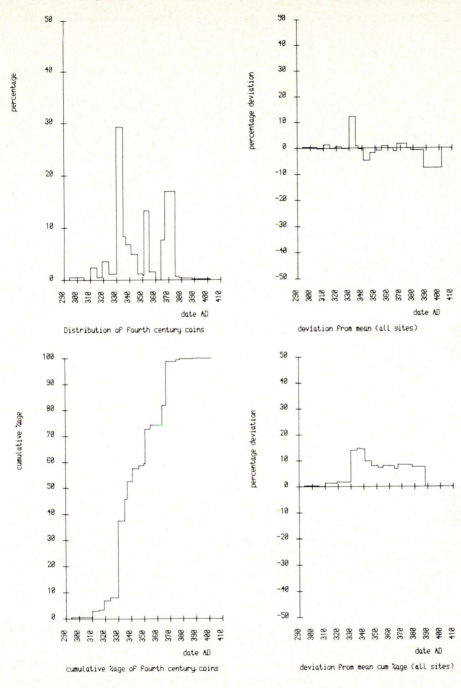

Distribution of fourth century coins

deviation from mean (all sites)

cumulative %age of fourth century coins

deviation from mean cum %age (all sites)

BARNSLEY PARK, GLOS.
SP 4083 2087

7.4 Graphs produced using GINO-F

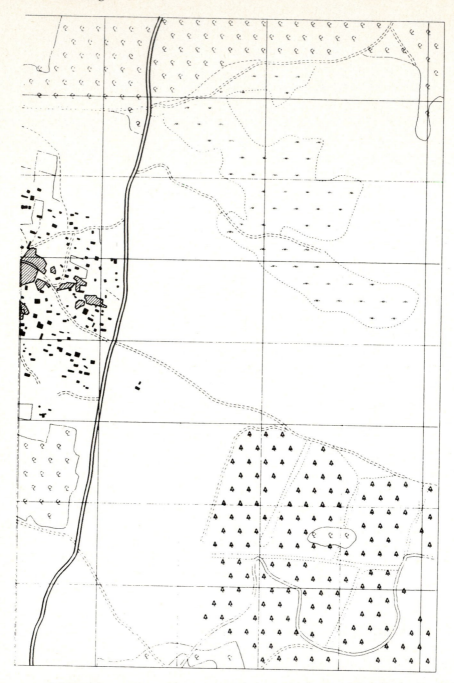

7.5 MYLIB: example map (reproduced from *Computer Applications* 8, by permission of the editors)

7.33 **SYMAP**

The **SYMAP** graphics package (Laboratory for Computer Graphics and Spatial Analysis 1975) provides facilities for drawing contour and chloropleth plots using a line printer. These have been used extensively by archaeologists (see, for example, Redman and Watson 1970), particularly in the years before plotters became widely available.

Line printer maps produce varying densities of shading by superimposing characters. The resolution is therefore limited by the fixed positions in which characters may be printed. The results are extremely crude when compared with maps produced on a plotter, but if shading is required, then the line printer has the advantage of being considerably faster.

Users interested in applying this and similar packages, perhaps because of limited access to plotting facilities, are referred to the collection of papers edited by Upham (1979), in which a number of contributors discuss the use and limitations of line printer graphics. Indeed, this volume contains much of value to anyone interested in the use of graphics in connection with spatial analysis.

7.34 **CP/M Graphics**

Many users of micro-computers equipped with graphics displays develop their own graphics software using the built-in commands supplied with the machine. Although satisfactory for developing programs for restricted local use, they must invariably be completely rewritten if it is ever required to run them on a different machine. This lack of portability of graphics software between different micro-computers has restricted the use of graphics in available software packages which are designed to be run on a variety of machines.

CP/M Graphics represents an attempt to standardise graphics I/O on micro-computers. It consists of a basic set of extensions to the conventional CP/M operating system, called **GSX**, and a range of subroutine libraries and interactive packages. GSX provides control over displays, plotters and so forth. This is the part of the system which ensures portability of software between machines running CP/M Graphics. **GSS-KERNEL** and **GSS-PLOT** are both libraries of graphics commands which can be linked to programs written in BASIC, FORTRAN, Pascal or PL/1. GSS-KERNEL provides a range of basic facilities for drawing lines, polygons and text. It conforms to the increasingly widespread ISO graphics standard, and thus provides for portability of graphics applications over a wide range of computers and operating systems. GSS-PLOT is intended for display of statistical information in graphical form. It contains routines for generating histograms, pie charts and scattergrams.

Two interactive graphics packages which can be used by non-programmers are available: **GSS-GRAPH** and **GSS-DRAW**. GSS-GRAPH can be used to produce graphs, histograms, pie charts, etc, whilst GSS-DRAW is intended as a general-purpose drawing tool. Finally, **GSS-4010** allows any suitably equipped micro-computer to emulate the popular Tektronix 4010, 4012 and 4014 graphics terminals.

7.4 **Word processing**

Word processing is the term applied to the handling of text by computer. A computer may be used like a typewriter to produce letters, reports, papers, and even complete books. However, word processing makes typing easier in several respects:

1) Changes, insertions, or deletions, can be made at any time, even after an entire document has been typed.

2) Words, sentences, paragraphs, or even entire chapters, may be moved from one location to another.

3) Once a document has been stored it can be used again and again. For example, if it is necessary to send more or less the same letter to several different people, the same text can be used, with different names and addresses added later.

Therefore, word processing offers substantial labour-saving possibilities to all archaeologists. Furthermore, it demands little knowledge of computing, as all of the operations are under the control of the word processing system. Full treatments of word processing, aimed especially at commercial applications, but of interest to all potential users, may be found in Morgan and Wood (1981) and Simons (1981).

There are three possible approaches to word processing: text formatting programs, dedicated word processors, and word processing packages.

Text formatting programs are the most primitive method, but may be all that is available on a mainframe computer which was not intended for word processing. The user normally types in text using a standard editor (cf. section 5.421). The computer is used as a normal typewriter but the user need not worry about the spacing and layout of the document at this stage, and may type it as a continuous stream of text, hitting the return key as each line is filled simply to keep all the document on the screen. Special text formatting commands must then be inserted into the file before it is processed by a text formatting program to produce the final document. These commands tell the computer how it should format the document: for example, where a new paragraph should start, where to underline, what line spacing to use, etc. For most text formatting programs these instructions take the form of two characters preceded by a full stop in the first column of a line. For example, '.DS' may indicate double spacing, '.BR' may instruct the computer to break to a new paragraph. A text formatting program will usually allow a user to right justify a piece of text so that there are no ragged margins, and to specify a heading which will be printed at the top of each new page. However, it does not incorporate the sophisticated editing facilities expected of a word processor. Examples of this type of **text run-off** program include **nroff** and **troff**, available on Unix systems. Nroff is designed for use with ordinary printers whilst troff may be used with appropriate typesetting equipment. Additionally, **pre-processors** known as **tbl** and **eqn** are available on Unix to produce tables and to typeset mathematical equations.

A **dedicated word processor** is a machine designed specifically for word processing. Word processors are relatively cheap, very powerful, and since they are intended for use by untrained office personnel, are user friendly. On the other hand, they cannot generally do anything other than word processing.

The third approach is to use a word processing package. This is a complex program which allow a normal computer to emulate a word processor. When the word processing has been completed the computer can revert to its other functions. Word processing packages are available for most computers. Those which run on mainframes tend to be relatively primitive, and the archaeologist may be discouraged from using them as it may be regarded as an inefficient use of resources. Micro- and mini-computers, on the other hand, are extensively used for word processing, and a wide range of packages is available. To indicate the value of word processing to archaeologists we shall examine the facilities offered by one such package: **WordStar**. This book was prepared entirely with WordStar.

7.41 **WordStar**

WordStar is a well established package which has gained a reputation as a standard.[2] It will run on most micro-computers with CP/M operating systems, and some others. As well as the User's Guide, which may appear somewhat overwhelming at first, there is an easy-to-use WordStar Training Guide available with the package.

There are some major differences between typing on a typewriter and using a word processing package. To begin with, the words that are entered are not printed out immediately, but are stored in the computer's memory. The user can see an image of a small segment of that memory displayed on the screen. Any mistakes may be corrected, and when the document is complete it may be saved as a file on disc, and printed.

When WordStar is used, a menu of instructions is displayed on the upper half of the screen (fig. 7.6). There are several menus, governing text formatting, printing, moving blocks of text, and so on. When the user has become proficient in using WordStar the menu may be suppressed, and the document to be edited then occupies the full screen. We shall now consider some of the facilities offered by WordStar, although most packages have comparable features:

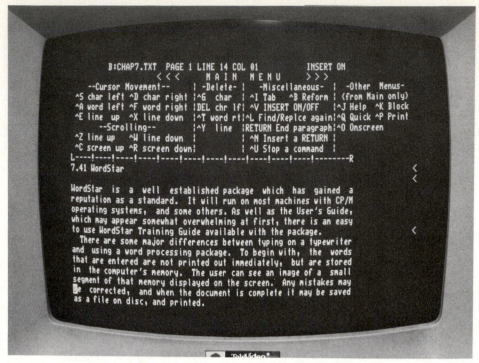

7.6 VDU screen with WordStar word processing session in progress (reproduced by permission of MicroPro International Corporation)

Automatic word-wrap. To enter text the user simply types it in and it appears on the screen. There is no need to worry about line length, as words that are too long are automatically taken over to the next line. WordStar also incorporates a **soft-hyphen** feature which hyphenates long words and splits them over two lines, if desired. Therefore return characters need be entered only when a new line is required, for a new paragraph, for example.

Margin settings and justification. If required, the text may also be right-justified, so that there are no ragged edges at the right margin. Once a line is complete the word spacing is automatically adjusted so that all the lines line up on the right as well as the left side. Whilst WordStar assumes A4 paper size, any paper size, and any margin settings, may be specified.

Editing. If a mistake has been made then the cursor may be moved to that position, and the error rectified. Control of the cursor, and over most WordStar functions, is by use of the control key on the keyboard. Control characters are typed by depressing the control key and another key simultaneously. For example, Control-G deletes a character; Control-T deletes a word; and Control-Y a whole line. The keys governing cursor movement are logically arranged so that their position on the keyboard reflects the movement of the cursor (fig. 7.7). Once a paragraph has been amended it may be

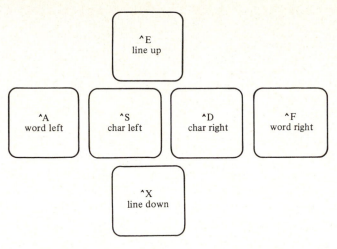

7.7 Section of a keyboard illustrating WordStar cursor control commands

necessary to reform it, bringing each line back into alignment, with a Control-B.

Automatic centring. Further commands give the user automatic centring of characters, which may be useful for formatting headings.

Conditional paging. Instructions may be inserted to begin a new page, for example at the start of a chapter, or to begin a new page conditionally, such as when a sub-heading occurs too close to the foot of a page.

Printer control. For printed output, further commands may be used to control features such as the exact line width, and to invoke printing features such as bold type face, and underlining.

Block moves. The user may mark blocks of text, with a pointer at beginning and end. The block may then be deleted, or copied to another location, or completely moved there.

Search and replace. It is possible to perform a **global** search for all occurrences of a character, or group of characters, throughout a document, and to replace them by something else. This may be useful, to convert abbreviations to full phrases, for example, or for changing American spellings to English ones, if a spelling checking program is unavailable.

Spelling checker. There is an extra package available to run with WordStar called **SpellStar**. This holds a dictionary of correct spellings, and scans the text for spellings it does not recognise, giving the user the option of correcting them. A useful feature of SpellStar allows the user to add new words to the dictionary, so that it may be customised to special interests.

Mailing program. A second additional package called **MailMerge** can be used with WordStar. This takes names and addresses, or other information, from a separate file, and inserts them for example in a circular letter. A merge facility may be used to produce letters assembled from standard paragraphs.

This summary by no means exhausts the facilities offered by WordStar. For instance, it should be noted that whilst we have concentrated on the uses of WordStar for word processing, the package can also be used for entering programs and data. In this case, the file is set up as a non-document file when WordStar is loaded, and all the options for automatic justification, word-wrap, etc, are switched off.

7.5 **Data management**

There exists a wide variety of packages designed to aid the storage and manipulation of data in information retrieval applications. These range from simple file management programs, which provide facilities intended to simplify data capture and report generation, to complex database management systems (DBMS). As with the rest of this chapter, it is impossible to refer to more than a few of the more popular packages. Those selected either have been used in, or would appear to be appropriate to, archaeological applications. The following sections are divided between those packages which run on mainframe and mini-computers, and those which are available for micro-computers. Although this division reflects general differences in complexity between the packages described, it is not altogether satisfactory. Many of the comments on the simpler file management packages which appear in the section on large computer systems are equally applicable to this type of software irrespective of the size of machine on which it runs.

In the space available it is impossible to present a detailed description of each package. Indeed, to do so would be inappropriate to the aims of this book. Rather, we shall concentrate on describing the range of available packages and assessing the ease with which they might be applied by archaeologists. A number of authors (e.g. George and Sarkar (1981), Mayne (1981) and, for micro-computer applications, Kruglinski (1983)) have devoted entire books to comparative reviews of database management software, and the reader with an interest in this topic, or who is in a position to select a system for an application, is recommended to consult one of these.

In addition to those mentioned below, there exist a number of integrated packages which combine simple data management facilities with word processing and calculating programs, such as the MicroPro products DataStar and CalcStar, which are both compatible with WordStar. Users of larger computers should also be aware of the wide range of utility programs which are available under many operating systems. These will include sorting and merging routines, but some operating systems, such as Unix, provide many extra routines including the relational database 'join' and a range of indexing facilities. Many simple data management requirements may be fulfilled using these programs.

7.51 **Packages for large computers**

Archaeologists using mainframes and larger mini-computers will rarely be in a position to select a system for their applications. Software for this type of machine is invariably expensive and it is unlikely that many installations will have more than a few different systems available. In many cases these will include both simple information retrieval packages and a DBMS.

The simpler packages range from report generators, which allow information contained in files to be presented in a required format, to general purpose file management systems designed to ease the tasks of data capture and information retrieval. The range of facilities provided varies widely, but most will generally include the basic essentials of sorting, merging and indexing of files as well as permitting the searching for occurrences of particular values within specified fields. An editing facility may be provided, but, with a number of systems, users will be expected to employ a separate utility program for this purpose. Additional facilities will depend largely on the type of applications for which the package was designed. For example, **Famulus** (Shaw 1978) includes routines for producing a thesaurus and a Key Word In Context (KWIC) index of words occurring in the file, and is therefore particularly suited to producing catalogues of bibliographic material for research groups or small libraries.

In recent years there has been an increasing interest in small, self-contained data handling systems. This type of package has been promoted as a means of storing and retrieving data particularly suited to managerial requirements. Although a number of suppliers misleadingly refer to their products as relational database systems (see section 6.63), they are nonetheless quite adequate for many applications. Some of these systems work on only a single file at a time, and thus although it is possible to perform two of what Elbra (1982) has called the 'relational DBMS acid-tests', they fail to qualify on the third. The basic operational functions are **SELECT**, **PROJECT** and **JOIN**. SELECT is the ability to retrieve on some predefined search criterion. PROJECT is analogous with report generation in that it allows data to be extracted and summarised. The third function, JOIN, which allows two files or **tables** to be joined on the basis of mutual occurrence of values within a shared field, is crucial to the concept of a relational DBMS and clearly impossible with a single file system. In addition, a true relational DBMS will provide the ability to represent different logical views of the same data without duplication in storage – that is, with minimal redundancy.

ICL's **PDS** or Personal Data System (ICL 1981) is one example of this type of data management package which, whilst strictly not a relational DBMS, does provide the basic functions of SELECT, PROJECT and JOIN. Its main strength lies in the ease with which an application may be set up and maintained by users with a minimum of computing experience. PDS provides sixteen commands which cover data definition, input and output, etc. Frequently used command sequences, up to 255 characters in length, may be saved as **macros**, which are subsequently used as normal commands whenever required. Although macros may call other macros, this approach is not as flexible as the programmable query languages used on some other systems.

Effective use of most of the simpler data management packages should be well within the capabilities of any archaeologist who has developed the basic data processing skills outlined in this book. Indeed, most applications may be satisfied provided the user has a clear understanding of the nature of the data and the functional requirements of the application. Many of these packages require little or no programming expertise, although those which provide a sophisticated query language may often serve as a useful introduction to these skills. In this way, an inexperienced user may begin by making simple interactive queries and progress by stages to writing application programs. Unlike the conventional approach to programming this may be achieved using real data.

The establishment and maintenance of the large databases used in administrative and commercial environments requires a team of specialist analysts and programmers under the direction of a database administrator. If a sites and monuments system were to be integrated as one small part of a local government computer-based information system, then these tasks would be performed by existing data processing staff. In the majority of applications, archaeologists are unlikely to be able to enlist such specialist services. Fortunately, most archaeological applications tend to be more limited and specialised, hence the task of setting up a database will frequently be within the capability of an experienced programmer. As with much other software, the greatest problems are often in understanding the documentation.

A number of the DBMS available for large computer systems are based on the specifications developed by **CODASYL**, the Conference on Data Systems Languages (CODASYL 1971). This organisation, based in the USA, includes representatives of both manufacturers and users, and was responsible for the development of the COBOL language. It follows therefore that the notation and syntax of the proposed data definition and manipulation languages closely follow that of COBOL. In some cases, interfaces to other languages may be provided, but in general, data manipulation is performed by calling external DML procedures from within COBOL applications programs. The CODASYL family of DBMS supports both the network and hierarchical data models (see section 6.63). Data is described in terms of **sets**, and relationships are expressed by specifying entities as either **owners** or **members** of sets. **IDMS** (Integrated Database Management System) is an example of the CODASYL family of DBMS which has been widely implemented on ICL and other mainframes. As with other implementations of the CODASYL Database Task Group's recommendations, IDMS is a subset of the full CODASYL specification, with a number of additional features.

The various members of the CODASYL family differ largely in the extent of these additions, but it is a relatively easy task for a programmer versed in one to adapt to any other member of the family. An archaeological application in which IDMS has been used to store and manipulate sites and monuments data is described by Sheppard (1977 and n.d.).

In addition to the DML procedures which are used within applications programs, many DBMS suppliers provide query languages which enable users to extract and manipulate data with a minimum of programming involvement. ICL provide a program called Query Master for this purpose, together with Report Master, which is usually employed to produce hard-copy. This latter is simply a report generator which is able to access data stored in an IDMS database.

As is often the case, the approach taken by IBM to DBMS appears at first to be quite different from that of the rest of the computer industry. However, from both the user's and programmer's viewpoint, the differences between IBM's **IMS-DL/1** system and the CODASYL family are principally in the terminology and syntax of data description and data manipulation languages. For example, an IMS database is defined in a number of **DataBase Definition modules (DBD)** which are collectively equivalent to a CODASYL schema. There are three types of DBD which are used to describe physical storage, logical views of the data and indexing arrangements. Each logical DBD describes a group of hierarchical **segments** and is thus similar to a CODASYL sub-schema. A segment is similar to a CODASYL set in that it represents a logical record with dependent repeating sub-records. In IMS terminology, the owner record is known as a **parent**, and the members are called **children**.

A number of academic computing departments have experimental DBMS, and in some cases their originators may be only too pleased to cooperate in new applications. Although databases are traditionally associated with large organisations, there has in recent years been increased interest in the use of DBMS in smaller, more specialised, environments. The CODD relational DBMS and its associated retrieval languages SALT and CHIPS (King and Moody 1983) were developed originally for a specific anthropological project involving the demographic study of an English village (Harrison *et al* 1982). It may prove possible for archaeologists to benefit from similar cooperation.

7.52 Micro-computer packages

With the increasing use of micro-computers for information storage and retrieval there has been a proliferation of packages described by their vendors as database management systems. As with many of those running on larger machines, few genuinely merit such description and are more correctly described as file management programs. Most of these packages provide a range of facilities similar to those which have been discussed above. The major differences lie in the capacity of the associated hardware to store large quantities of data and the speed with which it can be accessed, rather than in the flexibility of the software. As was stated above, it would be wrong to dismiss these simpler systems just because they do not offer the advanced facilities of a DBMS. There are many applications where the ability to handle a single file is all that is required.

The packages described in this section are all available to run under the CP/M operating system on eight bit micro-computers, and other versions are available for sixteen bit machines using either CP/M-86 or MS-DOS. They represent examples of the range of available software rather than specific recommendations. The prospective purchaser should compare a number of suitable packages before making a final choice. Major considerations in choosing a package should include ease of use, retrieval speed and the limitations which may be imposed on field length, record length and file size.

The **Cardbox** program produced by Caxton Software Ltd is a good example of the simpler single file systems. It allows the user to set up a 'form' on the VDU screen for data input, and to extract records from the file in any required format. Up to 99 search criteria may be used in any retrieval session. Cardbox thus provides a computer-based equivalent to a conventional manual card index. In addition to the obvious speed advantages over a typical manual system, its main strengths are in the ability to index selectively the file on any number of keywords, and to display part or all of the stored records in any desired format.

MDBS is a general purpose database system, produced by Micro Data Base Systems Inc., which will run under a number of operating systems, including CP/M, on a variety of micro-computers. Although the system is based on the CODASYL recommendations, there are a number of important differences. The syntax of the DDL and DML are somewhat simpler than the CODASYL specification, and the programmer is not restricted to using COBOL for applications programs, as language interfaces are also available for BASIC, FORTRAN, Pascal and a number of different processor machine codes. Other differences from the CODASYL specification include the ability to include directly a many-to-many relationship in the data definition rather than needing to specify two one-to-many relationships.

DBASE II is an implementation of the relational DBMS produced by Ashton-Tate (1981), available for use on eight and sixteen bit micro-computers using CP/M or MS-DOS. It provides all of the facilities which were described above for ICL's PDS. The combined data definition and query language may be used either interactively, or in combination to produce macro commands. There is however no restriction on the length of macros, and thus the language may be used to produce applications programs of any length. DBASE II may be regarded as an interpreted programming language which provides extensive facilities for handling data stored in relational files. Although the language provides no direct means of incorporating subroutines or procedures, this problem is easily overcome by writing the required sections as separate macros which are then called from the main program. A further improvement over systems like PDS lies in the ability to index a file or table on any one field or combination of fields. PDS is limited to presenting a table in a predefined order on the basis of a single key. With DBASE II, indexes may be created at any time, which allow the table to be viewed in any required order. For instance, in a table which contained bibliographic references, two indexes could be maintained to permit retrieval in order either of author name or of journal name. To change between these two views of the data it is necessary only to tell the system to use a different index.

NOTES

(1) SPSS is a trademark of SPSS Inc. of Chicago, Illinois, for its proprietary computer software. No materials describing software may be produced or distributed without the written permission of SPSS Inc.

(2) WordStar is a registered trademark of MicroPro International Corporation, 33 San Pablo Ave, San Rafael, CA 94903.

8

THE FUTURE

8.1 Where do we go from here?

In this final chapter we consider the question of where the archaeologist goes from here, in terms both of individual computing requirements, and of how current developments in computer hardware and software are liable to affect applications in archaeology. As other writers have noted, attempting to predict the future is at best a precarious business:

> History attests to the fact that some expectations have been overly optimistic about the potential of new techniques or technology and have fallen victim to the vicissitudes of the real world. At the same time, even the most visionary predictions have tended to underestimate grossly the rapid growth in the use of computers in all aspects of our society. (Gaines and Gaines 1980, 462)

At the same time, it is possible that by concentrating on particular applications to the exclusion of others, would-be prophets may be guilty of constraining rather than contributing to future work. We will therefore restrict our discussion to general trends in the development of computer systems and their likely effect on archaeological applications.

It is often suggested that applications are limited only by the user's imagination. Given the appropriate expertise, there may be some truth in this assertion, but the availability of, and freedom of access to, suitable hardware and software may prove to be limiting factors for most archaeologists. To those with little or no previous computing experience these factors may appear as daunting obstacles, and for this reason we include a number of suggestions on how to obtain the required facilities.

It is most unlikely that any archaeological organisation in the forseeable future would ever need, or be able to justify the expense of purchasing, a mainframe computer entirely for its own use. It follows therefore that such facilities must be sought at some existing installation. In the case of micro- and small mini-computers, the situation is very different. These machines are well suited to a number of types of archaeological and administrative applications, and their cost lies well within the budgets of many archaeological organisations. Existing owners of such machines are most unlikely to have sufficient spare capacity to be able or willing to share them, and archaeologists must therefore consider the purchase of their own systems. Our discussion of developments in these smaller machines will include a number of points to be borne in mind when selecting the appropriate hardware and software for an application.

8.2 **Current and future developments in computer systems**

Before turning to the questions of access to large machines and choosing a micro-computer for archaeological applications it is necessary to consider current and potential developments in hardware and software. Although many of these affect all types of machines, users of small computers are more likely to be affected by the rapid pace of development.

This section does not attempt to provide a full statement of the current state of the art in computer systems. Instead we have selected a number of areas which would seem to hold the greatest potential to affect what we as archaeologists do with computers, and how we do it.

8.21 **Hardware development**

The dominant trends in hardware development are towards increasing complexity and decreasing relative costs. As was noted in section 3.22, the distinction between micro-, mini- and mainframe computers has become blurred as new machines are introduced. Many sixteen bit micro-computers, costing little or no more than their eight bit predecessors, can now provide similar computing power to small mini-computers. The ICL PERQ machine shown in fig. 8.1 uses microprocessor technology to provide a single user with a high level of local processing power. Similarly, the Hewlett Packard HP9000 is designated as a 'super' mini-computer by its manufacturers, yet in little more space than a typical micro it provides equivalent power to that of a small mainframe. This machine uses what is claimed to be the first thirty-two bit CPU to be produced on a single integrated circuit. The cost, however, is in the mini-computer range: nevertheless, these machines give a clear indication of current moves in hardware development.

In parallel with developments in processors and memory units, the cost of storing data on backing store is decreasing rapidly. New varieties of disc drives and recording media are frequently announced, allowing fuller use of the increasing processing power, often at no greater cost than existing equipment. Thus the cost per byte of on-line storage is steadily diminishing. There is every indication that these trends will continue.

For the mainframe user the implications are that more data can be held on disc rather than having to be loaded from tape whenever needed. Thus there is an increasing potential for the application of rapid on-line information retrieval from large data banks. It is, however, the micro-computer user who is liable to benefit most.

In chapter 3 we discussed the increasing popularity of the sixteen bit micro-computers, and the imminent arrival of even more powerful thirty-two bit machines. The advantages offered by these over their eight bit predeces-

8.1 The ICL PERQ computer in use in a drawing office environment (photo ICL)

sors lie in their ability to access larger internal memory units, and the greater speed with which a given program may be executed. For archaeologists this trend has two major implications. Firstly, the use of many programs which were previously too big to fit into the available storage space of a micro-computer, or too complex to be executed in a reasonable time, is now becoming feasible. This applies particularly to statistical analysis. Many multivariate statistical problems which previously required at least a mini-computer can now be approached with the smaller machines. Secondly, the rapid increase in capacity of backing storage devices needed to keep pace with the developments in processors opens the possibility of on-line storage of much larger data banks than was possible using only floppy discs. The development of small Winchester discs with a capacity of from five to twenty megabytes marked the first phase of this trend. Subsequent advances in disc media and drive units have produced devices using exchangeable cartridges which have the capacity of the Winchester.

The cartridge disc drive, a miniature equivalent of the exchangeable disc packs used on larger machines, currently exists in several different forms. It is too early to determine which, if any, of these will eventually become the standard. Indeed there is much disagreement as to the future relative importance of floppy, Winchester and cartridge discs; some writers would have us believe that the fixed Winchester disc is doomed by the appearance of the cartridge, others that the cartridge will supersede the floppy disc for backing-up Winchesters. It seems likely that the method of data storage used will make it easier to transfer cartridges from one machine to another (provided of course that they are fitted with the same type of cartridge unit) than is currently possible with floppy discs.

The increasing capacity of floppy discs and the appearance of cartridges make it possible to use the same machine for a number of applications, each with their own large data sets. With older equipment this is often only possible if each data set is loaded on to a Winchester from a number of floppy discs whenever it is needed. Before a different application can be run, it is first necessary to back-up the Winchester on floppy discs before loading the new data set. This process may be extremely time-consuming.

A further important development in computer hardware lies in the use of networks. Many university computer installations are now employing networks to connect a range of hardware from terminals, through micro-computers, to mainframes. Such systems provide local processing power and access to larger machines when needed.

8.22 Software development

Whilst there are continuing developments in all aspects of software, we shall be concerned here only with micro-computer operating systems and applications packages. Development continues in programming languages, but, other than the probability of more widespread implementation of languages such as APL and LISP on small computers, it is unlikely that any will significantly affect archaeological applications in the near future. Many developments are closely linked with those in hardware which we have considered above. As the physically smaller machines become capable of handling larger quantities of data and approach the processing power of previous generations of larger computers, so the software controlling these processes tends to become more complex.

On the one hand there is a demand for more sophisticated system utilities to be added to the operating systems, and on the other a demand that these systems should be easier to use. The former comes principally from those who are used to running similar applications on larger machines and who are now changing to micro-computers. The same process was seen during the development of mini-computers from their early use as scientific tools to their more general role as data processing machines. The desire for greater simplicity comes from the increasing use of such machines by people with no formal training in computing. Both of these demands have constantly arisen and been met during the history of computing, but the relative importance of ease of use has increased dramatically with the widespread application of micro-computers.

On the whole, these demands are met simply by providing more of the facilities which a user of a larger machine would have come to expect. Thus the small machines gradually acquire a legitimacy as 'real' computers amongst established users. Innovative changes are much rarer and their acceptance is not so easily guaranteed. Market acceptance has not normally been achieved simply by providing sophisticated facilities or ease of use. Adoption by a major hardware manufacturer and the availability of a wide range of compatible software appear to have been the major factors affecting the success of operating systems.

The CP/M operating system developed by Digital Research for eight bit micro-computers owes much of its continued acceptance to the commercial availability of a wide range of software which uses it, rather than to a high degree of either sophistication or user-friendliness. A timely introduction ensured its initial position and the compatibility of subsequent versions has tended to limit the establishment of alternative operating systems.

Since the introduction of sixteen bit micro-computers, a version of CP/M known as CP/M-86 has shared this market with Microsoft's MS-DOS. Both of these operating systems work with the 8086 and 8088 processors produced by Intel, although versions of CP/M are being developed for other processors. A large quantity of software was rapidly produced to run under one or other of these operating systems, although much of this was simply converted from existing eight bit software. This has served to establish both operating systems and the processors on which they run. The continuing popularity of MS-DOS is guaranteed by its adoption by IBM (under the name PC-DOS) for their 'Personal Computer'. Subsequent versions of both operating systems have offered improved facilities aimed at allowing a number of applications or users to share the same system and backing store. Concurrent CP/M permits several tasks to be performed simultaneously, with the display switched from one to another as required by the user. MS-DOS 2 provides a hierarchical directory structure similar to that found on some mini and mainframe operating systems. However, in both cases it is still the availability of software and their widespread popularity which recommend these operating systems rather than sophistication or user-friendliness.

Although the power of operating systems such as CP/M and MS-DOS increases with each new release, they do not yet compare with the facilities offered by many of those used on larger machines. A number of versions of the Unix operating system, originally developed for mini-computers, are now available on some of the more powerful micros. Many programmers who are used to developing software in a mainframe or mini-computer environment find these systems preferable to those which have grown with micro-computer hardware.

An alternative approach to operating systems has been taken by the micro-computer manufacturer Apple in their 'Lisa' system. This attempts to separate the user from the complexities of conventional computing by presenting an image of the system in terms of sheets of paper and filing cabinets, rather than files and disc directories. This approach is clearly directed at the casual user who is familiar with a traditional office environment and has no wish to become involved in the detailed aspects of computing.

As with operating systems, applications packages are being developed to take advantage of the increased speed and storage capacity of the hardware. This is particularly noticeable in the steady increase in data management software. Here, the development of hardware has reached a point where it is worthwhile, rather than merely possible, to store large quantities of data on a micro-computer and to retrieve information rapidly from it. Although current systems are still quite slow in comparison to data management systems on larger machines, they now represent a suitable alternative for many applications.

As each new hardware development has been introduced, the effective costs of equipment have been reduced. The first generation of sixteen bit machines cost little more than their eight bit predecessors. This process is not always reflected in software costs. With both operating systems and applications programs, increased complexity invariably means increased cost. This is particularly true in the case of software for the more powerful micro-computers which are capable of performing tasks which were previously the domain of larger machines. Applications packages for mini-computers frequently cost thousands rather than hundreds of pounds, and there is every indication that this price level will apply to the most sophisticated micro-computer packages. However, as the general purpose operating systems become more sophisticated their users seem likely to demand more from their applications software, and it is possible that an increase in demand may serve to reduce the cost of the more expensive packages.

8.3 Access to large machines

How then can an individual or an archaeological organisation obtain access to mainframe computing facilities? The answer depends largely on individual circumstances and the facilities required. Nevertheless, it is possible to make a number of general observations.

In educational establishments the solution is usually quite simple. The local computer services unit will normally have a person who is responsible for answering inquiries from new and prospective users. It may be necessary to fill in a questionnaire indicating the range of facilities and storage space required. The new user will be given a **user number** and, probably, a **password** to be used when logging in at the start of a session. Many computer centres provide their own introductory manuals containing instructions on how to log in and make use of the system. Courses may be held at intervals to give an introduction to the system or to provide tuition in the more advanced use of facilities. Often the quickest way of getting started is to ask a colleague who knows the system to demonstrate how to log in and perform simple tasks such as creating, editing and listing of files. Thereafter the best way to learn is through experience. Attempting to read the manuals from cover to cover before actually using the machine is often a guaranteed route to confusion.

For archaeologists working in other environments, such as local or national government agencies, availability of computing facilities is likely to vary widely, according to departmental policy. An informal approach to the computer services unit, and discussions with colleagues who use the computer for other purposes, may help to clarify the local position. If the archaeological application can be integrated with the other activities of the organisation, such as in a local government planning department, there may be positive encouragement for the adoption of computer-based information systems. In recent years considerable experience has been gained in implementing information retrieval systems for regional sites and monuments registers in Britain (see, for example, Sheppard 1977, NYCC 1982), and for cultural resource management in the USA (Gaines 1981a). Anyone considering similar applications is strongly advised to evaluate the suitability of existing systems. The authors and users of these systems are perhaps best equipped to advise potential users of the problems of their implementation and of gaining access to suitable facilities.

A number of museum and excavation units have made use of commercial time-sharing computer systems (e.g. Brown *et al* 1981) although, usually for economic reasons, most seem eventually to have transferred their work to an educational computer installation. Indeed, collaborative arrangements between archaeological organisations and educational institutions can often prove to be the most economical means of gaining access to large scale computing facilities.

In Britain, the Museum Documentation Association provides extensive facilities for the storage of data on museum objects. The MDA supplies a number of standardised recording cards which museums and other institutions can use for cataloguing purposes. Using the GOS program package the MDA is able to prepare cross-reference indexes and catalogues for users of their system. Some work has also been done on the production of basic statistics from excavation records (Stewart 1982b). At present the system is suitable for applications where on-line retrieval facilities are not required. Users of this service can gain many of the advantages of using a computer to produce indexes and catalogues without becoming involved in the operation and management of the computer system. Thus the MDA may be able to provide an alternative approach for those who are unable to obtain the necessary computing facilities locally. The GOS package is also available to those who wish to implement it on their local computer installation, and a micro-computer version is currently under development. The MDA produces an extensive range of publications covering their activities and services, most of which are listed by Stewart (*ibid*).

8.4 **Choosing a micro-computer system for archaeological applications**
Prior to the introduction of sixteen bit micro-computers, the task of choosing a system was relatively straightforward. If graphics facilities were required then this might limit the choice, but, in general, almost any machine with between 48 and 64KB of memory and two floppy disc drives which used the CP/M operating system would suffice. The wide range of applications programs, compilers and interpreters available to run under CP/M have made it the obvious choice of operating system. Useful work can be done with many of the simpler machines, such as the BBC micro, the Apple or the Commodore PET. Each of these machines has a wide range of software available, but each of these has its own unique operating system. Although it is possible to use CP/M on a number of these machines, this can be achieved only by purchasing additional hardware. There is as yet no single specification for sixteen bit micro-computers which is clearly superior to the rest. As with the smaller machines, the best approach is to select a popular operating system for which a large body of applications software is available, and then to consider the range of hardware.

In order that archaeologists may exchange programs and data, some degree of standardisation of hardware and software is obviously required. The MDA recommendations (Stewart 1980) stressed the importance of hardware compatibility, with data and software being exchanged on floppy disc. The proliferation of different disc formats makes this an unwelcome constraint on the choice of suitable systems. In individual cases there may be a strong incentive to select a system which other archaeologists have used and for which specialised software has been developed. As a general rule, however, the question of compatibility should be approached from the view of standard high-level languages, and communication facilities.

Programs and data may be exchanged by a variety of means other than by discs. At the simplest level, two machines may be connected together by a serial link and the use of modems and telephone lines can obviate the need to transport equipment. At a more advanced level, common access to network facilities can provide an appropriate means of communication. Whilst these approaches may impose constraints on the choice of a suitable operating system, they provide a ready means of transferring high-level source programs between different machines. Archaeologists are not alone in their need for adequate communication between machines, and the choice of a widely used operating system should ensure that communication software will be readily available. The BSTAM and BSTMS programs produced by Byrom Software provide these facilities for CP/M systems. BSTAM enables two micro-computers to exchange files and BSTMS is designed to simplify communication between mainframe and micro-computers. These programs incorporate error checking and recovery functions which permit reliable communication even when using noisy telephone lines.

In order to determine whether a particular micro-computer represents the most appropriate means of implementing the envisaged applications, it is necessary to examine the availability of suitable software. It is only once this has been done, and alternative solutions have been discounted, that attention should turn to selecting the hardware. For many archaeologists selecting software will amount to comparing a number of commercial packages to determine which, if any, is the most suitable for each application. In addition, compilers or interpreters will be needed for software development and to implement published programs. In many cases, BASIC and Pascal will suffice, but, particularly if statistical work is to form an important part of the application, FORTRAN may prove useful.

The development of major applications software should be avoided if at all possible. If suitable software is not available, then there may be no alternative, but software development is extremely time-consuming and, therefore, expensive. The initial cost of purchasing software needs to be offset against the possible labour costs in developing a similar system. However, this should not be taken as an excuse for not trying to write programs. The need for short programs to re-arrange data or to perform simple statistical tests may arise quite frequently, and will present an ideal opportunity to develop programming skills.

As we have seen in section 8.22, the 'best' operating system need not be the most sophisticated or the most user-friendly of those currently available. Software support may often be a far more important consideration in choosing an operating system. In the case of single-user eight bit machines, the established position of CP/M makes it the obvious choice. In the case of sixteen bit machines, the position is not yet so clear. If software development by experienced programmers is to play a major role in the applications, then the facilities offered by one of the Unix based systems may be appreciated. For most users, however, the wide range of software available to run under CP/M and MS-DOS make either of these operating systems a suitable choice. A number of the machines which use these can be fitted with an extra processor to allow software written for the eight bit version of CP/M to be used, thus extending their general purpose capabilities. Indeed, for applications which do not require the advanced capabilities of the more powerful sixteen bit processor, it may prove more economical to use this additional hardware with the often less expensive eight bit software. This would also provide a degree of compatibility with software developed by archaeologists using eight bit CP/M machines. Experienced programmers may well prefer a Unix-based system, whilst many novices may be attracted by the user-friendly approach of systems like the Apple Lisa. However, unless there are very strong reasons for choosing one of these, considerations of software availability, cost and compatibility with other computer systems tilt the balance strongly in favour of the CP/M and MS-DOS systems. The Unix operating system and its imitators are becoming more widespread on the more powerful micro-computers, and the range of software is increasing rapidly. This development may well tilt the balance in favour of such systems within the near future.

8.41 **Choosing the hardware**

Once suitable software has been found, attention can be turned to selecting an appropriate machine. As a general rule, hardware selection should be influenced by the range of machines already in use by other archaeologists. Users with similar applications will often have a far clearer idea of the strengths and weaknesses of their machines than any computer salesman who is mainly concerned with selling machines for standard commercial applications. Machines may vary quite considerably in their processing and disc accessing speeds. For this reason it is advisable to compare the performance of the chosen software on a number of suitable machines.

With these considerations in mind, the following may be suggested as alternative basic specifications for micro-computer systems. The recommendations which resulted from the MDA seminar on micro-computers in archaeology (Stewart 1980, 2-3) remain generally appropriate for eight bit machines, although the suggested disc format can now be seen to have been a premature attempt at standardisation. Note that in the case of sixteen bit machines the type of processor is effectively determined by the chosen operating system.

1. General purpose single-user eight bit micro-computer

Processor:	Z80A or Z80B.
Memory:	minimum of 48KB, preferably 64KB.
Backing Store:	two 5.25 inch floppy discs
	or
	Winchester plus single floppy disc.
Operating System:	CP/M version 2 or 3.
Languages:	BASIC and Pascal.

2. Sixteen bit micro-computers

(a). Basic general purpose single-user system.

Processor:	8088 or 8086 (the 8086 will usually be faster).
Memory:	minimum of 128KB, preferably 256KB.
Backing Store:	two 5.25 inch floppy discs or Winchester plus single floppy disc.
Operating System:	CP/M-86 or MS-DOS 2.
Languages:	BASIC and Pascal.

(b). Basic single or multi-user system for intensive software development.

Processor:	68000.
Memory:	minimum of 256KB, preferably 512KB.
Backing Store:	Winchester plus single floppy disc.
Operating System:	Unix type.
Languages:	FORTRAN, Pascal, COBOL, C, as required.

It is almost inevitable that initial estimates of required memory size and backing store capacity will prove to be too low. Consequently some consideration should be given to the cost and ease with which the chosen system may be expanded to suit future requirements. Where a number of different people may need to use the system independently, the possibility of adding similar machines in a network configuration should be investigated. Indeed, for many applications, a micro-computer network may represent an economic solution from the outset. For applications where data may be collected in the field, a small portable computer may prove a useful addition to the system. Some of those now available have provision for communicating with other machines and most have either non-volatile memory or a small cassette system for storing data until it can be transferred to a larger machine.

The choice of a printer for use with a micro-computer will depend principally on two factors: cost and requirements. Where the machine is to be used primarily for the preparation of documents such as reports, the high quality output of a daisy-wheel printer may be the principal consideration. However, a large proportion of the printing performed in such applications may consist of rough drafts of articles. In such cases, the daisy-wheel printer may prove an expensive and slow means of output. Where a significant amount of program development or analytical work is envisaged, the higher speed of a dot-matrix printer will be an advantage. Here, the major demand will be for **listings** (printed copies) of programs, data files and results. In most cases, high print quality will not be needed for such material.

Many archaeologists will probably have mixed requirements, making the choice of printer type a difficult one. The final decision, for those who cannot justify the expense of two printers, will therefore be a matter of the individual priorities and budget. Daisy-wheel printers are generally more expensive than the dot-matrix type. Although a number of manufacturers produce daisy-wheel printers at a comparable price to that of many dot-matrix machines, these are often extremely slow and lack many of the facilities provided on the more expensive printers. It is perhaps worth noting that the print quality of some of the better dot-matrix devices is constantly being improved, and many users will consider these machines to be quite adequate for all purposes. A number of the more recently introduced models have the ability to produce near daisy-wheel quality print when running at a relatively slow speed, yet retaining a high speed mode for use when quality is of less importance. The cost of such printers is, however, comparable with that of the more sophisticated daisy-wheel machines.

Consideration should be given to the general comfort and health of those who will use the system. Fortunately, the rapid growth in use of office computers has led many manufacturers to consider seriously the ergonomic factors of their products. This is seen for instance in the trend towards green or orange VDU screens and separate keyboards. A number of recommendations on such related matters as lighting and seating arrangments for users are presented by Morgan and Wood (1981).

A question often overlooked when a system is purchased is that of maintenance. Manufacturers and dealers should be able to provide routine and emergency servicing, but this will invariably add to the cost of the system. Maintenance, as well as general running costs such as supplies of discs and paper, should be included when considering the costs of a system. Institutional users may be able to benefit from bulk purchasing and servicing arrangements.

Finally, anyone who has examined any of the many magazines dedicated to small computer systems cannot fail to notice the variety of new equipment which appears each month. There is a strong temptation to wait until the latest new product is available. This temptation should be avoided. Rapid developments will continue, but new products are invariably advertised many months before they are readily available. It is far better to purchase an adequate system which has been available for some time and has had its major problems ironed out than to have to wait several months for delivery of a system which has yet to be fully developed.

8.5 Future developments in archaeological computing

In section 1.2 we discussed the manner in which the development of computer applications has been driven by developments in hardware. This process may be identified in each of the four principal applications areas: information retrieval, statistics, ancillary data processing and modelling. There is no reason to doubt that it will continue. In each area, the initial developments have been the result of the work of a small number of specialists. Subsequently these techniques have become more widely adopted by archaeologists, particularly in the areas of information retrieval and statistics. This process has recently been repeated in the increasing use of micro-computers. The widespread availability of these machines suggests that they will play an important role in future developments.

Pioneer users of micro-computers invariably chose the equipment which appeared to offer the widest range of facilities commensurate with their requirements and budget. Thereafter, applications were developed within the constraints imposed by the hardware. Programs were developed locally or adapted from published examples, frequently being derived from those originally developed on mainframes. Just as with many of the earlier mainframe applications, these developments were driven as much by an enthusiasm for computers and a belief in their applicability to archaeological problems as by any specific desire to provide a solution to particular problems. This period of initial experimentation is now largely over, and we are entering a mature phase where the majority of users will view their machines as convenient tools for the solution of research and management problems.

Of course, as further hardware developments occur, there will probably always be a small number of people who, because of their specialist knowledge and interests, will continue to pioneer new applications. For these people, a thorough knowledge of developments in related disciplines is essential if they are to avoid attempts to '... re-invent hexagonal wheels which bump down the problem road as if nothing has ever been done before... ' (Scollar 1982,196).

For the majority of archaeologists, that is, those who regard the computer merely as a tool in their work, the increasing complexity and decreasing costs of micro-computers will mean that more and more problems which previously required mainframes for their solution can be tackled on the smaller machines. Using published or commercially available software archaeologists can gain a large degree of independence from central computer installations. Those who would not otherwise have access to machines, or who can only command limited use of facilities, stand to gain most, although the convenience of desk-top machines for many of the more mundane tasks, such as word processing, can be appreciated by all. It is generally agreed that micro-computers are less intimidating than their larger counterparts and hence a number of people who would not otherwise attempt to use a machine take to them quite readily. Projects that previously went unfinished, or were simply not tackled because they required electronic data processing, can be undertaken by people who once regarded them as the province of specialist 'computer archaeologists'.

Independence from a large computer installation may have its disadvantages, however. Archaeologists using a large computer installation can often call upon professional advice when needed. This may not be so easy for independent users. As long as applications can be satisfied by published or commercial software, then there need be few problems. If difficulties arise, the author of the program, or the supplier from whom it was purchased, should be able to provide assistance. However, many who begin by using only existing software quite rapidly progress to developing their own programs. At first, this may amount to little more than simple routines to alter the format of data files or to perform repetitive calculations. As greater confidence is acquired, many more archaeologists may begin to develop quite complex applications. It is at this stage that the problems of independence are most likely to arise.

The lack of information about what archaeologists are doing with computers, particularly micro-computers, has been addressed by Litvak King (1982). Suggested solutions included a greater number of meetings and a newsletter through which such matters could be discussed. This type of approach has had only a limited success in the past, as many archaeologists have regarded such meetings and publications solely as a forum for specialists. Perhaps a more valuable suggestion (*ibid*) is the formation of centralised sources of information concerning the availability of software, and users' experiences with it. This could easily be realised and would provide a valuable service to both specialist and non-specialist users. With suitable public networking facilities there is no reason why any programs or data which individuals may wish to share need not be made available to others. Software catalogues and other information could readily be disseminated via such a network.

A growth in the number of data banks used for information retrieval in individual and group research projects was identified in section 1.21 as a current trend which is likely to continue in the future. Other applications, particularly in the fields of statistics and modelling will continue to be important, but their relevant data will be increasingly derived from data banks. As Scollar (1982, 194) has noted, there is currently a trend away from the large data bank held on a mainframe towards more specialised applications using micro- and small mini-computers. Many of these data banks will be quite restricted in scope, although not necessarily in size. Decreasing storage costs are allowing a move away from tightly packed coded data towards a greater use of natural language. Hardware developments should ensure that facilities will be available to store whatever data our archaeological applications require. Probably the greatest restraint upon this growth in archaeological data banks will be the availability of time and people for the data capture. In the long term, advances in the fields of speech recognition, optical character recognition and artificial intelligence may make this less of an obstacle.

Perhaps the most significant development in archaeological computing has already begun. The use of computers by archaeologists is rapidly increasing. More and more archaeologists require their computers to produce meaningful results, rather than simply to demonstrate their possibilities. Computers are increasingly being accepted as everyday working tools, and archaeological computing is now becoming the province of the archaeologist rather than the computer specialist. This process has begun largely through the efforts of individual archaeologists who have taken it upon themselves to acquire the necessary skills. The widespread acknowledgement that an introduction to computing should form an essential part of an archaeological training will ensure that it continues.

BIBLIOGRAPHY

Alcock,D. 1977. *Illustrating BASIC, A simple programming language*. Cambridge University Press, Cambridge.

 – 1982. *Illustrating FORTRAN, The portable variety*. Cambridge University Press, Cambridge.

Aldenderfer,M.S. 1981a. 'Computer simulation for archaeology: an introductory essay', in Sabloff,J.A. (ed.), 1981, 11-49.

 – 1981b. 'Creating assemblages by computer simulation: the development and uses of ABSIM', in Sabloff,J.A. (ed.), 1981, 67-117.

Alvey,N.G. *et al* 1977. *GENSTAT: a general statistical program*. Rothamsted Experimental Station.

Alvey,N.G., Galwey,N., and Lane,P. 1982. *An introduction to Genstat*. Academic Press Inc (London) Ltd.

Ammerman,A.J. and Cavalli-Sforza,L.L. 1973. 'A population model for the diffusion of early farming in Europe', in Renfrew,C. (ed.), 1973, 343-57.

Angell,I.O. 1981. *A practical introduction to computer graphics*. Macmillan Press Ltd, London.

Arnold,J.B. III 1982. 'Archaeological applications of computer graphics', in Schiffer,M.B. (ed.), 1982, *Advances in archaeological method and theory*, **5**,179-216.

Ashley,R. 1980. *Structured COBOL: a self-teaching guide*. John Wiley & Sons Inc, New York.

Ashton-Tate 1981. *User's guide for dBaseII*. Ashton-Tate, Culver City, USA.

Aspinall,A. and Warren,S.E. (eds.) 1982. *Proceedings of the micro-computer jamboree*, University of Bradford.

Benson,D.G. and Jefferies,J.S. 1980. 'Microprocessors and archaeological records', in Stewart,J.D. (ed.), 1980, 5-12.

Berry,B.J.L. 1964. 'Approaches to regional analysis: a synthesis', *Annals of the Association of American Geographers*, **54**, 2-11.

Bishop,S. and Wilcock,J.D. 1976. 'Archaeological context sorting by computer: the STRATA program', *Science and Archaeology*, **17**, 3-12.

Booth,B.K.W. 1982. 'Some projects to store and process data from survey and excavation with the aid of a computer', in Graham, I. and Webb,E. (eds.), 1982, 20-5.

Borillo,M. 1971. 'Formal procedures and the use of computers in archaeology', *Norwegian Archaeological Review*, **4**, 2-27.

Bourelly,L. 1972. 'Quelques aspects de la notion moderne de simulation', in Borillo,M. (ed.), 1972, *Les méthodes mathématiques de l'archéologie*, 186-99.

Brew,J.O. 1946. 'The use and abuse of taxonomy', in *Archaeology of Alkali Ridge, southeastern Utah*. Papers of the Peabody Museum of American Archaeology and Ethnology, Harvard University, no. 21, 44-66. Harvard University Press, Cambridge, Mass.

Brown,J.A., Clayton,C., Wendt,T., and Werner,B. 1981. 'The Koster Project information retrieval application', in Gaines,S.W. (ed.), 1981a, 67-79.

Buckland,P. 1973. 'An experiment in the use of a computer for on-site recording of finds', in proceedings *Computer Applications in Archaeology* Conference, published as *Science and archaeology*, **9**, 22-4.

213

Burton,V., Bonin,A., Lourie,J., and Spiselman,T. 1970. 'The computer and archaeology', *American Journal of Archaeology*, **74**, 221-3.

CADC 1975. *GINO-F user manual*. Computer Aided Design Centre, Cambridge.

Calderbank,V.J. 1969. *A course on programming in FORTRAN IV*. Science Paperbacks. Chapman & Hall Ltd, London.

Carey,D. *et al* 1979. *How it works - the computer*. Ladybird Books Ltd, Loughborough.

Catton,J.P.J., Jones,M.U., and Moffett,J.C. 1982. 'The 1965-1978 Mucking excavation computer database', in Graham,I. and Webb,E. (eds.), 1982, 36-43.

Chamberlain,M.P. and Haigh,J.G.B. 1982. 'A microcomputer system for practical photogrammetry', in proceedings *Computer Applications in Archaeology* Conference, 142-9, University of Birmingham.

Chandor,A. *et al* 1977. *The Penguin dictionary of computers*. Second edition. Penguin Books Ltd, Harmondsworth.

Chenhall,R.G. 1967. 'The description of archaeological data in computer language', *American Antiquity*, **32**, 161-7.

– 1968. 'The impact of computers on archaeological theory: an appraisal and projection', *Computers and the Humanities*, **3(1)**,15-24.

– 1971a. *Computers in anthropology and archaeology*. IBM Corporation publication no.GE20-0384.

– 1971b. 'The archaeological data bank: a progress report', *Computers and the Humanities*, **5(3)**, 159-69.

Clark,G.A. and Stafford,C.R. 1982. 'Quantification in American archaeology: a historical perspective', *World Archaeology*, **14(1)**, 98-119.

Clarke,D.L. 1968. *Analytical archaeology*. Methuen & Co Ltd, London.

– (ed.) 1972. *Models in archaeology*. Methuen & Co Ltd, London.

CODASYL 1971. *CODASYL data base task group report, 1971*. Association for Computing Machinery, New York.

Codd,E.F. 1970. 'A relational model of data for large shared data banks', *Communications of the Association for Computing Machinery*, **13(6)**, 377-87.

Collin,W.G. 1978. *Introducing computer programming*. National Computer Centre Publications, Manchester.

Cook,R.M. and Belshé,J.C. 1958. 'Archaeomagnetism: a preliminary report on Britain', *Antiquity*, **32**, 167-78.

Cooke,K.L. and Renfrew,C. 1979. 'An experiment on the simulation of culture changes', in Renfrew,C. and Cooke,K.L. (eds.), *Transformations: mathematical approaches to culture change*, 327-48, Academic Press, New York.

Coombs,C.H. 1953. 'Theory and methods of social measurement', in Festinger,L. and Katz, D.(eds.), *Research methods in the behavioral sciences*, 471-535, Holt, Rinehart, and Winston, New York.

Cowgill,G.L. 1967a. 'Computer applications in archaeology', *Computers and the Humanities*, **2(1)**, 17-23.

– 1967b. 'Computer applications in archaeology', *AFIPS Conference Proceedings: 1967 Fall Joint Computer Conference*, **31**,331-7.

– 1968. 'Computer analysis of archaeological data from Teotihuacan, Mexico', in Binford,S.R. and Binford,L.R. (eds.), *New perspectives in archaeology*, 143-50, Aldine, Chicago.

Crowther,D.R. and Booth,B.K.W. 1982. 'A microcomputer catalogue for excavation small finds', in Graham,I. and Webb,E. (eds.), 1982, 44-50.

Date,C.J. 1975. *An introduction to database systems*. Addison-Wesley Publishing Company Inc, New York.

Day,A.C. 1972. *FORTRAN techniques, with special reference to non- numerical applications*. Cambridge University Press, Cambridge.

Deetz,J. 1965. *The dynamics of stylistic change in Arikara ceramics*. University of Illinois Press, Urbana.

– 1967. *Invitation to archaeology*. American Museum Science Books, The Natural History Press, New York.

Dixon,W.J. and Brown,M.B. 1979. *BMDP-79: biomedical computer programs P-series*. University of California Press, Berkeley.

Doran,J. 1970a. 'Systems theory, computer simulations and archaeology', *World Archaeology*, **1**, 289-98.

– 1970b. 'Archaeological reasoning and machine reasoning', in Gardin, J.-C. (ed.),1970, 57-69.

– 1972a. 'Automatic generation and evaluation of explanatory hypotheses', in *Proceedings of a colloquium on mathematical methods in archaeology, October 1971*, CADA, CNRS, Marseilles.

– 1972b. 'Computer models as tools for archaeological hypothesis formation', in Clarke, D.L. (ed.), 1972, 425-51.

– 1973. 'Explanation in archaeology: a computer experiment', in Renfrew, C. (ed.), 1973, 149-53.

– 1982. 'A computational model of sociocultural systems and their dynamics', in Renfrew, C., Rowlands, M.J. and Seegraves, B. (eds.), 1982, *Theory and explanation in archaeology*, 375-88, Academic Press Inc, London.

Doran, J. and Hodson, F.R. 1975. *Mathematics and computers in archaeology*. Edinburgh University Press, Edinburgh.

Dunnell,R.C. 1971. *Systematics in prehistory*. The Free Press, New York.

Ebdon,D. 1977. *Statistics in geography: a practical approach*. Basil Blackwell, Oxford.

Elbra,T. 1982. *Database for the small computer user*. National Computing Centre Publications, Manchester.

Everitt, B. 1974. *Cluster analysis*. Heinemann Educational Books Ltd, London.

Fasham,P.J. and Hawkes,J.W. 1980. 'Computerised recording systems and analysis in an archaeological unit: some observations', in Stewart,J.D. (ed.), 1980, 21-4.

Findlay,W. and Watt,D.A. 1981. *Pascal: an introduction to methodical programming*. Second edition. Pitman Books Ltd, London.

Fletcher,R. 1977. 'Settlement studies (micro and semi-micro)', in Clarke,D.L. (ed.), 1977, *Spatial archaeology*, 47-162, Academic Press Inc, London.

Ford,J.A. 1954. 'On the concept of types', *American Anthropologist*, **56**, 42-54.

Forsström,M. 1972. 'On automatic data treatment as an aid to the recording and processing of archaeological finds', *Norwegian Archaeological Review*, **5**, 28-44.

Foskett,A.C. 1970. *A guide to personal indexes using edge- notched, uniterm and peek-a-boo cards*. Second edition. Bingley, London.

Fry,T.F. 1981. *Computer appreciation*. Third edition. Butterworth & Co Ltd, London.

Gaines,S.W. (ed.) 1981a. *Data bank applications in archaeology*. The University of Arizona Press, Tucson, Arizona.

– 1981b. 'Computer data bank application at a remote site location', in Gaines,S.W. (ed.), 1981a, 80-9.

Gaines,S.W. and Gaines,W.M. 1980. 'Future trends in computer applications', *American Antiquity*, **45**, 462-71.

Gardin,J.-C. 1956. 'Le fichier mécanographique de l'outillage', *Institute Francais d'Archéologie de Beyrouth*,1-20.

– 1958. 'Four codes for the description of artifacts: an essay in archaeological technique and theory', *American Anthropologist*, **60**, 335-57.

– 1967. 'Methods for the descriptive analysis of archaeological material', *American Antiqui-ty*, **32**, 13-30.

– (ed.) 1970. *Archéologie et Calculateurs*. Editions du CNRS, Paris.

– 1971. 'Archaeology and computers: new perspectives', *International Social Science Jour-nal*, **23(2)**, 189-203.

– 1980. *Archaeological constructs*. Cambridge University Press, Cambridge.

George,F.H. and Sarkar,P.A. 1981. *Practical database for major mini and micro computers*. Chiltern Educational and Time-Share Services, England.

Gifford,D.P. and Crader,D.C. 1977. 'A computer coding system for archaeological faunal remains', *American Antiquity*, **42**, 225-37.

Graham,I. 1976. 'Intelligent terminals for excavation recording', in proceedings *Computer Applications in Archaeology* Conference, 48-52, University of Birmingham.

– 1980. *Microcomputers for archaeological excavation recording*, British Library Research Development Report 5600.

Graham,I. and Webb,E. (eds.) 1982. *Computer applications in archaeology 1981*. Institute of Archaeology, University of London.

Green,P.E. 1976. *Mathematical tools for applied multivariate analysis*. Academic Press, New York.

Hammond,R. and McCullagh,P.S. 1978. *Quantitative techniques in geography: an introduc-tion*. Second edition. Clarendon Press, Oxford.

Hardy,E. 1982. 'A microcomputer-based system of recording bones from archaeological sites', in Aspinall,A. and Warren,S.E. (eds.), 1982, 11-15.

Harris,E.C. 1975. 'Stratigraphic analysis and the computer', in proceedings *Computer Ap-plications in Archaeology* Conference, University of Birmingham.

– 1979. *Principles of archaeological stratigraphy*. Academic Press Inc (London) Ltd.

Harrison,S.J., Jardine,C.J., King, J.E., King,T.J. and Macfarlane, A.D.J. 1982. *The records of an English Village*. Microfiche publication, Chadwyck-Healey, Cambridge.

Hill, J.N. and Evans,R.K. 1972. 'A model for classification and typology', in Clarke, D.L. (ed.), 1972, 231-73.

Hodder,I. (ed.) 1978. *Simulation studies in archaeology*. New directions in archaeology series. Cambridge University Press, Cambridge.

Hodder,I. and Orton,C. 1976. *Spatial analysis in archaeology*. Cambridge University Press, Cambridge.

Hodson,F.R. 1970. 'Cluster analysis and archaeology: some new developments and applica-tions', *World Archaeology*, **1**, 299-320.

Hodson, F.R., Kendall, D.G., and Tautu, P. (eds.) 1971. *Mathematics in the archaeological and historical sciences*. Proceedings of the Anglo-Romanian Conference, Mamaia 1970. Edinburgh University Press, Edinburgh.

Hosler,D., Sabloff,J.A., and Runge,D. 1977. 'Situation model development: a case study of the Classic Maya collapse', in Hammond,N. (ed.), *Social processes in Maya prehistory*, 553-90, Academic Press, London and New York.

ICL 1981. *The personal data system (PDS56)*. RP0121, International Computers Ltd, London.

Ihm,P. 1978. 'Statistik in der Archäologie: Probleme der Anwendung, allgemeine Methoden, Seriation und Klassifikation', *Archaeo-Physika*, **9**.

Jardine,N. and Sibson,R. 1971. *Mathematical taxonomy*. John Wiley and Sons Ltd, London.

Jefferies,J.S. 1977. *Excavation records: techniques in use by the Central Excavation Unit*, Directorate of Ancient Monuments and Historic Buildings, Occasional Paper no.1, Department of the Environment.

Jensen,K. and Wirth,N. 1978. *Pascal user manual and report*. Second edition. Springer-Verlag, New York.

Johnston,R.J. 1978. *Multivariate statistical analysis in geography*. Longman & Co Ltd, London.

Jolley, J.L. 1968. *Data study*. World University Library, Weidenfeld and Nicolson, London.

Kenrick,P.M. 1980. 'Vector MZ microcomputer used for cataloguing pottery by the Colchester Archaeological Trust', in Stewart, J.D. (ed.), 1980, 35-7.

Kenworthy,J.B., Stapleton,J.R. and Thurston,J.H. 1975. 'The Fife Archaeological Index – a computer implementation', in proceedings *Computer Applications in Archaeology* Conference, 41-8, University of Birmingham.

King,T.J. and Moody, J.K.M. 1983. 'The design and implementation of CODD', *Software-Practice and Experience*, **13**, 67-78.

Klecka,W.R., Nie,N.H., and Hadlai Hull,C. 1975. *SPSS primer*. McGraw-Hill Book Company, New York.

Krieger,A.D. 1944. 'The typological concept', *American Antiquity*, **9**, 271-288.

Kruglinski,D. 1983. *Database management systems: a guide to micro-computer software*. McGraw Hill/Osborne.

Laboratory for Computer Graphics and Spatial Analysis 1975. *SYMAP user manual*. Harvard University.

Leach,E. 1973. 'Concluding address', in Renfrew,C. (ed.), 1973, 761-71.

Lee,B. 1979. *Introducing systems analysis and design*. National Computer Centre Publications, Manchester.

Levison, M., Ward,R.G. and Webb, J.W. 1972. 'The settlement of Polynesia: a report on a computer simulation', *Archaeology and Physical Anthropology in Oceania*, **7**, 234-45.

Litvak King,J. 1982. 'Microcomputers in archaeology: yesterday, today and tomorrow?', in Aspinall,A. and Warren,S.E. (eds.), 1982, 1-4.

Lock,G.R. forthcoming. 'The computing', in Cunliffe, B.W., *An Iron Age hillfort in Hampshire*. CBA Research Report.

Longacre,W.A. 1964. 'Sociological implications of the ceramic analysis', in P.S. Martin and others, *Chapters in the prehistory of eastern Arizona*, I, 148-67. Fieldana: Anthropology, vol. 53. Chicago Natural History Museum, Chicago.

Lyons,N. 1980. *Structured COBOL for data processing*. Glencoe Series in Computer Science and Data Processing. Glencoe Publishing Co, Inc, California.

McCracken,D.D. 1972. *A guide to FORTRAN IV programming*. Second edition. John Wiley and Sons Inc, New York.

– 1976. *A simplified guide to structured COBOL programming*. John Wiley and Sons Inc, New York.

McNett,C.W. 1981. 'Computer graphics in the analysis of archaeological data', in Gaines,S.W. (ed.), 1981a, 90-9.

Maddison,R. *et al* 1980. *Computer-based Information Systems*. The Open University Press, Milton Keynes.

Main,P.L. 1981. 'A method for the computer storage and comparison of the outline shapes of archaeological artefacts.' Unpublished PhD thesis. North Staffordshire Polytechnic.

– 1982. 'SHU - an interactive graphics program for the storage, retrieval and analysis of artefact shapes', in Graham, I. and Webb, E. (eds.), 1982, 75-82.

Mather,P.M. 1976a. *Computational methods of multivariate analysis in physical geography*. John Wiley and Sons, London.

– 1976b. *Computers in geography: a practical approach*. Basil Blackwell, Oxford.

Mayne,A. 1981. *Database management systems: a technical review*. National Computing Centre Publications, Manchester.

Millington,D. 1981. *Systems analysis and design for computer applications*. Computers and their Applications Series no.12, Ellis Horwood Ltd, Chichester.

Moffett,J.C. and Webb,R.E. 1982. 'Database management systems and radiocarbon dating',in proceedings *Computer Applications in Archaeology* Conference, 76-8, University of Birmingham.

Monro,D.M. 1977. *Computing with FORTRAN IV: a practical course*. Edward Arnold Ltd, London.

– 1978. *Basic BASIC: an introduction to programming*. Edward Arnold Ltd, London.

– 1982. *FORTRAN 77*. Edward Arnold Ltd, London.

Moore,D. 1978. 'Simulation languages for archaeologists', in Hodder, I. (ed.), 1978, 11-19.

Moore,L. 1980. *Foundations of programming with Pascal*. Computers and their Applications Series no.6, Ellis Horwood Ltd, Chichester.

Morgan,R. and Wood,B. 1981. *Word processing*. Oyez Publishing Ltd, London.

Morris,G. and Scarre,C.R. 1982. 'Computerised analysis of the shapes of a class of prehistoric stone tools from west central France', in Graham, I. and Webb,E. (eds.), 1982, 83-94.

Myers,G.J. 1975. *Reliable software through composite design*. Van Nostrand Reinhold Company, New York.

NCC 1977. *Data processing documentation standards*. National Computing Centre Ltd, Manchester.

– 1980. *Introducing data processing*. National Computer Centre Publications, Manchester.

Newell,R.R. and Vroomans,A.P.J. 1972. *Automatic artifact registration and systems for archaeological analysis with the Philips P1100 Computer: a Mesolithic test-case*. Anthropological Publications Oosterhout, The Netherlands.

Nie,N.H., Hadlai Hull,C., Jenkins,J.G., Steinbrenner,K. and Bent,D.H. 1975. *Statistical package for the social sciences*. McGraw-Hill Book Company, New York.

Nie,N.H. and Hadlai Hull,C. 1981. *SPSS update 7-9: new procedures and facilities for releases 7-9*. McGraw-Hill Book Company, New York.

NYCC 1982. *Archaeological record system*. North Yorkshire County Council Computer Services, Northallerton.

Oldenburg,E. and Møllerop,O. 1969. 'An attempt to code grave descriptions', *Norwegian Archaeological Review*, **2**, 78-85.

Orna,E. and Pettitt,C. 1980. *Information handling in museums*. K G Saur-Clive Bingley, New York.

Orton,C. 1980. *Mathematics in archaeology*. William Collins Sons and Co Ltd, London.

Palmer,R. 1976. 'A method of transcribing archaeological sites from oblique aerial photographs', *Journal of Archaeological Science*, **3**, 391-4.

– 1977. 'A computer method for transcribing information graphically from oblique aerial photographs to maps', *Journal of Archaeological Science*, **4**, 283-90.

– 1978. 'Computer transcriptions from air photographs', *Aerial Archaeology*, **2**, 5-9.

Petrie,W.M.F. 1899. 'Sequences in prehistoric remains', *Journal of the Anthropological Institute*, **29**, 295-301.

Pitt-Rivers (Augustus Henry Lane-Fox) 1887-98. *Excavations in Cranborne Chase, near Rushmore, on the borders of Dorset and Wiltshire (vols 1-2, 4); - in Bokerly and Wansdyke, Dorset and Wiltshire (vol 3)*. Privately printed, London.

Plog,F. 1975. 'Systems theory in archaeological research', *Annual Review of Anthropology*, **4**, 207-24.

– 1981. 'SARG: The computer in a cooperative effort', in Gaines,S.W. (ed.), 1981a, 46-56.

Plog,S. 1980. *Stylistic variation in prehistoric ceramics*. Cambridge University Press, Cambridge.

Powlesland,D. 1983. 'Pots, pits and portables', *Practical Computing*, **6(6)**, 144-6.

Pryor,F. 1980. 'Maxey, micros and myself - a personal assessment from the archaeologist's viewpoint', in Stewart, J.D. (ed.), 1980, 99-102.

Redman,C.L. and Watson,P.J. 1970. 'Systematic, intensive surface collection', *American Antiquity*,**35**,279-91.

Renfrew,C. (ed.) 1973. *The explanation of culture change: models in prehistory*. Gerald Duckworth and Co Ltd, London.

Richards,J.D. 1982. 'Micro-measurement', in Aspinall, A. and Warren,S.E. (eds.), 1982, 19-25.

Rieger,A. 1981. 'AZSITE: The Arizona State Museum site survey data base', in Gaines, S.W. (ed.), 1981a, 27-45.

Roberts,D.A. 1980. 'Data standards for archaeology', in Stewart, J.D. (ed.), 1980, 87-97.

Robinson,W.S. 1951. 'A method for chronologically ordering archaeological deposits', *American Antiquity*, **16**, 293-301.

Rouse,I. 1960. 'The classification of artifacts in archaeology', *American Antiquity*, **25**, 313-23.

  – 1970. 'Classification for what?', *Norwegian Archaeological Review*, **3**, 4-12.

Ryan,T.A., Jr., Joiner,B.L., and Ryan,B.F. 1976. *MINITAB student handbook*. Duxbury Press, North Scituate, Massachusetts.

  – 1981. *MINITAB reference manual*.

Sabloff,J.A. (ed.) 1981. *Simulations in archaeology*. University of New Mexico Press, Albuquerque.

Sammet,J.E. 1969. *Programming languages: history and fundamentals*. Prentice Hall Inc, New Jersey.

Scollar,I. 1959. 'Einführung in die Widerstandsmessung', *Bonner Jahrbücher*, **159**, 283-313.

  – 1968. 'Automatic recording of magnetometer data in the field', *Prospezioni Archeologiche*, **3**, 105-10.

  – 1969. 'Some techniques for the evaluation of archaeological magnetometer surveys', *World Archaeology*, **1**, 77-89.

  – 1974. 'Interactive processing of geophysical data from archaeological sites', in proceedings *Computer Applications in Archaeology* Conference,75-80, University of Birmingham.

  – 1975. 'Transformation of extreme oblique aerial photographs to maps or plans by conventional means or by computer', in *Aerial reconnaissance for archaeology*, CBA Research Report, **12**, 52-8.

  – 1977. 'L'informatique appliquée à la photographie aérienne', *L'archéologie*,**22**,78-87.

  – 1982. 'Thirty years of computer archaeology and the future', in proceedings *Computer Applications in Archaeology* Conference, 189-98, University of Birmingham.

Scollar,I. and Krückeberg,F. 1966. 'Computer treatment of magnetic measurements from archaeological sites', *Archaeometry*, **9**, 61-71.

Scollar,I. and Weidner,B. 1979. 'Computer production of orthophotos from single oblique images or from rotating mirror scanners', *Aerial Archaeology*, **4**, 17-28.

Scott,J.E. 1982. *Introduction to interactive computer graphics*. John Wiley and Sons, Inc, New York.

Shaw,A. 1978. *Famulus reference manual*. University College London Computer Centre.

Sheppard,B. 1977. *Handbook 1: recording the evidence*. Archaeological Survey of Merseyside, Merseyside Archaeological Society, Liverpool.

  – n.d. *Computer handling of sites and monuments records: user's handbook*. Archaeological Survey of Merseyside.

Shorter,E. 1971. *The historian and the computer: a practical guide*. Prentice Hall Inc, New Jersey.

Siegel,S. 1956. *Nonparametric statistics for the behavioral sciences*. McGraw-Hill Book Company, New York.

Simons,G.L. 1981. *Introducing word processing*. National Computing Centre Publications, Manchester.

Sneath,P.H.A. 1982. 'Classification and identification with incomplete data', in proceedings *Computer Applications in Archaeology* Conference, 182-7, University of Birmingham.

Sneath,P.H.A. and Sokal,R.R. 1973. *Numerical taxonomy: the principles and practice of numerical classification*. W.H. Freeman and Co, San Francisco.

Spaulding,A.C. 1953. 'Statistical techniques for the discovery of artifact types', *American Antiquity*, **18**, 305-313.

– 1960. 'Statistical description and comparison of artifact assemblages', in Heizer,R.F. and Cook,S. (eds.), *The application of quantitative methods in archaeology*. Viking Fund Publications in Anthropology no. 28.

SPSS Inc. 1983. *SPSS-X user's guide*. McGraw-Hill Book Company, New York.

Stevens,S.S. 1946. 'On the theory of scales of measurement', *Science*, **103**, 677-80.

Stewart,J.D. (ed.) 1980. *Microcomputers in archaeology*. Museum Documentation Association Occasional Paper 4, Duxford, Cambs..

– 1982a. 'MDA, MDS and computerised archaeology', in Graham, I. and Webb, E. (eds.), 1982, 101-11.

– 1982b. 'Computerising archaeological records - a progress report on the work of the MDA', in proceedings *Computer Applications in Archaeology* Conference, 4-10, University of Birmingham.

Taylor,W.W. 1948. *A study of archaeology*. American Anthropological Association Memoir no. 69.

Thomas,D.H. 1972. 'A computer simulation model of Great Basin Shoshonean subsistence and settlement patterns', in Clarke, D.L. (ed.), 1972, 671-704.

– 1973. 'An empirical test for Steward's model of Great Basin settlement patterns', *American Antiquity*, **38**, 155-76.

Upham,S. (ed.) 1979. *Computer graphics in archaeology: statistical cartographic applications to spatial analysis in archaeological contexts*. Anthropological Research Papers No.15, Arizona State University, Tempe.

Whallon,R. 1972a. 'A new approach to pottery typology', *American Antiquity*, **37**, 13-33.

– 1972b. 'The computer in archaeology: a critical survey', *Computers and the Humanities*, **7(1)**, 29-45.

Wilcock,J.D. 1970a. 'Prospecting at South Cadbury: an exercise in computer archaeology', *Science and Archaeology*, **1**, 9-11.

– 1970b. 'Petroglyphs by computer', *Science and Archaeology*, **2-3**, 27-9.

– 1971. 'Non-statistical applications of the computer in archaeology', in Hodson,F.R., Kendall, D.G., and Tautu, P. (eds.) 1971, 470-81.

– 1973a. 'A general survey of computer applications in archaeology', in proceedings *Computer Applications in Archaeology* Conference, published as *Science and Archaeology*, **9**, 17-21.

– 1973b. 'The use of remote terminals for archaeological site records', in proceedings *Computer Applications in Archaeology* Conference, published as *Science and Archaeology*, **9**, 25.

– 1982. 'STRATA - the microcomputer version', in Graham,I. and Webb,E. (eds.), 1982, 112-4.

Wilcock,J.D. and Coombes,T. 1982. 'A television camera interface for the automatic capture of artefact shapes by microcomputer', in Aspinall,A. and Warren,S.E. (eds.), 1982, 27-33.

Wilcock,J.D. and Shennan,S.J. 1975. 'Shape and style variation in Central German Bell Beakers : a computer-assisted study', *Science and Archaeology*, **15**, 17-31.

Wilcock,J.D., Short,T., and Greaves,A. forthcoming. 'The Harwell low level measurements laboratory microcomputer network', in proceedings *Computer Applications in Archaeology* Conference, University of Bradford.

Wilson, I.R. and Addyman, A.M. 1978. *A practical introduction to Pascal*. Macmillan Computer Science Series, Macmillan Press Ltd, London.

Wishart,D. 1978. *CLUSTAN user manual*. Third edition. Program Library Unit, Edinburgh University.

Wobst,H.M. 1974. 'Boundary conditions for Palaeolithic social systems: a simulation approach', *American Antiquity*, **39**, 147-78.

Wright,H and Zeder,M. 1977. 'The simulation of a linear exchange system under equilibrium conditions', in Earle,T.K. and Ericson, J.E. (eds.), *Exchange Systems in Prehistory*, Academic Press, New York.

Yoeli,P. 1982. 'Cartographic drawing with computers', *Computer Applications*, **8**, Special Issue. Department of Geography, University of Nottingham.

Yourdon, E. and Constantine,L.L. 1979. *Structured design: fundamentals of a discipline of computer program and systems design*. Prentice-Hall Inc, New Jersey.

GLOSSARY

Acoustic coupler: inexpensive form of modem used with conventional telephone handset, rather than being directly connected to the telephone lines (section 3.53).

Address: location in memory at which an item is stored.

Algorithm: sequence of operations required to perform a specific task (section 1.1).

Alphameric: see alphanumeric.

Alphanumeric: field of characters which may be numeric or alphabetic (section 2.73).

ALU: Arithmetic and Logical Unit. That part of the CPU which performs arithmetic and logical operations.

Application package: a program or suite of programs designed to perform a specific type of work, usually with a large number of users in mind (section 4.1).

Application program: a program written by, or for, an individual user to perform a particular task (section 4.1).

Archiving: process of making back-up copies of programs or data (section 3.41).

Array: an arrangement of items of data, each identified by a subscript (section 4.517).

ASCII: American Standard Code for Information Interchange. A character code adopted as standard by the American National Standards Institute in 1963 (section 2.72, 3.21).

Assembler: program which translates assembly language into machine executable code.

Assembly language: low level programming language which is specific to a particular processor. Individual machine operations are represented by mnemonics.

Back-up: (1) duplicated copies of programs or data; (2) reserve hardware.

Batch processing: operating mode in which instructions are stored in a file and executed at a later time. Instructions from a number of users are placed into a batch queue and processed in order.

Baud: unit of speed for serial data transmission. Represents bits per second, a character when transmitted with start and stop bits usually occupies about ten bits, therefore, 300 Baud is roughly 30 characters per second (section 3.5).

Benchmark: standard program used to test the speed of execution of different machines.

Binary: number system to the base two, in which numbers are represented by the digits 0 and 1 (section 3.21).

Boolean algebra: uses algebraic notation to express logical relationships (section 4.525).

Bootstrap: the technique of loading a program into a computer by means of preliminary instructions which in turn call in instructions to read programs and data (section 4.61).

Branch: an optional sequence of program instructions following a conditional jump instruction.

Buffer: section of memory used as a temporary store of data between communicating processes or devices, enables data to be moved in large blocks (e.g. line by line) rather than character by character.

Bug: an error or malfunction of a computer program or system.

Bus: system of parallel connections employed between hardware components (section 3.5).

Byte: unit of storage equivalent to eight bits (section 3.21).

Call: a program instruction which causes program control to branch to a subroutine.

CPU: Central Processing Unit, that part of the computer which contains the memory, ALU and control units (section 3.3).

Character: one of a set of symbols used in data processing to denote, for example, the digits 0-9, or the letters of the alphabet (section 2.72).

Code: the representation of data or programs in symbolic form.

Coding book: a catalogue of all possible attribute states and the codes used to represent them (section 5.23).

Coding sheet: a pre-prepared form designed to ease the coding of data (section 5.41).

Compatibility: is said to exist between two computers if programs can be run on both without alteration.

Compiler: a complex computer program which translates the instructions of a source program into machine code (section 4.5).

Conditional jump: a jump which occurs if a specified condition is true.

Copy: to reproduce programs or data without alteration.

Core: the immediate access store or memory of a computer (section 3.3).

Corrupt: to spoil a record of program or data.

CRT: Cathode Ray Tube, the display tube in a VDU.

Daisy wheel printer: printer which produces high quality output similar to that of many electric typewriters (section 3.733).

Data: recorded observations (section 1.1).

Data bank: a comprehensive file of data, or a group of files treated as a unit (section 2.76).

Database: often used as a synonym for data bank, but strictly is a collection of data which is accessed and maintained by a Database Management System or DBMS (section 6.6).

Data capture: the collection of computer input data (section 5.422).

Data processing: manipulation of data to produce a more useful form (section 1.1).

Data processing cycle: recursive sequence of data input, data processing, and output of information for input into next sequence (section 1.1).

Debugging: technique of identifying and correcting errors which occur in hardware and software (section 4.6).

Delete: any operation to remove a file, or eliminate a record or group of records from within a file.

Digitiser: device for capturing graphical data using either a stylus or cursor device (section 3.65).

Direct access: mode of access to a file in which each record may be accessed with equal ease (section 6.4).

Directory: or catalogue: a list of files held on a disc or other storage medium (section 6.22).

Disc: magnetic storage medium (section 3.42).

Display: visual representation on a VDU.

Documentation: written descriptive material accompanying a program (section 4.5).

Dot-matrix printer: printer which creates characters out of a matrix of closely spaced dots (section 3.732).

Down: term used to indicate computer equipment which is out of order.

Drum plotter: form of plotter on which the paper is located on a drum which provides motion in one axis. Motion in the other axis is provided by moving the pen across the drum (section 3.75).

Dump: to write an area of memory to a peripheral unit.

Edit: to arrange data into the form required for data processing.

Editor: a program used to edit data or programs (section 5.421).

Encode: to apply a code to data or instructions.

Error listing: a list of programming errors produced by a compiler.

Execution: the execution of a program occurs when its compiled object code is run on the computer.

Field: a subdivision of a record containing a unit of information (section 2.73).

File: organised collection of data (section 1.1, 2.75, 6.2).

Fixed length record: each record occupies a fixed number of character positions (section 5.3).

Floppy disc: flexible magnetic disc used for storage on many smaller computers (section 3.42).

Flowchart: diagrammatic representation of a sequence of events, usually drawn according to conventional symbols which indicate different classes of event and their interrelationship (section 4.41).

Format: the arrangement of data.

Hands-on: using a computer directly at a terminal.

Hard copy: information presented in the form of print or drawings on paper.

Hardware: all the electronic and mechanical equipment used as part of a computer system (section 1.1, chapter 3).

Hexadecimal: number system to the base 16. Uses the digits 0-9 and A-F. Frequently used by programmers working in low-level languages as a convenient means of representing numbers. One hexadecimal digit corresponds to four binary digits or bits (section 3.21).

High-level language: a language in which each instruction corresponds to several machine code instructions (section 4.5).

Information retrieval: branch of data processing relating to the storage and categorisation of large quantities of data, and the automatic retrieval of specific items (section 1.21).

Input: data or programs introduced into a computer system.

Input/output device: a device, such as a teletype-writer, which can be used to both accept and deliver messages (section 3.5).

Integer: a whole number without any fractional component (section 2.65).

Intelligent terminal: a form of terminal which is capable of some local processing.

Interactive: a mode of operating a computer whereby each action of the user generates an immediate response.

Interpreter: a program which translates a source program into machine code for immediate execution (section 4.5).

Job: a unit of work for a computer (section 4.6).

Job control language: language used to give instructions to the computing system. It is a subset of the operating system (section 4.62).

Jump: to depart from the normal sequence of program instructions.

Keyword: in a coding system a keyword is the set of characters which the computer accepts as representing a given attribute state (section 5.2).

KiloByte: 1024 bytes (section 3.21).

Label: (1) character(s) used to identify a file, record, or single data item; (2) character(s) used to tag a program instruction.

Language: a code for communicating with a computer which consists of a set of characters and well-defined rules for combining them (section 4.5).

Left-justified: describing data formatted so that it occupies consecutive spaces starting at the left hand end of the area allocated to it.

Library: a collection of subroutines and programs written for a given computer, and usually designed for incorporation into other programs.

Light pen: light-sensitive device which may be used to point a locations on a VDU screen. Used to provide an alternative means of interaction with the user to that available with a keyboard (section 3.74).

Line printer: a device which prints a complete line of characters simultaneously (section 3.731).

Load: to put data or programs into computer memory, ready for execution.

Log: a record of events in the course of a computer run.

Loop: a series of instructions which are performed repeatedly until some specific condition is satisfied.

Low-level language: a language in which each instruction has a single corresponding machine code equivalent (section 4.5).

Machine code: a code in which binary digits directly convey the basic instructions to a computer.

Macro-instruction: a composite instruction, which is of value when a particular sequence of operations tends to be repeated. It is called by the macro name.

Memory: that part of the computer in which data and programs are stored during program execution.

Menu: display giving a choice of operations to the user.

Modem: device used to connect a terminal or a computer to a telephone line so as to enable communication over long distances (section 3.53).

Multi-access: operating mode in which a number of users may work apparently simultaneously on one machine.

Network: system in which a number of computers may be connected together in order to share each others' hardware resources and to enable users to access data and programs on any machine as if they were all on one large machine (section 3.23).

Number-crunching: use of computers to perform tasks involving considerable mathematics, and consequently great computational power (section 1.22).

Object program: a program in machine language translated from a source program by a compiler (section 4.5).

Off-line: a device not connected to the central processor.

On-line: a device is on-line when it is connected to a computer.

Operating system: the set of programs, typically supplied with a computer, which provide the interface between the hardware, the user, and the user's program (section 3.9, 4.6).

Operator: a person who operates computer equipment.

Output: information which is produced by the computer system.

Password: a character combination keyed in by the user to indicate he or she is properly authorised (section 4.62).

Peripheral equipment: a general term for devices which may be connected to a computer's central processor.

Plotter: device used to produce line drawings under program control (section 3.75).

Portability: a feature of a program or data which can be used on more than one computer system (section 4.5).

Printer: device for producing printed output (section 3.73).

Print-out: hard copy output from a printer.

Program: a set of instructions designed to perform a given task by computer (section 1.1, chapter 4).

Programmer: one who writes programs.

Pseudo-code: a code which represents the steps in an algorithm in narrative form (section 4.42).

Punched card: a card punched with a pattern of holes to represent data (section 3.61, 3.71, 5.41).

Punching error: mistake made in tranferring data from coding sheets to punched cards (section 5.41).

Random access: (1) see direct access. (2) used to describe Random Access Memory, a slightly confusing term which simply means that any randomly chosen elements of memory may be accessed with equal ease (section 3.3).

Read: to copy data from some source and bring it into a central processor without destroying the original record.

Real number: a decimal number with a fractional component (section 2.65).

Real time: a mode of operation in which input data is received and processed as it is generated.

Record: a unit of data representing a basic element of a file, consisting in turn of a group of fields (section 2.74).

Remote access: the use of a computer via a terminal situated at some distance away (section 5.42).

Right-justified: describing data formatted so that it occupies consecutive positions starting from the right hand end of the location assigned, so that the right hand margin is straight (section 5.41).

Run: the execution of a program or routine (section 4.51).

Scanner: optical device used to convert graphical information such as photographs into a machine storeable form.

Security: arrangements to see that data or programs (1) will not be lost or corrupted; (2) do not become available to unauthorised users.

Simulation: the mathematical representation of problems, allowing physical situations to be represented on a computer (section 1.24).

Software: in its most general form refers to all the programs which are used on or by a computer system (section 1.1, chapter 4).

Source program: a program written in a programming language (section 4.5).

Stand-alone: having the ability to function without connection to a central processor.

String: sequence of characters.

Structure diagram: a diagrammatic representation of the structure of a problem (section 4.42).

Structured programming: collection of techniques designed to be used to make programming more rigorous (section 4.42).

Subroutine: small program which is called up to execute some chosen operation.

Suite: a collection of computer programs with related use.

Systems analysis: analysis of what is to be done, and the best way to achieve it (section 4.3, 4.4).

Tape: magnetic tape, a storage medium generally used for long term storage on large machines. Some small portable machines also use cassette tapes for backing store (section 3.41).

Tele-typewriter: form of computer terminal consisting of a keyboard and small printing unit (section 3.52).

Terminal: device through which the user usually communicates with the machine. Consists of a keyboard for input and either a printer or visual display for output (section 3.51).

Test data: a set of data developed to test the adequacy of a program or computer system.

Time-sharing: operating mode in which a large number of users or processes are each sequentially allocated short periods of CPU time.

Track: annular section of a magnetic disc on which data is stored (section 3.42).

User: one who uses a computer.

User-friendly: a feature of a computer system which is easy to use (section 4.6, 5.422).

Utility program: program which performs standard procedures common to many applications (section 4.1).

Validation: automatic checking of input data by a computer program (section 5.422).

Verification: double-checking input data, for example, by punching cards twice, or running through a verifier (section 5.41).

VDU: Visual Display Unit, the display section of a terminal etc (section 3.51).

Word processing: the processing of alphabetic data (section 7.4).

Word processor: a stand-alone device capable of word processing (section 7.4).

INDEX